# ENDING THE CYCLE OF VIOLENCE

◆

*We dedicate this book to our parents:*
*Yonah and Shmuel Peled*
*Immy and Bernard Jaffe*
*Leah Rae and LeRoy Edleson*

# ENDING THE CYCLE OF VIOLENCE

◆

## Community Responses to Children of Battered Women

Einat Peled
Peter G. Jaffe
Jeffrey L. Edleson
editors

**SAGE** Publications
*International Educational and Professional Publisher*
Thousand Oaks   London   New Delhi

*For information address:*

SAGE Publications, Inc.
2455 Teller Road
Thousand Oaks, California 91320

SAGE Publications Ltd.
6 Bonhill Street
London EC2A 4PU
United Kingdom

SAGE Publications India Pvt. Ltd.
M-32 Market
Greater Kailash I
New Delhi 110048 India

Printed in the United States of America

**Library of Congress Cataloging-in-Publication Data**

Ending the cycle of violence : community responses to children of
  battered women/edited by Einat Peled, Peter G. Jaffe [and] Jeffrey
  L. Edleson.
       p. cm.
    Includes bibliographical references and indexes.
    ISBN 0-8039-5368-2.—ISBN 0-8039-5369-0 (pbk.)
    1. Children of abused wives—Mental health services. 2. Children
  of abused wives—Services for. 3. Family violence—Prevention.
  I. Peled, Einat.  II. Jaffe, Peter G.  III. Edleson, Jeffrey L.
  PJ507.F35E53  1994
  362.82'92—dc20                                                94-27938

95  96  97  98  99  10  9  8  7  6  5  4  3  2  1

Sage Production Editor: Diana E. Axelsen

# Contents

# Acknowledgments

The three of us first met in July 1992 at the National Conference on Intervention With Children of Battered Women held in Minneapolis. The 3-day conference was organized by the Domestic Abuse Project with support from the Emma B. Howe Memorial Foundation. It attracted more than 350 people from 32 U.S. states, Canada, and three other countries.

The conference participants helped us recognize the need for more information on new programs for children of battered women. In the lobby of the hotel, as conference participants stopped by to talk, we sketched out the plan for this book.

With our plan in hand, we approached conference presenters and others across North America working in innovative programs for children of battered women. At the same time, we approached Marquita Flemming, then the social work editor at Sage Publications, with the initial prospectus of this book. She enthusiastically supported our plan and brought Sage's impressive resources to bear. Terry Hendrix, the interpersonal violence editor, took over for Sage when Marquita moved on to another area of the company's operations. Terry helped shepherd the project with his experienced advice throughout the writing and production process.

The chapter authors, 27 professionals living in three countries, worked hard to produce excellent chapters. The outcome of all of our efforts is this book, *Ending the Cycle of Violence: Community Responses to Children of Battered Women*. It is the first book to feature chapters on the growing number of innovative programs that aim to improve the situation of children exposed to violence against their mothers and to address the many critical issues that must be considered when designing such programs.

Our work could not have been achieved without the support of the boards, staff, and clients of the Domestic Abuse Project in Minneapolis, Minnesota, and the London Family Court Clinic in Ontario, Canada. These two organizations deserve more detailed acknowledgement here.

## Domestic Abuse Project

Einat Peled and Jeffrey Edleson received inspiration and tremendous support from the staff of the Domestic Abuse Project, where much of our work and research with children of battered women took place. We specifically thank Diane Davis, who coordinates the DAP Children's Program, and the therapists and interns who work with her in that endeavor. We also thank Carol Arthur, Joan Bilinkoff, Ellen Altman, and Ann Moore, all senior DAP staff who lent vision, time, and resources to these efforts.

The Domestic Abuse Project (DAP) was established in 1979 and began from a perspective that the response to violence required a multisystems intervention. This response required providing (a) immediate protection, support, and advocacy for battered women and their children; (b) education and accountability for violent men; (c) ongoing support, education, and healing for battered women and their children; and (d) coordinated intervention in and monitoring of social institutional responses to battering. In 1979, shelters in the metropolitan Twin Cities area were providing immediate protection, support, and advocacy. Consequently DAP focused on developing the later three areas.

The agency grew rapidly in the 1980s and now comprises five major units: (a) community intervention, (b) clinical services, (c) marketing and communication, (d) evaluation and research, and (e) administrative services. The majority of DAP resources now are focused on intervention in the criminal justice system, working both on behalf of individual battered women and on changing system responses to all battered women and their children. DAP also devotes considerable resources to providing support and education groups for battered women and for their children, psychoeducational groups for men who batter, individual and family counseling when appropriate, and a network of aftercare and self-help groups for those who have completed more structured programs at the agency or elsewhere. DAP's children's program is located within clinical services and has a full-time coordinator who draws on other staff for leadership of children's groups and individual or family services as needed (see Chap. 5 for more detail).

Community intervention and clinical services are supported by three smaller units. The marketing and communication unit provides publications and training to professional and community groups worldwide. Extensive in-house training is offered to interns from a variety of graduate professional programs and to staff of other agencies who arrange extended visits to

Minneapolis. Publications include a collection of handbooks that describe DAP services in detail, a large number of research and clinical practice articles that have appeared in numerous journals, and a regularly scheduled *Research Update* newsletter that provides news of DAP's evaluation and research findings. The evaluation and research unit operates in close relationship with the University of Minnesota's School of Social Work faculty and students. The unit is a model of collaborative, practice-based research. The administrative services unit supports the general operation of the agency.

In 1993, DAP provided information to more than 13,000 people. Agency staff provided direct advocacy services to 3,287 victim/survivors, and direct treatment services to 577 men, 237 women, 54 children, and 47 adolescents; 28 full- and part-time staff and 12 interns provided these services.

## London Family Court Clinic

Peter Jaffe is indebted to the board and staff of the London Family Court Clinic, who have facilitated his work in a number of ways, including creating a caring and supportive environment. The clinic's climate has always fostered the integration of clinical and research excellence and a vision of zero tolerance of violence. Karen Rhiger has undertaken a major task in helping to organize the manuscript, in addition to all of her other responsibilities as an administrative officer at the clinic, and the editors gratefully acknowledge her contribution.

The London Family Court Clinic (LFCC) is a children's mental health center committed to advocate for the special needs of children and families involved in the justice system. The clinic's advocacy includes assessment, counseling, and prevention services, as well as research and training for the community.

The clinic recognizes that children and families involved in the justice system are in crisis and at a major turning point in their lives. Clinic staff believe that the justice system has an opportunity to be part of a healing and conflict resolution process when it is responsive to the real needs of children and families. The staff believes that the clinic can play a role in making the justice system more sensitive and responsive to the people it serves. The Clinic plays this role by (a) providing clinical assessments for the court, (b) acting as a bridge between the justice system and helping agencies, (c) promoting positive adjustment through early identification of childhood problems and through prevention programs, (d) offering training and community education programs, (e) ensuring child victims or witnesses to violence are not revictimized or further traumatized by court proceedings, (f) conducting research in collaboration with community partners to make services, policies, and legislation more responsive to the needs of children and families in the justice system, and (g) sharing information through publications and workshops.

In the year ending in June, 1993, almost 400 referrals were made to the clinic. During that same period, more than 150 workshops and presentations were offered throughout Canada, the United States, and in two other countries. The clinic also produced 17 publications, received 15 research grants, and fielded almost 400 requests for information during this period.

Throughout the clinic's 20-year history, violence against women and children has been the organization's central focus. A large proportion of the children referred to the clinic have lived with violence that has gone unnoticed by the community until their emotional and behavioral problems can no longer be ignored. Good examples include the following: Adolescent boys who are assualtive to their girlfriends after many years of witnessing their father abuse their mother, children with nightmares and flashbacks after visitation with a father who terrorrized their mother for a decade before she finally fled to a shelter, and children too terrified to testify against a sexually abusive stepfather because they know all the different forms of violence that they witnessed at home. These children are a constant reminder that we are a long way from ending the cycle of violence.

## Personal Acknowledgments

Einat Peled and Jeffrey Edleson received extensive intellectual and material support from the faculty and staff of the University of Minnesota's School of Social Work and College of Human Ecology.

Einat Peled was and is inspired by her ever-loving and supportive family and wholeheartedly thanks the many children who trusted her with their feelings and thoughts about life and violence. Peter Jaffe's partner, Deb, has been a constant reminder that there is more to life than writing and presenting workshops. Personal relationships, family, and fun were always presented as important priorities. The book would have been published earlier without her . . . but life wouldn't have been the same. Jeffrey Edleson's two sons, Daniel and Eli Edleson-Stein, and his partner of 20 years, Marcie Stein, have taught him to be sensitive to the needs of children and about how important a violence-free and nurturing home, community, and world environment is to the healthy development of all children.

# PART ONE

# Living in a Violent Culture

# 1

# Introduction

EINAT PELED
PETER G. JAFFE
JEFFREY L. EDLESON

The world in which we raise our children is extremely violent. Millions of children are victims of child physical and sexual abuse every year (Dubowitz, 1986; Straus & Gelles, 1986). Many more children are frequent witnesses of violence: They watch it, hear it, read about it, and play with it. Violence is a major theme in television shows, movies, newscasts, music, sports, literature, and children's toys (Miedzian, 1991); it is rampant in many North American cities (Garbarino, Dubrow, Kostelny, & Pardo, 1992; Kotlowitz, 1991); and it is a constant presence in families in which the mother is being abused.

In this book we focus on children who witness violence directed at their mothers by their intimate partners. The phenomenon of children witnessing violence directed at their mothers, as described by professionals or studied by researchers, encompasses a wide range of experiences (see Jaffe, Wolfe, & Wilson, 1990; Peled, 1993). Children may observe this violence directly by seeing their fathers (or other intimate partners of their mothers) threaten or hit their mothers. One 13-year-old girl recalled the following violence:

> He choked her for a minute or so and then he stopped. . . . She cried and coughed, tried catching her breath. And then she called the police. (Peled, 1993, p. 102)

A 12-year-old girl, referring to her mother and her stepfather, recalled:

> He picked her up off the bed, they were fighting, and then he picked her up off the bed and threw her against the wall. (Peled, 1993, p. 103)

3

Children may not see, but rather hear the sounds of violence from another part of their home, such as these 10-year-old boys:

The only time I remember is when my dad, he broke down the, did my mom tell you that? That he broke down that door? . . . The bathroom one. I was about four. I don't know where I was. I think I was, I might have been in their room watching TV. . . . After it happened, I asked my mom what happened. Then she told me. (Peled, 1993, p. 102)

He went downstairs, so did Mom. And on the steps he turned back and said something to Mom but I don't know. And he went downstairs and they, I heard all this banging and the floor, the floor was, just kept on, there's so much, there's like bangs in the floor and on the walls and stuff like that. But, and then there was all this yelling. (Peled, 1993, p. 114)

Children also may be exposed to the results of this violence without either hearing or seeing the acts of aggression. One mother of a 6- and a 4-year-old recalled her experience:

After he was arrested and stuff, I wanted to get out of here. I called the police and they said, "Oh yeah, he's posted his bail, he'll be out in an hour." And I was, "An hour? I gotta get out of here." So I called a girlfriend at like two in the morning. My brother and my girlfriend and I went and had to wake those guys up. You know it was January, it was freezing out. Pack up, try and explain to them we gotta leave and why and pack up a few things and get out of here. And that was really hard on them. (Peled, 1993, p. 135)

## CHILDREN OF BATTERED WOMEN

It is estimated that between 3.3 million (Carlson, 1984) and 10 million (Straus, 1991) children in the United States are at risk of exposure to woman abuse each year. These children are at increased risk of being abused themselves (Stark & Flitcraft, 1985) and are thought to suffer from an array of behavioral, emotional, and cognitive problems (Fantuzzo & Lindquist, 1989; Goodman & Rosenberg, 1987; Jaffe et al., 1990).

Studies have found child witnesses to have more overall externalizing problem behavior (Jaffe, Wolfe, Wilson, & Zak, 1986), more overall internalizing problem behavior (Christopherpoulos et al., 1987), and less social competence (Wolfe, Zak, Wilson, & Jaffe, 1986). Children of battered women also were found to show more anxiety (Forsstrom-Cohn & Rosenbaum, 1985; Hughes, 1988), more aggression (Westra & Martin, 1981), more temperamental problems (Holden & Ritchie, 1991), more depression (Christopherpoulos et al., 1987), less empathy (Hinchey & Gavelek, 1982), less self-esteem (Hughes, 1988), and lower verbal, cognitive, and motor abilities (Westra & Martin, 1981) than children who did not witness violence at home. Further, there is some support for the notion of cross-generational transmission of violence by which children from violent families of origin are suggested to carry violent and violence-tolerant roles to their adult intimate relationships (Cappell & Heiner, 1990; Rosenbaum & O'Leary, 1981; Widom, 1989).

The high number of children witnessing woman battering is not, most likely, a recent development. Some evidence suggests that children have been witnessing their mothers being abused for a long time (Edleson, 1991; Gordon, 1988; Pleck, 1987). Until recently, children's witnessing violence in their home was not recognized as a problem requiring intervention. For example, the pediatrician Ira S. Wile wrote in *The Survey* in 1924:

> It is undoubtedly true that the brawling home has little advantage compared with the equable atmosphere secured by divorce. Yet, so long as cruelty and animosity are not directed upon the children, they are at least free from the internal stresses that exist when divorce breaks up the home and wraps or tears those intangible ties termed home influences. (p. 474)

The predicament of children who witness their mothers being abused began to attract professional and public attention in the late 1970s. Professional interest seemed to have been contingent on the relatively recent construction of marital violence as a social problem (Loseke, 1987; Straus, Gelles, & Steinmetz, 1980) and to draw on existing public and professional awareness of the problems of child abuse in general (Nelson, 1984) and child psychological abuse in particular (Brassard, Germain, & Hart, 1987; Garbarino, Guttmann, & Seeley, 1986).

Battered women and the advocates, clinicians, and researchers who worked with them were the first to report on children of battered women (e.g., Dobash & Dobash, 1979; Hilberman & Munson, 1977; Martin, 1976; Stacy & Shupe, 1983; Walker, 1979). Professionals, faced with battered women's concerns for their children and the difficulties experienced by the children themselves, described emotional and physical difficulties experienced by children residing in shelters for battered women (e.g., Elbow, 1982; Hilberman & Munson, 1977; Layzer, Goodson, & DeLange, 1986; Levine, 1975; Moore, 1975).

Although there is a growing body of research on children of battered women, scant information has been available on interventions to help these children.

## OVERVIEW OF THE BOOK

This book presents the work and thoughts of authors from across North America who are working in a variety of ways to both prevent future violence and intervene to lessen the effects that current violence has on children. The book is organized into four parts covering the following: (a) living in a violent culture, (b) shelters and domestic violence counseling, (c) child protection services and the criminal justice system, and (d) prevention and education in schools and communities.

The book begins with Myriam Meidzian's detailed discussion in Chapter 2 of how our societies teach boys to consider violence an acceptable behavior and then maintain these teachings into adulthood. This chapter sets the context in which the rest of the programs and issues are discussed.

Part Two focuses on shelters and domestic violence counseling. Chapter 3 and 4 both focus on individual assessment and counseling in cases of trauma. The authors are all psychiatrists and psychologists working directly with traumatized children. In Chapter 3, William Arroyo and Spencer Eth offer a framework for assessing the effects of trauma. Louise Silvern and her colleagues at the University of Colorado Department of Psychology provide a step-by-step framework in Chapter 4 for helping children overcome the effects of witnessing violence.

The next three chapters in Part Two focus on work with children, their mothers, and their fathers. Einat Peled and Jeffrey Edleson describe in Chapter 5 both the Domestic Abuse Project's Children's Program and the results of their multiyear investigation into its effects. Joan Bilinkoff, the Director of Therapy for the Domestic Abuse Project, offers in Chapter 6 guidelines for working with battered women as single mothers. David Mathews, from the Wilder Community Assistance Program in St. Paul, Minnesota, follows with a chapter devoted to how one works on parenting skills with men who batter. This part ends with Honore Hughes and Michele Marshall's chapter on the work of children's advocates both within and outside battered women's shelters.

Part Three focuses on child protection issues when mothers are also battered women. In Chapter 9 Joan Zorza, a lawyer with the National Center on Women and Family Law in New York, offers a concrete guide of legal remedies for those working with battered women and their children to use when seeking protection from abusers. Carole Echlin and Larry Marshall, both working in child protection services in Ontario, provide an overview in Chapter 10 of assessment and intervention in child protection and then touch on some current controversies over protecting children of battered women. Part Three ends with Chapter 11, in which Martha McMahon, a sociologist at the University of Victoria, and Ellen Pence, from the Duluth Domestic Abuse Intervention Project, describe a supervised visitation center and then address many of the serious philosophical concerns that arise in providing services to perpetrators and victims/survivors.

The final section of the book, Part Four, addresses school and community efforts to prevent and educate about violence. Denise Gamache, a long-time innovator in domestic violence programs, and Sarah Snapp, a counselor currently offering prevention education programs, review current efforts at the elementary level and then illustrate the practical issues one faces when implementing a statewide project. In Chapter 13, Marlies Sudermann and her colleagues at the London Family Court Clinic describe their efforts to provide violence prevention programming in secondary schools. Chapter 14 follows with David Wolfe and his colleagues at the University of Western Ontario focusing on programs for high-risk youth. Chapter 15 is written by Claudette Dumont-Smith, an aboriginal activist in Canada. Dumont-Smith describes both the problems her people face and how traditional methods of healing are being used to end violence. The book ends with Chapter 16, in which the editors discuss the future of efforts to assist children of battered women.

## REFERENCES

Brassard, M. R., Germain, R., & Hart, S. N. (Eds.). (1987). *Psychological maltreatment of children and youth.* New York: Pergamon.

Cappell, C., & Heiner, R. B. (1990). The intergenerational transmission of family aggression. *Journal of Family Violence, 5,* 135-152.

Carlson, B. E. (1984). Children's observations of interparental violence. In A. R. Roberts (Ed.), *Battered women and their families* (pp. 147-167). New York: Springer.

Christopherpoulos, C., Cohn, A. D., Shaw, D. S., Joyce, S., Sullivan-Hanson, J., Kraft, S. P., & Emery, R. E. (1987). Children of abused women: I. Adjustment at time of shelter residence. *Journal of Marriage and the Family, 49,* 611-619.

Dobash, R. E., & Dobash, R. (1979). *Violence against wives.* New York: Free Press.

Dubowitz, H. (1986). *Child maltreatment in the United States: Etiology, impact, and prevention* (Background paper prepared for the Congress of the United States, Office of Technology Assessment).

Edleson, J. L. (1991). Social workers' intervention in woman abuse: A study of case records from 1907 to 1945. *Social Service Review, 65,* 304-313.

Elbow, M. (1982). Children of violent marriage: The forgotten victim. *Social Casework, 8,* 465-468.

Fantuzzo, J. W., & Lindquist, C. U. (1989). The effects of observing conjugal violence on children: A review and analysis of research methodology. *Journal of Family Violence, 4,* 77-94.

Forsstrom-Cohn, B., & Rosenbaum, A. (1985). The effects of parental marital violence on young adults: An exploratory investigation. *Journal of Marriage and the Family, 47,* 467-472.

Garbarino, J., Dubrow, N., Kostelny, K., & Pardo, C. (1992). *Children in danger: Coping with the consequences of community violence.* San Francisco: Jossey-Bass.

Garbarino, J., Guttmann, E., & Seeley, J. W. (1986). *The psychologically battered child: Strategies for identification, assessment, and intervention.* San Francisco: Jossey-Bass.

Goodman, G. S., & Rosenberg, M. S. (1987). The child witness to family violence: Clinical and legal considerations. In D. J. Sonkin (Ed.), *Domestic violence on trial: Psychological and legal dimensions of family violence* (pp. 97-126). New York: Springer.

Gordon, L. (1988). *Heroes of their own life: The politics and history of family violence: Boston 1880-1960.* New York: Viking.

Hilberman, E., & Munson, K. (1977). Sixty battered women. *Victimology, 2,* 460-471.

Hinchey, F. S., & Gavelek, J. R. (1982). Empathic responding in children of battered women. *Child Abuse and Neglect, 6,* 395-401.

Holden, G. W., & Ritchie, K. L. (1991). Linking extreme marital discord, child rearing, and child behavior problems: Evidence from battered women. *Child Development, 62,* 311-327.

Hughes, H. M. (1988). Psychological and behavioral correlates of family violence in child witnesses and victims. *American Journal of Orthopsychiatry, 58,* 77-90.

Jaffe, P., Wolfe, D. A., & Wilson, S. (1990). *Children of battered women.* Newbury Park, CA: Sage.

Jaffe, P., Wolfe, D. A., Wilson, S., & Zak, L. (1986). Similarities in behavioral and social maladjustment among child victims and witnesses to family violence. *American Journal of Orthopsychiatry, 56,* 142-146.

Kotlowitz, A. (1991). *There are no children here: The story of two boys growing up in the other America.* Garden City, NY: Doubleday.

Layzer, J. I., Goodson, B. D., & DeLange, C. (1986). Children in shelters. *Response to Victimization of Women and Children, 9*(2), 2-5.

Levine, M. B. (1975). Interpersonal violence and its effect on children: A study of 50 families in general practice. *Medicine, Science and Law, 15,* 172-176.

Loseke, D. R. (1987). Lived realities and the construction of social problems: The case of wife abuse. *Symbolic Interaction, 10,* 224-243.

Martin, D. (1976). *Battered wives.* New York: Simon & Schuster.

Miedzian, M. (1991). *Boys will be boys: Breaking the link between masculinity and violence.* Garden City, NY: Doubleday.

Moore, J. G. (1975). Yo-yo children: Victims of matrimonial violence. *Child Welfare, 54,* 557-566.

Nelson, B. J. (1984). *Making an issue of child abuse: Political agenda setting for social problems.* Chicago: University of Chicago Press.

Peled, E. (1993). *The experience of living with violence for preadolescent child witnesses of woman abuse.* Unpublished doctoral dissertation, University of Minnesota, Minneapolis.

Pleck, E. H. (1987). *Domestic tyranny: The making of a social policy against family violence from colonial times to present.* New York: Oxford University Press.

Rosenbaum, A., & O'Leary, D. K. (1981). Children: The unintended victims of marital violence. *American Journal of Orthopsychiatry, 51,* 692-699.

Stacy, W., & Shupe, A. (1983). *The family secret: Domestic violence in America.* Boston: Beacon.

Stark, E., & Flitcraft, A. (1985). Women-battering, child abuse, and social heredity: What is the relationship? In N. Johnson (Ed.), *Marital violence* (pp. 147-171). London: Routledge & Kegan Paul.

Straus, M. A. (1991, September). *Children as witnesses to marital violence: A risk factor for lifelong problems among nationally representative sample of American men and women.* Paper presented at the Ross Roundtable on Children and Violence, Washington, DC.

Straus, M. A., & Gelles, R. J. (1986). Change in family violence from 1975-1985. *Journal of Marriage and the Family, 48,* 476-479.

Straus, M. A., Gelles, R. J., & Steinmetz, S. K. (1980). *Behind closed doors: Violence in the American family.* New York: Anchor.

Walker, L. E. (1979). *The battered woman.* New York: Harper & Row.

Westra, B., & Martin, H. P. (1981). Children of battered women. *Maternal Child Nursing Journal, 10,* 41-54.

Widom, C. S. (1989). *The intergenerational transmission of violence.* New York: Harry Frank Guggenheim Foundation.

Wile, I. S. (1924). Children and this clumsy world. *The Survey, 51,* 471-486.

Wolfe, D. A., Zak, L., Wilson, S., & Jaffe, P. (1986). Child witnesses to violence between parents: Critical issues in behavioral and social adjustment. *Journal of Abnormal Child Psychology, 14,* 95-104.

# 2

# Learning to Be Violent

## MYRIAM MIEDZIAN

In recent years we have grown more and more aware of and concerned with violence in our streets and in our homes.[1] The women's movement has focused our attention on wife battering, child battering, sexual abuse of children, and rape. In some urban centers the evening news begins with a tally of the dead and wounded in local "war zones."

Our suburbs and small towns, too, are often settings for outbursts of rageful, gruesome acts. In the last decade we have witnessed children and teachers being assaulted and killed in their schools, workers being murdered by disgruntled former employees, endless vengeful killings of former wives and former girlfriends, and increases in racist, anti-Semitic, and homophobic acts of violence. We hear increasingly about crimes committed "for fun" or out of curiosity—like the boys in a small Missouri town who wanted to see what it would feel like to kill someone, so they bludgeoned one of their schoolmates to death. Homicide rates have more than doubled in the last 30-odd years, going from 4.7 homicides per 100,000 in 1960 (U.S. Bureau of the Census, 1990) to 10 homicides per 100,000 in 1991 (FBI *Uniform Crime Reports,* 1991). Perpetrators are getting younger and younger. From 1965 to 1990, arrests for homicide among juveniles increased by 332% (FBI *Uniform Crime Reports,* 1991).

Although factors such as poverty, racism, breakdown of the family, and inadequate societal support systems for working parents all play roles in these staggering rates of violence, they cannot account for the fact that, year after year, close to 90% of the persons arrested for violent crimes are males. For example, the 1991 *Uniform Crime Reports* revealed a figure of 88%. In 1988, according to that year's report, it was 89%. Females suffer from these conditions as much as do males, yet they commit only a fragment of the violent crimes. Why?

It is the thesis of this chapter that a major contributing factor to male violence is a still prevailing, obsolete definition of masculinity centered on toughness, dominance, extreme competitiveness, eagerness to fight, and repression of empathy. As demonstrated in the following pages, the socialization of boys has increasingly encouraged this concept of masculinity, instead of moving away from it. Although a small percentage of men have moved toward increased sensitivity, empathy, and involvement in child rearing, more than ever most boys and men are encouraged to act in accordance with this obsolete set of values that I refer to as "the masculine mystique." These values play a major role in criminal and domestic violence and underlie the thinking and policy decisions of many of our political leaders.

The masculine mystique manifests itself differently in different environments, but the end result is the same: For a poor ghetto youth, proving that he is a man might involve a willingness to rob, assault, or kill someone. Homicide is the major cause of death among young African American males (Centers for Disease Control and Prevention, 1990). For a group of middle- or upper-class boys, it might mean participating in a gang rape or going on a 100-mile-per-hour "joy ride." Automobile accidents are the major cause of death among young white males (U.S. Bureau of the Census, 1990). For the men in our National Security Council, proving manhood might mean showing how tough they are by going along with a military intervention that is not really necessary for our national security. In the case of Vietnam, this intervention led to the death of at least 58,000 Americans and well over 1 million Vietnamese.

Men are still the most frequent victims of violence. From 1980 to 1991 about three times as many men as women were murdered per year (FBI *Uniform Crime Reports,* 1975-1991). But whereas most men are murdered by other men, 9 out of 10 female murder victims are murdered by males— 30% are slain by their husbands or boyfriends. More than 100,000 rapes are reported annually (FBI *Uniform Crime Reports,* 1991). According to the National Family Violence Survey (Gelles & Straus, 1988), every year approximately 1.8 million women suffer one or more severe assaults inflicted by their husbands or male partners.

This chapter represents an attempt at understanding how the way we socialize boys in the United States encourages violent behavior. Some recommendations for change are outlined. But I first address the common objection that "boys will be boys" and that nothing much can be done to diminish male violence because it grows out of an inexorable aggressive instinct.

## RESEARCH ON MALE VIOLENCE

The research and writings of sociobiologists often are used to buttress the view that the male of the species, through natural selection, has developed highly aggressive and territorial drives that are unalterable and that have led to conflict and violence throughout human history. Hormonal studies are marshalled to support this "killer instinct" view of male aggression. Here the culprit is perceived as being the male hormone testosterone. But it is a far cry from the implications of some of the popularized versions of these theories to what the most respected researchers in the field are saying. In fact, the broad consensus among them is that although violent behavior is based in human biology, it can in no way be considered an inexorable instinct or drive.

For example, in his book *Sociobiology: The New Synthesis,* E. O. Wilson (1975) tells us that aggression is not an active drive or instinct constantly seeking release. Instead of picturing it on this hydraulic model of a fluid constantly applying pressure against the walls of its containers, we should picture aggression as a preexisting mix of chemicals that can be transformed by specific catalysts if they are added at some later time. This is the culture-pattern model, which is based on the interaction of genetic potential and learning.

In their book *Man and Woman, Boy and Girl,* a study of the influence of hormones on male and female behavior, Money and Ehrhardt (1972) are intent on emphasizing the role of the environment in human development: They devote an entire chapter to this topic. In several articles Ehrhardt (1985a, 1985b) argues that behavior and environment can have a strong and direct influence on hormone levels and suggests that testosterone levels may well be affected by environmental factors.

In brief, there is considerable agreement among experts that although human beings, particularly men as a group, have a potential for learning violent behavior, environment can make all the difference in terms of encouraging or discouraging such behavior. The belief that "boys will be boys" and so the killing and fighting will go on regardless of what we do has no foundation in the best available knowledge. It is based on the erroneous belief that violent behavior grows out of a drive or an instinct akin to hunger or sex.

But to say that violence is not an instinct or a drive is not to deny that it has a biological basis. We are physical beings, and so all human behavior is grounded in biology. If we were not biologically programmed with the ability to learn to be violent, violent behavior could never have developed. As hard as some of us might want to fly like birds, we will never be able to do so because we do not have the biological potential for flight. Intensive efforts have been made in recent years to teach language to chimps. These attempts have failed. Chimps are not biologically wired to be able to learn more than a few concrete terms; conceptualizing and abstracting are beyond their potential. They are not beyond our potential, nor is violence. We must begin to move beyond simplistic analysis of violence that focuses exclusively on biology or on socialization.

Violence is best understood as developing out of an interaction between a biological potential and certain kinds of environments. In comparing males and females, the differential treatment of boys and girls from birth makes it difficult to assess what is due to biology and what is due to socialization. It is the *combination* of evidence from diverse and independent sources—studies in the U.S., cross-cultural studies, hormonal and animal studies—that leads to the conclusion that the potential for violence appears to be greater in males than females.

The violence gap between boys and girls is enlarged further by the fact that boys, more frequently than girls, suffer from physical conditions such as attention deficit disorder with hyperactivity (ADDH or ADHD), mild mental retardation, and learning disability, which put them at greater risk for behaving violently. It appears that ADDH is approximately six to nine times as prevalent in boys as in girls. It is a predisposing factor for antisocial personality disorder, whose distinguishing characteristics include delinquency, theft, vandalism, repeated physical fights or assaults, and repeated drunkenness or substance abuse. Mental retardation is nearly twice as prevalent among males as females. Children who are mentally retarded are three to four times as likely to suffer from ADDH as the general population. Some experts have estimated that up to 30% of criminal offenders are mentally retarded.

Whereas boys are at least twice as likely to be identified by teachers as suffering from learning disability, recent research suggests that dyslexia (the most common of the learning disabilities) is, in fact, as prevalent in girls as in boys. But boys tend to act more impulsively and to be frustrated more easily than girls, which makes it more difficult for boys to deal with a learning disability. Their tendency to act out captures teachers' attention. Also there is significant overlap of ADDH and learning disability. It is estimated that approximately 40% of the jail population in the United States suffers from learning disability. (See Miedzian, 1991, for more detail on these data.)

Nevertheless, when we speak of male-female differences with respect to violence, we must remember that we are referring to tendencies that are more pronounced in one group than the other, rather than tendencies among

separate, non-overlapping groups. Research informs us that despite socialization that encourages them to be more aggressive, a substantial number of
boys are no more aggressive than girls. The fact that a majority of men lead
essentially nonviolent lives, despite living in a society that applauds the
values of the masculine mystique, testifies to the lack of any intense inclina-
tion toward violent behavior on their part.

Whether a boy becomes violent depends on the interaction between
potential and environment. It is precisely because males as a group have a
greater potential for learning violent behavior than do females that we should
be doing everything possible to create a social environment that discourages
violence among males.

The enormous influence society has in encouraging or discouraging the
potential for violence is clear both from changes that take place within the
same culture and differences between societies. How can we explain the fact
that homicide rates in the United States increased by more than 100%
between 1960 and 1991 (FBI *Uniform Crime Reports,* 1991; U.S. Bureau of
the Census, 1990) except by pointing to societal changes? The only other
possible explanation would be widespread genetic mutations.

Anthropologist Peggy Sanday's cross-cultural study of 95 societies revealed that 47% of them were free of rape (Sanday, 1981). Psychologist
Robert R. Holt reported that in at least 33 societies, war as well as interpersonal violence are extremely rare (Holt, 1987).

People who live in violent societies often assume that high levels of violence
are inevitable. We all tend to take for granted our society's deeply set cultural
traits and view them as normal. To provide some distance from our tacit
assumptions and make it easier to examine those present-day cultural traits
that encourage violence in boys, in the following pages I take an anthropological perspective on our culture. I look at violence in American society
from the point of view of a group of visiting South Asian anthropologists.

## THE CULTURE OF VIOLENCE

Anyone who has ever taken a cultural anthropology course is aware that
different societies have different patterns of culture and that the different
threads—music, sports, children's games, drama, work, relations between
the sexes, religion, communal values, and so forth—making up the cultural
web of a society are usually intricately related. If a tribe's songs and dramas
are centered on violence and warfare, if its young boys play war games and
violently competitive sports from the youngest age, and if its paintings,
sculptures, and pottery depict fights and scenes of battle, it is a pretty sure

bet that this is not a peaceful, gentle tribe in which a serious fight rarely occurs and aggressive wars are unthinkable.

Every child in the world is born into a particular culture, and "from the moment of his birth the customs into which he is born shape his experience and behavior," we are told by anthropologist Ruth Benedict (1934/1946, p. 18). Throughout history people have known this intuitively, and so they have been careful to socialize their children from the youngest age into a pattern of behavior acceptable to the group. We have in our own society some very clear examples: Groups such as the Christian Hutterites and the Amish or the Jewish Chasidim want their children to grow up to be devoted primarily to religious rather than material values, to be sexually modest, chaste before marriage, and monogamous after marriage. These groups share a strong sense of community and commitment to taking responsibility for the well-being of all of their members. The Hutterites and the Amish place a strong emphasis on nonviolence. None of these groups allow their children to participate in the mainstream culture.

Sometimes societies develop customs that become highly detrimental to their members: A cultural trait that might be of considerable value in a limited form or that was of value at an earlier point of history is elaborated and continued in a form that is socially deleterious. Benedict (1934/1946) refers to this process as the "asocial elaboration of a cultural trait" (p. 42).

Prime examples are the incest taboos and marital customs of the Kurnai tribe of Australia. Benedict explains that all human societies have incest taboos but differ significantly with respect to whom the prohibitions refer. Over the centuries the Kurnai's incest taboos became so severe that there are virtually no mates available for young people, especially young men. This circumstance does not lead the Kurnai to change their incest taboos or rules of marriage. Quite to the contrary, they are stringently enforced. As a result, the only way that tribe members usually are able to marry is by eloping. As soon as the villagers find out about the marriage, they set out in pursuit of the newlyweds, who are killed if caught. The fact that possibly all of the pursuers were married in the same way does not bother anyone. Moral indignation runs high. If the couple can reach an island traditionally recognized as a safe haven, however, they eventually can be accepted by the tribe as married. Cultural webs and irrationalities are simpler and easier to see in small, isolated tribes or small communities than in large, industrial societies, but they exist in both. Industrialized societies are made up of different socioeconomic classes, often different ethnicities. In large countries, such as the United States and Canada, differing geography and climate affect people. Nevertheless, certain aspects of the culture—besides a common language— are widely shared. Children and adolescents from coast to coast play with the same toys, see many of the same television shows and films, listen to the same rock and rap music, and participate in many of the same sports activities.

I suspect that if the Kurnai were to send a few anthropologists over to study contemporary North American society, they would be as amused by our irrationalities as we are by theirs. On the one hand, they would find in the Declaration of Independence a deep commitment to life, liberty, and the pursuit of happiness. An examination of the Constitution would reveal that the goals of government include "justice," "domestic tranquillity," and "the general welfare." An examination of contemporary society would reveal that we deplore murder, assault, wife and child battering, sexual abuse of children, and rape.

On the other hand, our newspaper headlines, our television news with its daily roundups of murders and rapes, our shelters for battered women and their children, and our crime statistics (according to the FBI *Uniform Crime Reports,* in 1990 alone more than 1.8 million Americans were the victims of violent crime) would inform the visiting anthropologists just how deeply afflicted we are by these problems. Having established this strong contradiction between our professed goals and beliefs and our reality, they would wonder what it is we teach our boys that makes them become such violent men.

"Who are your young boys' heroes? Who are their role models?" they would want to know. Arnold Schwarzenegger, Sylvester Stallone, and Jean Claude Van Damme would be high on the list.

"Do your boys watch only violent adventure films?" they might ask. No. They like comedies, too, but when they reach adolescence, many of them become particularly fond of slasher films such as the *Texas Chain Saw Massacre* and *Nightmare on Elm Street* series in which they can watch people being chopped up, dismembered, decapitated, or burned alive. Wanting to experience all aspects of our culture, the Kurnai anthropologists undoubtedly would watch a few slasher films. They would discover that the perpetrators are practically all males and that the films frequently are centered on the victimization of females.

"What about the rest of their leisure time—what do your boys do with it?" Our young boys spend about 28 hours per week watching television (American Psychological Association, 1993). By the time they are 18 years old, they have watched thousands of television murders, a vast majority of them committed by men (*National Coalition on Television Violence News,* 1988).

As anthropologists, the Kurnai would be fully aware of how intricately linked culture is to behavior. In addition, consultations with American social scientists would inform them that more than 235 studies have been carried out in the last 45 years on the effects of viewing violence on the screen, with a large majority of them finding that boys who watch violent entertainment are at high risk of committing acts of violence (Miedzian, 1991).

"Do they listen to much music?" might be their next question. Our boys certainly do. They spend billions of dollars each year on records and tapes; they listen to radio and MTV. Rock and rap stars are adulated by millions of boys. The Kurnai anthropologists might be advised to turn on MTV to see what the young boys are learning there. They would find that the programming often consists of angry-looking young men singing lyrics and playing music that sound as angry as the men look. They soon would realize that some of the most popular heavy metal and rap songs include lyrics celebrating rape, racism, homophobia, violence, and the denigration of women.

From their survey of American television, they would learn that a considerable amount of television time—on cable, on major networks, and on independent channels—is devoted to sports. In the light of the fact that many American boys admire sports heros more than any other group of men, they would be particularly interested in the kind of behavior and values modeled by professional athletes.

They undoubtedly would be struck by the frequency of brawls and fistfights at basketball, baseball, hockey, and football games. Watching football, they might be perplexed about how the central activities of the game—tackling and blocking—differ from bodily assault. Their examination of media interviews with professional athletes would reveal that, as former Patriots football player Keith Lee put it, "Nothing's illegal unless you get caught" (Miedzian, 1991, p. 181). For example, taking out top players of the opposing team is a common practice. ("Taking out" a player is a euphemism for injuring a player so badly that he or she cannot finish the game.)

Looking at youth and high school sports, they would discover that whereas the avowed goals of these activities include teaching boys sportsmanship, fair play, and camaraderie and developing a healthy, fit body, boys, in fact, often learn as early as at the Little League or Pop Warner level that winning is the only thing. A reading of sociologist Fine's book *With the Boys: Little League Baseball and Preadolescent Behavior* (1987) would inform them that although moral factors often are emphasized at the beginning of the season, eventually "integrity takes a back seat to the pragmatic concern with *winning* baseball games. Players learn that integrity is a rhetorical strategy one should raise only in certain times and places. The adults involved with Little League tend to be oriented toward winning, losing, and competition" (Fine, 1987, p. 74).

In the light of the fact that violence against women is a major societal problem, the Kurnai would be particularly struck that already at this very young age, boys commonly insult each other by yelling "girl" or "wuss" (cross between *woman* and *pussy*) at each other. This early exercise in the denigration of women is commonly tolerated by coaches.

The Kurnai's survey of high school varsity sports would inform them that many boys are learning that anything goes in order to win a game. Boys who play football are often taught to take out top players of the opposing team.

Finally the Kurnai would not be surprised that athletes appear to be overrepresented in sexual assaults against women (O'Sullivan, 1993). After all, if one combines the denigration of women with the idea that winning is the only thing and that anything goes in order to win, then one easily might conclude that anything goes in order to score with women.

The anthropologists soon would find that our already high rates of violent crime have been further exacerbated by an ever-growing drug problem. In this light they would carefully register the fact that drug and alcohol abuse are common among the athletes and musicians that many young boys admire and emulate.

"What about your boys' toys?" the Kurnai might ask next. A trip to the playground or a look under Christmas trees—religious symbols used in the celebration of the birth of the deified founder of the nation's leading religion, who preached a gospel of love and nonviolence—would reveal that whereas little girls get dolls and carriages and dollhouses, little boys get "action figures" such as G.I. Joe, violent space age toys and games, and, of course, lots of guns. As anthropologists, the Kurnai would be well aware that children's play often represents a rehearsal for adult life. It no doubt would strike them that the (to them highly perplexing) lack of laws restricting the sale of guns to adults renders this boyhood gun play particularly dangerous.

The Kurnai certainly would want to study family relations in the United States. Having already established that most American boys grow up surrounded by a culture of violence that equates masculinity with toughness, dominance, and an eagerness to fight, they would not be surprised at the very high rates of wife and child battering. The process operating here would be quite clear: The media and the toys encourage violent behavior in boys. Most of these boys grow up to be husbands and fathers. Many of them also become batterers. Studies indicate that being battered intrinsically puts a boy at higher risk of violent behavior: In addition to the often repressed anger they experience, boys who grow up in a violence-filled home tend to view violence as a normal response to anger or frustration (Miedzian, 1991). This perspective then is corroborated by toys that encourage violent play, as well as by endless portrayals of angry, violent men in the media.

An examination of violent crime statistics would reveal to the Kurnai that the highest rates of violence in our society are found among those boys and men who were raised entirely by single mothers. According to some studies, approximately 70% of juvenile offenders come from single-parent families (FBI *Uniform Crime Reports,* 1991). The anthropologists would realize that this is due, in part, to the economic deprivation of so many single mothers. But they also would be aware of cross-cultural data indicting that the presence of a caring, involved, nonviolent father decreases the chances of a son being violent. Their readings in contemporary American psychology and sociology—especially the works of Dinnerstein (1977) and Chodorow (1978)—would provide them with a deeper psychological understanding of why it is so important for a boy to have a loving father (or father substitute) that he can identify with and model himself on.

Given how difficult it is for single mothers to raise sons, the Kurnai would be shocked at how little societal support these women get. Overworked and underpaid mothers who are the sole support of their children and themselves cannot even rely on quality, reliable day care or after-school programs for their children. This gap leaves millions of children unattended and emotionally deprived—a good breeding ground for anger and violence. In addition, instead of the media helping single mothers by providing their sons with positive male role models, movies saturate the boys with Arnold Schwarzenegger terminating people in high-tech style, Sylvester Stallone machinegunning them, and Jean Claude Van Damme chopping them up. They would see the fact that most single mothers succeed in raising decent sons in spite of this as a testimony to these women's courage, perseverance, love, and commitment to their children.

Delving deeper, the Kurnai would find that many boys who start out with fathers lose them along the way through divorce. They would hear divorced women, social workers, psychiatrists, and other professionals complain bitterly that a large percentage of divorced fathers never or rarely see their children, nor do they make child support payments.

Increasingly stunned by the irrationalities of our society, the anthropologists might inquire of these professionals: "Because of the lack of interest of so many of your men in nurturing and taking responsibility for their children, and because of the subsequent increases in rates of violence and other social problems, why don't you encourage your little boys to become good fathers by buying them dolls and baby carriages and dollhouses? Why don't you encourage them to play house instead of train them to become warriors?" "Parents would never stand for that," both professionals and parents would explain. "They are much too afraid that their sons might grow up to be gay if they played with 'wimpy' girls' toys." At this point the visiting anthropologists might emit a cry of disbelief at these homophobic fears that prevent American boys from rehearsing the fathering role.

Having established the deep contradictions and absurdities of our customs, the Kurnai would look for the origins. They would find that, like many warrior societies, we have a long tradition of raising our boys to be tough, emotionally detached, deeply competitive, and concerned with dominance. Under any conditions, this training encourages violence in boys. But because of a combination of factors, these traits, they would note, had gotten out of hand in recent years. The extreme emphasis on the rights of the individual without any concomitant sense of responsibility played a role in so many men's abandonment of their children. Social welfare laws that discouraged marriage and encouraged fathers to leave the home contributed to the approximately 350% increase between 1960 and 1987 in children born to single mothers (U.S. Bureau of the Census, 1985, 1990).

An extreme emphasis on shortsighted self-interest, especially financial gain, seems to have blinded some Americans to the fact that it takes a whole society to raise a child well and that the whole society profits from having children raised well. This moral and political climate discouraged the passage of profamily laws mandating parental leave, financial aid for families with young children, and flexible work hours and prevented the development of quality day care and after-school programs. As a result, millions of children are left unattended or very poorly cared for while their parents work.

The enormous escalation of violence that Americans are experiencing also seems to coincide with the development of a vast system of communications technology that has led to the creation of a culture of violence of unprecedented dimensions, much of it directed toward or available to children. This culture of violence now plays a major role in socializing American children who spend more time being entertained by media than they spend with their parents or in school.

Instead of treasuring their children as a precious national resource to be handled with utmost care, Americans have allowed them to be exploited as a commercial market. "How could they let this happen?" the Kurnai would wonder. Surely Americans must understand that one of society's most important tasks—the socialization of the next generation—cannot be left in the hands of people whose main concern is financial gain, people who do not hesitate to exploit other people for profit.

In their efforts to understand this puzzle, the Kurnai would be helped by their understanding of their own culture. Because their absurdly rigid and all-encompassing marriage regulations represent an asocial elaboration of an originally highly beneficial system of incest taboos, they would look to our past to see how useful traditions might have evolved into present-day absurdities. They would discover that our laissez-faire attitude toward children's entertainment could indeed be traced to the asocial elaboration of some of our most beneficial and admirable values.

A system of largely unfettered free enterprise led to the extraordinary economic development of the nation. The subsequent commitment to free enterprise is so deep that the economic exploitation of children is taken for granted. Even when companies manufacture children's toys that encourage reckless violence, sadism, and torture, their right to do so is accepted with little questioning.

The Kurnai would turn next to the First Amendment, the embodiment of the national commitment to free speech. It would not escape their attention that, regarding pornographic and "indecent" material, it has long been acknowledged that the First Amendment cannot apply equally to children and adults. A long-standing tradition of laws protects children from such material. Therefore, as the Kurnai would have already noted, there are no pornographic television programs on Saturday mornings.

For some strange reason, the Kurnai would conclude, these people have blinded themselves to the fact that what makes sense with respect to sex makes at least as much sense with respect to violence. And so they have allowed their children to be raised on tens of thousands of television murders, detailed depictions of sadistic mutilations on the screen, and song lyrics that advocate rape. What a perfect example of an asocial elaboration, they might exclaim! Everything is justified in terms of free enterprise and free speech. But this freedom as interpreted in their present-day society contributes to the nation's enslavement.

Don't these Americans see that boys raised in a culture of violence are not free? Their basest, most destructive tendencies are reinforced from the youngest age to the detriment of their altruistic prosocial tendencies. Then when they commit serious acts of violence, they are sent to prison. Don't they see that millions of Americans, especially women and elderly people, live in great fear of being battered, mugged, raped, or murdered and that many are afraid to leave their homes after dark?

A survey of national crime statistics published by U.S. government agencies would inform the Kurnai that more than 20,000 Americans each year suffer the greatest loss of freedom (FBI *Uniform Crime Reports,* 1975-1991). They are deprived of their lives through violent deaths. Their families and friends are permanently deprived of someone they love.

How long will it take these people, the exasperated anthropologists might wonder, until they realize that an interpretation of freedom that allows for no restraints with respect to the commercial exploitation of children is self-destructive? The Kurnai would have taken note of the fact that, despite their extreme emphasis on freedom and their tendency to neglect responsibility, in many areas Americans do acknowledge that there is no such thing as absolute freedom. Ordinances prohibit people from playing loud music in the middle of the night if in doing so they deprive others of the freedom to sleep. Laws restrict the freedom of chemical companies to dump pollutants into their waters so that people will not be deprived of clean drinking water and good health. But when it comes to the right to produce a culture of violence that pollutes the minds of their young and encourages violence, these strange people act as if freedom is an absolute!

## MOVING AWAY FROM VIOLENCE

The depressing portrait of American society that I have drawn in these pages is intended as a catalyst for change. We must begin to work toward a society that discourages antisocial, violent behavior and encourages the best in our children. We must effectively protect them from gratuitous exploitative violence in entertainment. This can be accomplished without any infringement on adults' first amendment rights. We have a long legal history of laws aimed at protecting children. Liquor laws prevent a 10-year-old from entering a bar and ordering an alcoholic beverage. Pornography laws prevent a 15-year-old from buying pornographic magazines that his or her parents are free to purchase. We must begin to extend these laws to protect children from entertainment that teaches them that violence is fun, exciting, and manly.[2]

We have in this country a double standard with respect to pornography and violence. Many parents who would not dream of taking their children to see a pornographic film do not hesitate to take them to films in which murder and mutilation are depicted in gruesome detail. We need a major educational campaign (comparable to the antismoking campaign) aimed primarily at parents to make them aware of the effects of violent entertainment on their children. Eventually every television set sold in the United States should be equipped with an electronic device that permits parents to control what their young children watch. Devices already being produced are sometimes referred to as "lock boxes."

We need to develop a Children's Public Broadcasting System devoted to top-quality television programming for children of all social classes. The existence of two such channels (one for 2- to 9-year-olds, another for 10- to 13-year-olds), combined with lock boxes, would create a separate television universe for children.

Our government spends billions of dollars each year to pay for emergency room care necessitated by acts of violence, to keep more than 1.2 million prisoners incarcerated, and to maintain a judiciary system that cannot deal adequately with our extraordinary crime rates. Although funds somehow are found for these *postviolence* expenses, programs that would serve to prevent violence are rejected or not even entertained because of the cost.

Our military budget still hovers around $270 billion per year. But in the last 18 years close to 400,000 Americans have been murdered, while in all our wars since and including Vietnam, fewer than 60,000 Americans have lost their lives. *We are suffering from a domestic national security crisis far more serious than any international crisis that confronts us.* In the light of this crisis, it would behoove us to take out of our military budget funding necessary to create and maintain a Children's Public Television Network that would help our children develop their highest potential instead of cater to their basest tendencies as commercial television so frequently does. We desperately need quality child care and other profamily measures. We need public school programs in conflict resolution, in antibigotry, and in child rearing (these classes encourage boys to view themselves as *future* responsible, caring fathers and discourage child battering).

The behavior of human beings is extremely malleable. Anthropological studies reveal the enormous variability of human behavior and values in different cultures. Studies in psychology and sociology show us how early childhood experiences, family peer groups, and culture mold the individual. History reveals that radical changes have taken place within a given culture in a very short period of time: Extremely violent groups have become peaceful, and vice versa.

If we want, we can decrease violence. Instead of just giving lip service to family values, we need laws and programs that will help families raise decent children. American boys must be protected from a culture of violence that exploits their worst tendencies by reinforcing and amplifying the atavistic values of the masculine mystique. Women's lives and freedom are threatened constantly by men raised in this culture. We all deserve better.

## NOTES

1. This chapter was adapted from *Boys Will Be Boys: Breaking the Link Between Masculinity and Violence* by Myriam Miedzian (Doubleday, 1991; Anchor, 1992).

2. For a detailed discussion of the recommendations made in this chapter and for other proposals aimed at changing the socialization of boys to decrease violence, see *Boys Will Be Boys.*

## REFERENCES

American Psychological Association. (1993). *Violence and youth: Psychology's response* (Summary report of the American Psychological Association Commission on Violence and Youth). Washington, DC: Author.

Benedict, R. (1946). *Patterns of culture.* New York: Mentor. (Original work published 1934)

Centers for Disease Control and Prevention. (1990). *Federal Centers for Disease Control report.* Atlanta, GA: Author.

Chodorow, N. (1978). *The reproduction of mothering: Psychoanalysis and the sociology of gender.* Berkeley: University of California Press.

Dinnerstein, D. (1977). *The mermaid and the minotaur: Sexual arrangements and human malaise.* New York: Harper & Row.

Ehrhardt, A. A. (1985a). Gender differences: A biosocial perspective. *Nebraska Symposium on Motivation 1984: Psychology and Gender, 32,* 37-57.

Ehrhardt, A. A. (1985b). The psychobiology of gender. In A. S. Rossi (Ed.), *Gender in the life course.* Hawthorne, NY: Aldine.

Federal Bureau of Investigation (FBI). (1975-1991). *Uniform crime reports.* Washington, DC: U.S. Department of Justice.

Fine, G. A. (1987). *With the boys: Little League baseball and preadolescent behavior.* Chicago: University of Chicago Press.

Gelles, R., & Straus, M. (1988). *Intimate violence.* New York: Simon & Schuster.

Holt, R. R. (1987, May). *Converting the war system to a peace system.* Paper presented at the Conference of the Exploratory Project on the Conditions of Peace, Cohasset, MA.

Miedzian, M. (1991). *Boys will be boys: Breaking the link between masculinity and violence.* Garden City, NY: Doubleday.

Money, J., & Ehrhardt, A. (1972). *Man and woman, boy and girl.* Baltimore: Johns Hopkins University Press.

*National Coalition on Television Violence News.* (1988, March/April). *9*(3-4).

O'Sullivan, C. (1993). Fraternities and the rape culture. In E. Buchwald, P. R. Fletcher, & M. Roth (Eds.), *Transforming a rape culture* (pp. 27-28). Minneapolis: Milkweed.

Sanday, P. R. (1981). *Female power and male dominance: On the origins of sexual inequality.* Cambridge, UK: Cambridge University Press.

U.S. Bureau of the Census. (1985). *Statistical abstract of the United States.* Washington, DC: Author.

U.S. Bureau of the Census. (1990). *Statistical abstract of the United States.* Washington, DC: Author.

Wilson, E. O. (1975). *Sociobiology: The new synthesis.* Cambridge, MA: Harvard University Press.

# PART TWO

# Shelters and Domestic Violence Programs

# 3

# Assessment Following Violence-Witnessing Trauma

WILLIAM ARROYO
SPENCER ETH

This chapter focuses on children and adolescents who have witnessed interpersonal violence. Violence perpetrated against a member of a child's or adolescent's social network (a parent, sibling, or close friend/relative) places the young witness at risk for developing a constellation of symptoms consistent with psychic trauma. This wide spectrum of symptoms is described later in this chapter and the next.

Mental health clinicians who serve traumatized children and adolescents are met with two daunting challenges. The first is to help children cope more effectively with their overwhelming thoughts and related anxiety. The second is to help them and their families reestablish activities of daily living that are conducive to normal child development.

The goals of this chapter are twofold: First, we discuss the research already completed in the area of children who witness extreme acts of violence. Second, we describe a clinical approach that can be used with traumatized children during the early aftermath of an event they witnessed.

## RESEARCH ON
## CHILDREN WHO WITNESS VIOLENCE

Violence is unbridled in the United States, particularly in urban areas. Today it is nearly impossible for any child to be completely shielded from major acts of violence.

A recent annual estimate of homicides in the United States according to the Federal Bureau of Investigation (FBI) (1991) is 24,703. In some urban areas, such as Los Angeles, it is estimated that as many as 10% to 20% of all homicides are witnessed by dependent children (Eth & Pynoos, 1985a). Nearly 25% of all murders are perpetrated by family members (Straus, 1986).

Family or domestic violence that includes wife battering is associated with psychological trauma in child witnesses. Straus and Gelles (1986) reported the overall incidence of "severe" husband-to-wife and wife-to-husband violence to be 11.3% and 3.0%, respectively, in a 1985 national telephone survey. Gelles and Cornell (1985), in their extensive research review, concluded that greater wife abuse occurs in households of lower socioeconomic status, larger families, and husband-dominant power. Mason (1992) reported that 25% to 50% of women who head homeless families had left their homes to escape domestic violence, but, unfortunately, their homeless situation probably compounds the psychological harm already suffered by their children. Children who often witness domestic violence are also at greater risk to become victims later in life of such violence. Kalmuss (1984) indicated that the most significant predictor of marital aggression is having witnessed domestic violence during one's childhood. According to Lewis and her colleagues (Lewis, Shanok, Grant, & Ritvo, 1983), the most important factor contributing to violence in a large group of homicidally aggressive children was having a father who behaved violently, often homicidally.

The most recent annual national estimate of forcible rape is 106,593 (FBI, 1991). Many of these acts are perpetrated by household members. Russell (1982), in her survey of households, found that 14% of all married women in the United States experienced marital rape at some time in their lives. Among these marital assaults, 11% were known to or had been witnessed by at least one child.

The frequency of exposure to extreme violence spirals in urban neighborhoods (Osofsky, Wewers, Hann, & Fick, 1993); such violence is often gang-related warfare (Hoffer & Cervantes, 1992). During the last two decades there has also been a tremendous influx of refugees to the United States from war-torn countries throughout the world. Symptomatic children and their families have fled from massive killings and other extreme related acts of violence in Southeast Asia, Central America, the Middle East, and Eastern Europe (Arroyo & Eth, 1985; Williams & Westermeyer, 1983).

## POST-TRAUMATIC STRESS AND ITS DEVELOPMENTAL IMPACT

Children who witness violence are at risk of developing numerous psychological symptoms and syndromes (Eth & Pynoos, 1985b). Because of space limitations, only psychic trauma is discussed in this section. In addition, we describe our impressions on the basis of our clinical experience regarding developmental implications of psychic trauma.

*Psychic trauma* or *post-traumatic stress* refers to those symptoms an individual experiences in the face of a life-threatening event; the individual may be a victim or witness of such an incident. The child's internal resources (coping skills) and external resources (intervention by caretaking adults or others) are overwhelmed and/or ineffective; there is also a concomitant physiological reaction. The subjective experience is that of utter helplessness (Freud, 1926). Terr (1991) conceptualizes psychic trauma as consisting of two types (Types I and II). Type I arises from a trauma caused by a single, discrete event. The more severe type, Type II, arises from repeated exposure to traumatic events; this exposure may apply, for example, to repeated episodes of witnessing extreme domestic violence. Children who are confronted often by life-threatening situations engage in coping mechanisms of "massive denial, repression, dissociation, self-anesthesia, self-hypnosis, identification with the aggressor, and aggression turned against the self" (Terr, 1991, p. 15). *Post-traumatic stress disorder* (PTSD) (American Psychiatric Association [APA], 1988) is the diagnostic category used most frequently to refer to a constellation of symptoms of psychic trauma. The primary symptom involves intense fear, helplessness, or horror; young children may instead exhibit disorganzed or agitated behavior. The remaining symptoms of PTSD can be categorized into three clusters relevant to all age groups: (a) reexperience phenomena, (b) avoidant symptoms, and (c) autonomic hyperarousal for all age groups.

Although, in general, there is considerable overlap among the various age groups of children with respect to symptoms of psychic trauma, there are some differences (Eth & Pynoos, 1985b; Pynoos, 1993). Despite the recent increase in empirical investigations of psychic trauma in children (Pynoos, 1993), much more research is needed.

### Infancy

Psychic trauma has differential developmental implications. The study of psychic trauma during infancy is a new frontier in the field of stress research. Children who are traumatized before 28-36 months of age are unable to "put their traumas to words" (Terr, 1988), which would suggest that it is virtually impossible to detect symptoms of post-traumatic stress in this age group. In addition, the rapid and complex developmental changes during this period pose further diagnostic challenges. Despite these factors, Drell and his colleagues (Drell, Siegel, & Gaensbauer, 1993) have postulated various symptoms that infants may manifest after being exposed to a traumatic event; some are similar to those found in older age groups. The postulated symptoms include hypervigilance, exaggerated startle responses, developmental regressions, clinging behavior, body dysregulation, and nightmares; this constellation may be colored further by the primary caretaker's response. A severely injured mother, for example, may be too impaired immediately after the assault to respond to the acute needs of the infant witness. Growth and developmental progress may be compromised by prolonged and severe symptoms.

## Young Children

Traumatized children 3-5 years of age who present with avoidant symptoms such as withdrawal may become unable to embark on the road to increased independence from parents and development of social skills. The attachment to their parents may become intensified. Related memories to psychic trauma after the age of 3 probably are made possible by a burst in left-brain development at around age 3 (Thatcher, Walker, & Giudice, 1987).

## School-Age Children

Young school-age children who are already toilet trained and have developmentally appropriate language skills may suffer developmental regressions and thus revert to their former patterns of bowel and bladder habits and communication. This behavior, in turn, may result in the ostracism of the child by classmates, thereby compromising his or her social development.

The reexperience phenomenon in young children may manifest itself as repetitive play (APA, 1994) in which youngsters repeatedly engage in dangerous behaviors related to the original trauma. If the original event involved an assault on her mother, the young girl who subsequently engages in this behavior with a classmate may injure herself or her classmate. Such recurrent problematic behavior may result in her rejection by her peers, which may have aversive implications for her social development.

The autonomic hyperarousal states of hypervigilance and impaired concentration may compromise the learning ability of most school-age and high school students. Marginal students who become traumatized may become at risk of school failure.

Although young traumatized children do not consolidate memories with the clarity found in older children, their experiences do tend to color their perceptions of their world, and the children may display fears, as well as a sense of a foreshortened future. Figure 3.1 is an example of this latter phenomenon: A traumatized 8-year-old girl projects her fear onto the girl in her drawing. This child emigrated from a war-torn country where she repeatedly was exposed to discrete acts of violence; she developed PTSD prior to her emigration. She then reunited with her parents in the United States; her parents frequently engaged in physical altercations. Her PTSD symptoms were exacerbated after being exposed to severe episodes of violence in her home. In response to the direction to draw anything she could tell a story about, she drew a young girl with tears streaming down her face. She commented that the girl "is crying because she knows she will die soon." Shortly thereafter she admitted that she believed she, too, would die soon.

Some school-age children spend considerable time in the retelling of the traumatic incident; some do so by dissecting the event into minute details. This incessant behavior may temporarily protect the child from overwhelming feelings of anxiety and fear. An obsessional defense is indicated by some of the children's preference for an unemotional, journalistic account of the violence offered in the interview. The reverse, however, is also possible. This is the case when the young traumatized witness remains in a continuous state of anxious arousal, as though he or she is perpetually anticipating imminent danger. This typical state of hyperalertness or hypervigilance serves to replace the child's real traumatic memories with self-initiated fantasies of some future imaginary threat. Such a case is illustrated in Figure 3.2. This third-grade Korean girl, who was an honor student, reported several symptoms of psychic trauma, including hypervigilance and nightmares, in addition to a deterioration in her school performance. The onset of these symptoms began within a few days after fires destroyed her neighborhood during an episode of civil unrest in Los Angeles. Her hypervigilance was related to her continual fear that she would be killed by a rioter. On the right in her drawing she depicts herself asleep; in the "dream bubble" on the left she is seen next to her assailant.

The assault of one family member by another may also affect moral development. If the assailant escapes "unpunished" by the judicial system, for example, the young child may conclude that, despite having been taught that it is wrong to hurt someone, it is not always wrong and that indeed in some instances aversive consequences are nonexistent.

During adolescence, psychic trauma tends to assume the adult form of post-traumatic stress disorder (Eth, 1989). Subsequent to the early phase following trauma, many adolescents engage in a variety of antisocial behaviors,

**Figure 3.1.**

including truancy, sexual acting out, substance abuse, and other delinquent acts. Some exhibit reenactment behavior that, at times, can be life-threatening through the use of automobiles, weapons, and ingestion of dangerous substances. Such behaviors have aversive implications for peer relations, personal safety, academic performance, and future employment.

## EMERGENCY EVALUATION

Pynoos and Eth (1986) devised a focused therapeutic interview protocol that originally was developed for use with youngsters who had witnessed a parental homicide (Pynoos & Eth, 1984). This protocol generally should be conducted within 1 week of the potentially traumatic event. It has been employed effectively primarily in clinical situations during the aftermath of numerous life-threatening events that youngsters have witnessed or in which they have been directly victimized. Such events include witnessed assaults in the community, a witnessed death of a relative or friend, and community disasters.

This interview protocol can serve several purposes. It can be used as a single therapeutic trauma-focused session as it was originally designed; this would be similar to crisis intervention. Typical settings for this intervention

**Figure 3.2.**

include emergency rooms, temporary shelters/placement of children, schools, and other agencies that serve children when an out-of-home placement is made. It can be used also as the initial session of psychotherapy that typically would be provided in outpatient, therapeutic group, or residential settings. This intervention is designed to provide the child who has witnessed trauma with the first opportunity to discuss the early emotional impact of the incident. Although the child already may have discussed the event (e.g., of intrafamily violence) with other adults, including law enforcement officers and relatives, this intervention would provide an opportunity for discussion with an unbiased adult who is trained in child development and who is a mental health professional. This technique also has been used effectively by the authors in a consultation format for a child who already is undergoing some other type of mental health intervention. In cases in which children have been both witness and victim, this technique has been used in pediatric hospital settings.

This semistructured, three-stage interview technique facilitates a spontaneous and complete exploration of the child's subjective experience. This subjective experience is a multifaceted perception that may be influenced by many sources, including the child's cognitive developmental level, prior trauma, coping skills, and general premorbid state. In the case of an assault on a child's mother, the mother's response and the severity of injury may also be influential. Ideally the session should take place shortly after the event. It can be administered readily in approximately 2 hours. Additional time must be allotted, however, for the gathering of information from the referral source and the family about the circumstances of the event and the child's emotional and behavioral responses. Such information will point to significant references or omissions in the child's account. It is not uncommon for children to distort duration of time, sequence of events, and other aspects of a traumatic circumstance. A more detailed discussion of this pertinent information is described in a subsequent section.

The components of the three-stage protocol are the opening, trauma, and closure phases. The necessary preparation, each of the three phases, the family interview component, and some cultural considerations are discussed in detail below.

**Interview Preparation**

Efforts to support the child emotionally are introduced at the time of the initial greeting by the clinician. The youngster generally is accompanied by a responsible adult unless he or she is an older adolescent. The youngster's level of trauma-related anxiety may become evident at this time of the first face-to-face contact. The invitation to accompany the clinician to the office usually is accepted by the child if the child has been prepared adequately by a parent or referral source prior to the interview. If this preparation has not taken place, however, it is strongly recommended that the goals of the visit be discussed with the child and the responsible adult. If, for example, this discussion already has taken place during a telephone conversation with an adult, then only the child would need to be informed. If the child appears to be particularly distressed and reticent at the time of introduction of the clinician, a brief explanation in the presence of a supportive adult of the goal of the visit may be stated in a reassuring manner to the anxious child.

It is advisable to offer the child the option to accompany the clinician alone to the interview room in a way that creates an atmosphere in which the child feels safe and in control of the situation. The traumatized child already has endured an event in which he or she was overwhelmed emotionally and rendered utterly helpless. Giving this "option" to the child will promote and support the child's sense of mastery. For example, a 5-year-old accompanied by an aunt might be asked, "Can we go to talk and draw in my office while your aunt waits for us here?"

On a rare occasion a very young child may vehemently protest entering a room alone with the clinician despite reassurances and promised rewards from the caretaker who is responsible for bringing the child to the session.

This reaction may be explained by severe separation anxiety in the case of a child who, for example, developed this clinical picture after having recently witnessed the severe beating(s) of his mother. In that case a person (other than the mother) who is viewed by the child as supportive can be invited to be present during the interview to serve as a quiet source of support. It is essential that this person remain as unintrusive as possible. On occasion the passive bystander may benefit from observation of an adult model effectively providing support to the traumatized child. However, there are also disadvantages. One is that the child may be inhibited by the person's presence in the interview because of perceived aversive potential ramifications. This reticence may become evident in the child's initial level of anxiety. If the child does not respond to initial attempts at reassurance (e.g., by exhibiting a lower level of anxiety), then the child should not be coerced into participating in the interview. The present caretaking adult may provide additional pertinent information regarding the child's anxiety. Another option is first to engage the child in a less structured play or to provide a snack until the child is apparently more relaxed.

On a few occasions we have been requested by legal authorities to videotape a session with the child witness that can be used in the subsequent trial of an assailant. It is not recommended, for various reasons, that this request be honored routinely. The most important reason is that this interview technique is designed primarily to provide a safe and therapeutic context for the child, who in most cases already has endured extreme emotional turmoil. The goals of this interview technique and that of an interview by an investigating party for legal purposes are often at odds with one another. The latter interview rarely provides any psychological help to a child, for it is intended to secure evidence for the arrest and trial of a criminal defendant.

The following step-by-step narration of the core of this interview technique is not meant to suggest a rigid structure; rather, the format is intended to allow for a natural flow of material, following the child's lead as closely as possible. What is most important in the session is that the child be encouraged to directly confront the violence and be secure in the knowledge that it can be done successfully. It may be an error for the therapist to collude with the child's resistance to explore the traumatic source of anxiety.

## Opening Phase

The first or opening stage of the interview commences with the entry into the office. It usually is reassuring to the youngster if the therapist comments that he or she has worked with other children in similar situations, if indeed this is the case. A genuinely expressed interest by the therapist in helping the child feel better can also be reassuring. At this juncture the clinician should mention that he or she has been informed by others about some of the details of the traumatic event. By so doing, the focus of the interview is established, and the child is informed that he or she will not be alone in contending with the painful memories of the violence. The child immediately is given art materials. Markers are the clear favorite of most children, but crayons and other writing utensils are also useful. Nearly any kind of unlined blank paper can be used.

Some toddlers may be more forthcoming in their descriptions of the traumatic events if a medium other than drawing utensils is used. They may have poorly developed fine motor skills or simply appear to be more comfortable with clay or some other very malleable play substance. This preference can be discerned during a prior family meeting.

The directions provided to the child as he or she prepares to embark on the drawing or clay activity is two-pronged. The first is that the child may draw or make anything at all that he or she wishes, regardless of how good an artist the child may be. The second is that the child is to relate a story about the picture or clay figurine or provide an explanation of the drawing or clay figurine. This free-drawing task or clay activity serves to initiate the active process of therapy by countering the passive, helpless stance of the traumatized victim and by producing useful clinical material for the session.

It often surprises some child therapists when adolescents willingly engage in a drawing activity. Although many adolescents will indeed be able to describe the circumstances of the events with minimal prodding, many are reluctant to accurately verbalize their thoughts. Their feelings about the event may be more readily accessible for discussion once they have been engaged in a drawing task. This seems to be particularly true when rapport has not been established, as is often the case during the first interview with teenagers.

**Trauma Phase**

The intrusive nature of the violent incident or its association usually is reflected somewhere in the drawing or clay figurines or in the story or explanation of the drawing or clay figurines. The second stage of the interview commences when the therapist identifies this traumatic reference and links it to the child's own art product. For example, if the drawing contained the figure of a law enforcement agent, the therapist could indicate, "It would have been so much better if the police had been there to protect your mother from being injured." This comment may trigger a powerful emotional response in the child. The therapist then would seek to comfort and reassure the traumatized child that he or she (the child) will not be overwhelmed with emotion. The latter therapeutic effort is achieved through a comfortable and safe atmosphere, as well as a sense of compassion and genuine interest on the part of the clinician. A therapist may have to proceed very slowly and gently with the child at this point and may have to physically comfort the child with a hand on the shoulder or an arm around the back of the child.

After the child has regained composure, the therapist can suggest, "Now is a good time to tell me everything that happened." This direction promotes a thorough recounting of the entire episode of violence, which is critical to achieving psychosocial mastery. A thorough reconsideration of the elements of a traumatic event by the traumatized child of the elements of a traumatic event can help reframe the event into a more adaptive perspective in which it is less anxiety provoking to the traumatized person. The child may respond with a verbal description of the traumatic incident or reenact the events in play or in art. The role of the therapist in the second stage of the interview is to facilitate a full description of the violence, its antecedents and its aftermath. It is beneficial to carefully question the child in order to explore the entire series of events surrounding the trauma and its manifold consequences. This work may be exhausting for both parties, and the child may be offered brief rest periods or even snacks to feel adequately nurtured during the emotional challenge of the session.

During the child's description of the violence, attention is refocused on the central action that embodies the continued intrusive imagery and traumatic reminders. The therapist may inquire about what the child considers the worst moment of the violence. Often surprising details are revealed that may portend identifications with the victim or the aggressor. For example, one teenager was horrified when she noticed that her mother was wearing the adolescent's own dress at the time her mother was shot to death by her father. The child's sensory experiences during and after the violence should be addressed. This may be elicited by such questions as, "How did you feel at the time?" or "Which parts of your body were hurting at that time (headache, chest pain, etc.)?" School-age children commonly complain of bodily aches and pains in the aftermath of violence, perhaps as physical concomitants of the recurrent memories of the violence. Although an increase in anxiety may accompany this material, afterward the child is emboldened in his or her resolve to confront these painful memories. This fortitude may be due, in part, to the process of desensitization in the act of retelling and to the atmosphere of safety and compassion in the therapeutic endeavor.

The child should be encouraged to verbalize any feelings of fear of harm by the perpetrator and to express any wishes for revenge. It is very common for children to have thoughts and feelings of revenge. A useful way for the therapist to elicit these feelings is through a statement such as "I bet it would feel good to hit (or kill) the bad man now even though it was impossible to have stopped him then." In the case of intrafamily violence, however, the child witness may be strongly conflicted by his or her seemingly contradictory feelings of hate and love. The challenge to the clinician in this latter circumstance is to acknowledge both contradictory positions by the child. The young teenager with a more developed cognitive skill level may be more capable of coping with this task than the younger child. If the assailant has not been captured, then the child's apprehension as a threatened eyewitness may be appropriate, and consultation with the police is advisable. The issues of violence and revenge implicitly call into question the child's own ability to control aggressive impulses. It could be important to ask the child what he or she does when angry and whether that has changed since the violent event. These data regarding coping style should be compared with information gathered from family members prior to the interview.

Some children may be preoccupied with feelings of self-reproach for not having acted successfully to prevent the violence, when in fact nothing more could have been done. The therapist can assist the child in restoring a more realistic sense of self-efficacy, thereby diminishing feelings of guilt. In situations of domestic violence, the child will struggle painfully with issues of responsibility and loyalty. As a witness to a potential crime, a child will be faced with the responsibility of making statements to law enforcement officers or later in court that he or she believes may have serious aversive implications for the parent(s) and family that directly conflicts with his or her conviction of "blind" loyalty to the particular parent and family. Furthermore, the sophisticated teenager, for example, may know that the therapist could be subpoenaed as a witness, or the young child already may have been advised by another family member not to comment on the event; this information would serve to discourage the youngster from engaging in this technique.

**Closure Phase**

The final or closure stage of the interview centers on the sensitive, crucial process of terminating the interview and separating from the child. It is helpful, in preparation for the session's end, to review and summarize the preceding discussion. By emphasizing how understandable, realistic, and universal their responses have been, children come to feel less stigmatized and isolated and are more willing to accept support from others. It may be convenient to return to the child's drawing or story in order to underscore a point or to articulate the continuity of the session. It may help some children to know what may be expected as they progress through the course of a post-traumatic syndrome. For instance, a child who has witnessed his or her mother injured by a gunshot may be reassured, "Although loud noises make you jittery each time you hear one, you will probably notice that this will begin to decrease over time."

Contrary to some psychotherapeutic practices, it may be valuable to compliment children on their bravery during the violence and their courage in sharing their thoughts and feelings in the session. On hearing these kind and truthful words, the child usually reacts in a proud manner. Children should be informed whether they will be seen again. However, even if the interview is a one-time consultation, it is advisable to hand the child a business card or telephone number and to provide assurance that the therapist can be reached if necessary. Children rarely call, but they do treasure the knowledge of the therapist's availability and concern.

On many occasions children will require a referral for further mental health intervention on the basis of the findings of this interview technique. Indications for referral include a general poor level of functioning, especially in the social, cognitive, and emotional areas, given the child's premorbid level of functioning and the child's developmental progress. Other factors include suicidal ideation or gesture, especially among adolescent male witnesses of marital violence (Carlson, 1990), and homicidal ideation. It is not uncommon, for example, for adolescents to want to seek revenge with the assaultive parent. Symptoms of various mental disorders related to stress, especially of PTSD, also are appropriate indications. Special circumstances related to intrafamily violence, such as out-of-home placement for a child or restraining orders regarding a parent, may also warrant further follow-up.

### Family Interview

Although it is desirable to obtain other background information from the family or parents in order to conduct the usual comprehensive interview of the child and the family (Steinhauer, 1990) in a clinical setting, it is not critical to do so in preparation for this trauma-focused technique. Potentially important information for the purpose of using this technique includes (a) circumstances prior to the event, (b) the observed reaction of the child, (c) the extent of injury to all parties, (d) initial medical treatment, (e) efforts made by the child to intervene or to avoid personal danger, (f) information shared with the child witness after the event, (g) the location of the assailant, (h) the relationships between the child and the victim and between the child and the assailant, and (i) proposed or new household living arrangements.

The younger and more dependent the child is on the parent, the greater the likelihood that the child will be influenced strongly by the mother's reaction.

Several factors may significantly affect a parental report in the case of intrafamily violence. A mother, for example, may be too traumatized or injured to give this information; another knowledgeable informant, such as a relative or even a law enforcement officer, may have to be summoned. Potential parental criminal and out-of-home placement ramifications also may introduce a bias. Furthermore, disparities among reported symptoms related to trauma by children and their parents are common (Nader & Pynoos, 1992). Parents will emphasize externalizing or outward behaviors, while children will also report internalizing or problematic thoughts and fears.

Information that will have treatment referral implications for the family are parental psychopathology, parental substance abuse patterns, and the degree and duration of marital discord.

## Cultural Considerations

Another special circumstance related to intrafamily violence involves cultural and linguistic issues. Customs and values in a non-European-based culture may not readily condone the mental health intervention practices of Western societies. In some Eastern cultures, such as in China, the disclosure of one's feelings and family problems (e.g., wife battering) is strongly discouraged. This practice is related to "the powerful sense of family shame and obligation" (Huang & Ying, 1990, p. 51). Therefore, in culturally traditional (non-Western) families this technique may not be readily applicable. It would be prudent to inquire among members of that particular community about their customs regarding procuring help for traumatized children, as well as information regarding common reactions of stress found among its members. In addition, Western-based information regarding psychic trauma should be shared with these community members. In a similar vein the issue of linguistic diversity is also an important factor in the assessment of children. It is optimal if the interviewer understands both the language and the culture of the child and the family (Malgady, Rogler, & Costantino, 1987; Olmedo, 1981).

## CONCLUSION

Exposure to violence continues to exert a heavy toll on children and adolescents. Family or domestic violence is a major source of this exposure. This psychological toll is manifested in myriad ways, both in the short term and the long term. Many of these youngsters aimlessly grapple alone with the related overpowering thoughts and feelings. The three-stage trauma-focused interview technique described in this chapter is an effective way of providing assistance to psychologically traumatized children in the early aftermath of a life-threatening event. A future challenge in trauma research is in the area of outcome studies as they relate to this and other methods of psychological intervention.

## REFERENCES

American Psychiatric Association (APA). (1987). *Diagnostic and statistical manual of mental disorders* (3rd ed. rev.). Washington, DC: Author.

Arroyo, W., & Eth, S. (1985). Children traumatized in Central American warfare. In S. Eth & R. S. Pynoos (Eds.), *Post-traumatic stress disorder in children* (pp. 103-120). Washington, DC: American Psychiatric Press.

Carlson, B. E. (1990). Adolescent observers of marital violence. *Journal of Family Violence, 5,* 285-299.

Drell, M. J., Siegel, C. H., & Gaensbauer, T. J. (1993). In C. H. Zeanah, Jr. (Ed.), *Handbook of infant mental health* (pp. 291-304). New York: Guilford.

Eth, S. (1989). The adolescent witness to homicide. In E. P. Benedek & D. G. Cornell (Eds.), *Juvenile homicide* (pp. 87-113). Washington, DC: American Psychiatric Press.

Eth, S., & Pynoos, R. S. (1985a). Developmental perspective on psychic trauma in childhood. In C. R. Figley (Ed.), *Trauma and its wake* (pp. 36-52). New York: Brunner/Mazel.

Eth, S., & Pynoos, R. S. (1985b). *Post-traumatic stress disorders in children.* Washington, DC: American Psychiatric Press.

Federal Bureau of Investigation (FBI). (1991). *Reports for the U.S.* Washington, DC: U.S. Department of Justice.

Freud, S. (1926). Inhibitions, symptoms, and anxiety. In S. J. London (Ed.), *The standard edition of the complete psychological works of Sigmund Freud* (Vol. 20, pp. 87-156). New York: Hogarth.

Gelles, R. J., & Cornell, C. P. (1985). *Intimate violence in families.* Beverly Hills, CA: Sage.

Hoffer, T.A.N., & Cervantes, R. C. (1992). Psychological effects of exposure to gang violence. In R. C. Cervantes (Ed.), *Substance abuse and gang violence* (pp. 121-135). Newbury Park, CA: Sage.

Huang, L. H., & Ying, Y. (1990). Chinese American children and adolescents. In J. T. Gibbs, L. N. Huang, & Associates (Eds.), *Children of color: Psychological interventions with minority youth* (pp. 30-66). San Francisco: Jossey-Bass.

Kalmuss, D. (1984). The intergenerational transmission of marital aggression. *Journal of Marriage and the Family, 46,* 11-19.

Lewis, D. O., Shanok, S. S., Grant, M., & Ritvo, E. (1983). Homicidally aggressive young children: Neuropsychiatric and experiential correlates. *American Journal of Psychiatry, 140,* 148-153.

Malgady, R. G., Rogler, L. J., & Costantino, G. (1987). Ethnocultural and linguistic bias in mental health evaluation of Hispanics. *American Psychologist, 42,* 228-234.

Mason, J. O. (1992). The dimensions of an epidemic of violence. *Public Health Reports, 108,* 1-3.

Nader, K., & Pynoos, R. S. (1992, May). *Parental report of children's responses to life threat.* Paper presented at the American Psychiatric Association meeting, Washington, DC.

Olmedo, E. L. (1981). Testing linguistic minorities. *American Psychologist, 36,* 1078-1085.

Osofsky, J. D., Wewers, S., Hann, D. M., & Fick, A. C. (1993). Chronic community violence: What is happening to our children? *Psychiatry, 56,* 36-45.

Pynoos, R. S. (1993). Traumatic stress and developmental psychopathology in children and adolescents. In J. M Oldham, M. B. Riba, & A. T. Tasman (Eds.), *Review of psychiatry* (Vol. 12, pp.205-238). Washington, DC: American Psychiatric Press.

Pynoos, R. S., & Eth, S. (1984). The child as witness to homicide. *Journal of Social Issues, 40,* 269-290.

Pynoos, R. S., & Eth, S. (1986). Witness to violence: The child interview. *Journal of the American Academy of Child and Adolescent Psychiatry, 25,* 306-319.

Russell, D. (1982). *Rape in marriage.* New York: Macmillan.

Steinhauer, P. D. (1990). Families and family therapy. In B. D. Garfinkel, G. A. Carlson, & E. B. Weller (Eds.), *Psychiatric disorders in children and adolescents* (pp. 537-554). Philadelphia, PA: Saunders.

Straus, M. A. (1986). Medical care costs of intrafamily assault and homicide. *Bulletin of the New York Academy of Medicine, 62,* 556-561.

Straus, M. A., & Gelles, R. J. (1986). Societal change and change in family violence from 1975 to 1985 as revealed by two national surveys. *Journal of Marriage and the Family, 48,* 465-479.

Terr, L. (1988). What happens to the early memories of trauma? A study of twenty children under age five at the time of documented traumatic events. *Journal of the American Academy of Child and Adolescent Psychiatry, 27,* 96-104.

Terr, L. (1991). Childhood traumas: An outline and overview. *American Journal of Psychiatry, 148,* 10-19.

Thatcher, R., Walker, R., & Giudice, S. (1987). Human cerebral hemispheres develop at different rates and ages. *Science, 236,* 1110-1113.

Williams, C. L., & Westermeyer, J. (1983). Psychiatric problems among adolescent Southeast Asian refugees: A descriptive study. *Journal of Nervous and Mental Disease, 171,* 79-85.

# 4

# Individual Psychotherapy for the Traumatized Children of Abused Women

LOUISE SILVERN
JANE KARYL
TOBY Y. LANDIS

Many children of abused women are traumatized by the violence they witness. In this chapter we describe individual psychotherapy that is specific to alleviating their post-traumatic psychopathology.

All theoretical models of post-traumatic stress disorder (PTSD) suggest that when children are traumatized by exposure to violence, they require an opportunity to explicitly disclose that violence in detail and to integrate it into an understanding of themselves and their world. Diverse models of PTSD provide complementary strategies for alleviating distress that follows trauma and for interrupting maladaptive defenses against that distress, so similar strategies are applicable, regardless of therapists' theoretical position. Treatment should vary, however, with individual differences among children in the complexity of their needs. We describe a hierarchy of increasingly specialized interventions to address increasingly complex needs.

Although this chapter focuses on trauma-specific therapy, witnessing abuse against their mothers places children at risk for many internalizing and externalizing problems, not only for post-traumatic symptoms (e.g., Cappell & Heiner, 1990; Carlson, 1990; Davis & Carlson, 1987; Jaffe, Wolfe, & Wilson, 1990; Jaffe, Wolfe, Wilson, & Zak, 1986). When children have multiple problems, treatment ideally should integrate other approaches with trauma-specific strategies.

That ideal, however, is far from the current state of the field. The literature about treatment is sparse, and it focuses on family (Hurley & Jaffe, 1990) or group counseling (Alessi & Hearn, 1984; Jaffe, Wilson, & Wolfe, 1988; Ragg, 1991). Almost nothing has been written about processes, such as trauma, that are best addressed through individual therapy (but see Silvern & Kaersvang, 1989). Thus this chapter addresses a gap in the literature, in the spirit of a tentative proposal that should be tested and integrated with other modalities.

## WITNESSING ABUSE
## AS A TRAUMATIC STRESSOR

Recently it has been noted that many battered women suffer from PTSD (Dutton, 1992; Herman, 1992; Kemp, Rawlings, & Green, 1991; Walker, 1991), but there has been little recognition that their children are also at great risk of traumatization. The essential element of traumatic stress is that victims are overwhelmed cognitively, affectively, and behaviorally; that is, sensations cannot be cognitively organized, "terror and helplessness" (American Psychiatric Association [APA], 1987, p. 247) cannot be modulated, and resources for coping behaviorally are inadequate.

Psychological trauma often results from witnessing threats or violence against others (APA, 1987; Figley, 1985), especially if the danger is due to human action (APA, 1987) by a familiar person and if violence occurs in situations the victims had expected to be safe (e.g., their homes). Such conditions profoundly violate expectations about the safety and goodness of the world (Foa, Steketee, & Rothbaum, 1989; Janoff-Bulman, 1985). Finally dissociative defenses characterize children more than adults, and these defenses render them more vulnerable to PTSD (Putnam, 1993). In summary, witnessing abuse of the mother by another caretaker is similar to known traumatic stressors and horribly well-suited to traumatize children (Silvern & Kaersvang, 1989).

In fact, evidence suggests substantial post-traumatic symptomatology among children who witnessed the murder or rape of their mothers (Malmquist, 1986; Pynoos & Eth, 1984, 1986; Pynoos & Nader, 1988). A similar finding emerged regarding less severe violence. In a small study of 20 children (ages 7 to 13 years) at battered women's shelters, half manifested "severe" PTSD on Frederick's (1988) Reaction Index (Landis, 1989; Silvern, Landis, & Karyl, 1990).

Results of a retrospective study of 270 university women suggest that relationships between childhood exposure to abuse against their mothers and trauma symptoms might extend into adult life. Reports of parental spouse abuse were associated with high levels of current, adult post-traumatic symptoms and with high depression and low self-esteem (Silvern et al., in press). Parental spouse abuse remained significantly associated with poor adult adjustment even after the effects of child abuse were statistically eliminated.

*Case Illustration:*

*Presenting Problem and History.* As an illustration of a child who indeed developed post-traumatic symptoms after witnessing abuse against his mother, in this section we present an initial description of "Josh," with a focus on his presenting problems and history. Later in this chapter, we repeatedly return to Josh for examples of post-traumatic symptoms and therapeutic process.[1]

Until age 6, Josh lived alone with his single mother, "Monica." Josh did well, according to Monica, and at the end of the first grade (age 7), the teacher described Josh as "friendly, outgoing, curious, and attentive."

That summer, Monica married "Gary." Within months, Gary began to abuse her physically and verbally. Both Josh and Monica reported that the boy and Gary had little relationship. Close to Josh's eighth birthday, after a brutal assault on her, Monica took Josh outside and ran with him across the parking lot and into the car. According to Monica, Gary chased them into the parking lot, and she swerved the car toward him "to scare him" as she drove off. She yelled that he would never see her or Josh again. Gary made threatening gestures and screamed: He would "search anywhere for them"; they would have "no place to hide." Monica and Josh stayed at a shelter for a few weeks. After it was confirmed that Gary had left the state, Monica filed for divorce and returned home.

Three months later, Monica sought psychotherapy for Josh. He had been suspended briefly from school because during the preceding weeks, on a few occasions, he had set fire on the playground to what the teacher described as a wad of paper and wires. Monica had noticed other problems immediately upon returning from the shelter. The first time Josh saw the parking lot, he threw a terrified "fit," and his mother almost had to carry him to the apartment, which he then refused to leave. She insisted that he go to school, but Josh quit his extracurricular activities. He "panicked" if his mother suggested leaving the house together, even for activities that Josh previously had enjoyed. Josh resisted going to bed, his appetite was poor, and he was "jumpy."

The teacher reported that Josh seemed disinterested and sullen, frequently daydreaming. Moreover, he claimed to be too "dumb" to do the classwork, and he gave up easily.

During an individual evaluation interview, Josh initially was quiet and hesitant. He did not play spontaneously. When he was asked directly, however, Josh answered that he tried not to think about the day Gary and his mom split up. Josh described nightmares about being chased by "someone, maybe Gary." He said he could not concentrate in school because he was busy planning how to "get" Gary if he "ever tried anything." In response to further questions, Josh said he was not sure how he would get Gary, why the parking lot bothered him, why he did not eat much, or why he had started the fires. Josh became acutely anxious in response to these topics. He said that he thought it was "fair" that he had gotten into trouble for lighting the fires and that he wanted to quit. During the session, Josh was startled occasionally by incidental sounds.

Josh clearly had symptoms of post-traumatic psychopathology. The clinical criteria for PTSD are detailed in a later section. For now, it is worth noting that Josh had symptoms in each of three categories that are necessary for a *DSM-III-R* diagnosis of PTSD.[2] First, *hyperarousal* was found in Josh's difficulty sleeping, his hypervigilance and exaggerated startle reactions, and probably in his loss of appetite and difficulty concentrating. Second, *avoidance* was evident in Josh's efforts to avoid thoughts or physical cues related to the violence (e.g., the parking lot), his withdrawal from activities, and his affective constriction. Third, indications of intrusive *reexperiencing* included intense distress on reexposure to cues of the trauma, recurrent traumatic dreams, and preoccupation with the violence. Reexperiencing can include post-traumatic play, in which children (re)enact a symbolized aspect of the trauma without apparent awareness of a connection to the event itself. In a later section we consider whether Josh's fire setting represented post-traumatic play.

A theoretically eclectic approach to trauma-specific therapy was employed with Josh. We describe the rationale for this approach in the next section, and later we describe more specifics about therapeutic technique, with examples from Josh's treatment.

## AN ECLECTIC MODEL OF POST-TRAUMATIC SYMPTOMS

The proposed eclectic rationale for therapy rests on the common assumptions and complementary implications for treatment that can be found among diverse models of PTSD.[3] The most fundamental shared assumption is that distress persists after a traumatic event. All models further agree that this distress then induces the formation of symptoms.

Some symptoms appear to be direct expressions of distress. These include the *DSM-III-R* category of "hyperarousal" and those examples of reexperiencing that involve *feeling* extreme distress, as if the trauma were recurring. Other symptoms are best viewed as defenses against distress. These include both the *DSM-III-R* "avoidance" category and examples of reexperiencing, such as post-traumatic play in children or reliving in adults, in which behavior reminiscent of symbolized aspects of the trauma can occur without felt distress about the traumatic event itself (Rose, 1991). Given these two "types" of symptoms, all *therapy strategies are intended to ameliorate distress that persists after traumatic events and/or to interrupt defenses.*

## Persistent Distress After Traumatic Events

Affective and cognitive processes contribute together to distress (Foa et al., 1989). However, different models of PTSD emphasize one aspect over the other.

A learning theory model (Deblinger, McLeer, & Henry, 1990; Keane, Zimmerling, & Caddell, 1985; Kilpatrick, Veronen, & Best, 1985), which is derived from Mowrer's (1960) two-factor learning theory, emphasizes the importance of traumatic affect. In learning theory terms, a traumatic event such as witnessing wife abuse presents children with an *unconditioned aversive stimulus,* which evokes intensely painful emotions in the absence of prior learning. In addition to this unconditioned stimulus, traumatizing events include stimuli that are initially emotionally neutral. Through classical conditioning, these additional stimuli become associated with the unconditioned traumatic stimulus, so they come to function as *conditioned* (learned) aversive stimuli. Then painful emotions are evoked by stimuli that did not have this power before the trauma.

In the midst of trauma, many stimuli typically become conditioned. These conditioned aversive stimuli can include perceptual details associated with the trauma, such as sights, sounds, locations, or thoughts and feelings (Kilpatrick et al., 1985). For example, the parking lot apparently had become associated with the emotionally painful violence that Josh witnessed in that location. In their daily lives, victims are confronted regularly with many conditioned stimuli that can evoke distress. The distress that was initially a response to the trauma itself comes to intrude persistently on victims' experiences.

Psychodynamic models are similar to learning theory in emphasizing the affect associated with trauma to explain why distress persists. From this viewpoint, intense traumatic affect is aroused by the traumatic event, and later partial repetitions of that affect can be evoked by cues (often unconsciously) reminiscent of the trauma.

In either model, victims often cannot understand the connection of a trauma to their later distress. Moreover, learning theory's concepts of stimulus generalization and higher order conditioning (Foa et al., 1989) or psychodynamic concepts of symbolization (Terr, 1983) are employed to explain that traumatic affect (e.g., terror) can be elicited by cues that are quite dissimilar to the obvious or manifest content of the initial trauma. For instance, Josh avoided not only the parking lot but also after-school soccer, which he previously had enjoyed.

Other models attribute persistent distress to the disruption of cognition or information processing that is inherent in the overwhelming quality of trauma (Hartman & Burgess, 1993; Horowitz, 1986). Fragmented, unintegrated impressions of traumatic memories cannot be integrated into the usual schema of long-term memory or understanding, and they are, instead, encoded in "active memory," which continuously intrudes on awareness and on the processing of new information. Pynoos and Eth (1984, 1986) noted children's preoccupation with fragmented details of violence against their mothers that they had witnessed. The most preoccupying detail symbolized the "worst moment" in terms of its personal meaning.

Rather than the fragmented quality of trauma, some models attribute persistent distress more to the content of the cognitions or dilemmas that are induced by trauma. Janoff-Bulman (1985) argued that trauma remains intrusive until it is integrated into victims' disrupted sense of themselves as worthy persons in a trustworthy world. As another example, Foa and Kozak (1986; Foa et al., 1989) claimed that traumatic events disrupt assumptions about safety. Traumatic affect generalizes along lines dictated by victims' beliefs about the implications of the trauma for their safety. Josh apparently believed that the violence he had witnessed had pervasive implications for his safety.

Children's cognitions about their helplessness and "failure" to protect their mothers are a further source of distress, especially for adolescents (Pynoos & Eth, 1984). Learned helplessness has been proposed to explain trauma (Donovan & McIntyre, 1990; Peterson & Seligman, 1983; van der Kolk, Greenberg, Boyd, & Krystal, 1985), although it applies best to symptoms of avoidance, depression, and low self-esteem (Foa et al., 1989). Helplessness is learned by exposure to inescapable, aversive events. If victims attribute the events to pervasive, unchangeable causes (e.g., "I'm a coward"), they develop impaired motivation to cope with new stressors, damaged self-esteem, and depression (Boggiano, Barrett, Silvern, & Gallo, 1991), for instance, Josh's readiness to give up in school.

Compensatory or defensive reactions against helplessness are common. Post-traumatic play often conveys a brittle bravado (Terr, 1990). Similarly many child witnesses are preoccupied with "plans of action"—that is, fantasies about protective actions they "should" have taken in the past or should be prepared to take in the future (Pynoos & Eth, 1986). Josh's plan about ways to get Gary is an example of such a plan.

Just as models of PTSD highlight complementary processes that induce persistent distress after trauma, the models suggest ways to reverse the distress. Psychodynamic and learning models focus on alleviating the aversive emotional reactions elicited by cues associated with the trauma. The learning model calls for *extinction* of the classically conditioned link between the unconditioned trauma and other stimuli. To secure extinction, victims must be psychologically reexposed to the conditioned emotional stimuli in a safe, nontraumatic setting so that the link between these stimuli and the trauma is unlearned (Deblinger et al., 1990; Keane et al., 1985; Koss & Harvey, 1991; Lipovsky, 1992). Similarly, psychodynamic models call for a conscious review of the traumatic event in a calm setting so that traumatic anxiety can be ascribed accurately to its source in the past, rather than the present (Rose, 1986). Cognitive models suggest the need to integrate the fragmented traumatic impressions with one another into a coherent event that can enter into a tolerable, continuous sense of self (Dye & Roth, 1991; Horowitz, 1986).

## Defenses Against Trauma

Until distress is alleviated successfully, trauma victims can calm themselves only by forming and maintaining maladaptive defenses. For example, Josh's avoidance of his usual activities allowed him to stay calm. If his mother tried to interrupt this defense, however, he experienced a return of trauma-related fear. Although avoidance and post-traumatic play are frequent indications of defense, dissociation is the defining constituent of defenses against trauma, and dissociation during the occurrence of a stressor increases the risk that symptoms will develop (Marmar et al., 1994). *Dissociation* is a psychobiological process that can include analgesic responses, trance states, amnesias, flashbacks, and cognitive fragmentation (Putnam, 1993). Fragmented experience is initially inherent in the traumatic experience of being overwhelmed. Dissociation is later actively maintained as a mode of coping with the pain related to the personal meaning of the trauma (Putnam, 1993).

The two-factor learning model views defenses as the second step in the development of PTSD, in which victims learn to escape from the distressing conditioned stimuli that develop during the first step. Escape includes cognitive suppression, affective constriction, dissociation, and behavioral avoidance.[4] Successful escape from distress serves as an operant reinforcement, which further strengthens the learning of the defensive escape. Analogously, from a psychodynamic perspective, defenses protect against traumatic anxiety in response to reminders of the trauma. In terms of the cognitive models, defenses develop to protect against painful, repetitive preoccupation with fragmented, dissociated impressions of the trauma (Hartman & Burgess, 1993).

Defenses and distress join in a self-sustaining, vicious circle (Figley, 1985; Horowitz, 1986; Putnam, 1993; Silvern & Kaersvang, 1989; van der Kolk et al., 1985). As long as distress persists, defenses are strengthened. The defenses, in turn, interfere with reexposure to or cognitive review of the traumatic event, both of which ultimately are needed to alleviate distress. Meanwhile the defenses do not consistently protect against continuing distress because traumatic memories that remain unintegrated are inherently intrusive and disruptive (e.g., Horowitz, 1986). Moreover, defenses minimize children's motivation for therapy.

Conversely, a "therapeutic" circle is possible. Strategies that ameliorate distress should weaken defenses, and strategies that interrupt defenses should make traumatic memories accessible for intervention. All therapy strategies are intended, first, to alleviate distress by modulating affective responses to reminders of the event and/or by facilitating cognitive integration, and second, to interrupt defenses. The goal is to interrupt the vicious circle between defense and distress.

## STRATEGIES FOR
## TRAUMA-SPECIFIC PSYCHOTHERAPY

Before implementing any strategies to relieve the psychological consequences of witnessing parental spouse abuse, interventions must focus first on securing the physical safety of the mother and children. Beyond the inherent value of safety, therapy is futile otherwise. Ongoing trauma would fuel distress, and defenses against that distress would continue to be needed. Defenses cannot be breached if they are called on by current rather than past experience. Therapy can ameliorate the residue of traumatic memories, but it cannot substitute for ending traumatic events. Moreover, safety is also crucial for children whose problems reflect processes other than trauma and who require interventions other than the one outlined below. As examples, children who model batterers' aggression or who are insecurely attached to abused mothers cannot be helped while the models or the sources of danger dominate their lives.

Assuming that safety has been established, treatment for trauma will concern relieving distress and interrupting defenses. However, individual differences in the type and intensity of defenses and distress create differences in the complexity of the symptom picture and therapy process. In the absence of an accepted typology, we propose a "hierarchy" of intervention strategies. Each "step" in this hierarchy addresses both distress and defenses, while the steps are intended to begin with strategies that are most generic and inclusive and to move to those that are more specialized and needed only for traumatized children who present more complex treatment needs.

The first, most inclusive step is to assess *all* children of abused women to identify traumatic and other symptoms. If trauma-related symptoms are *not* evident, then, although other needs may be identified, the concern with specifically post-traumatic psychopathology is resolved. If post-traumatic symptoms are found, then further steps in the proposed treatment hierarchy become relevant. Moreover, during treatment it will be necessary to (re)assess whether particular symptoms are trauma related.

At the second step, all psychologically traumatized children of abused women require the opportunity to disclose the violence to which they have been exposed. A strategy for straightforward, detailed therapeutic communication, described as "straight talk," is suggested to facilitate disclosure. If disclosure is nevertheless incomplete, then straight talk remains necessary but in combination with further, more specialized steps.

At a third step, the symptoms of some additionally traumatized children can be resolved by desensitization and cognitive restructuring. These strategies are used in combination with ongoing reassessment and repeated attempts to elicit disclosure.

At the last step, it may prove necessary to introduce interpretation intended to clarify the meaning of fragmented, dissociated impressions of the violence that have been expressed symbolically through symptom formation. Interpretation is interwoven with the more generic strategies.

## Step 1: Targeting Post-Traumatic Symptoms

As the first step in trauma-specific psychotherapy, *all* children of abused women should be assessed to identify trauma-related symptoms and distinguish them from others. If trauma or associated dissociation is overlooked, children can be misdiagnosed and treated inadequately (Putnam, 1993). Yet post-traumatic pathology should not simply be assumed from the presence of a high-risk stressor. Trauma-specific therapy should be used when, but only when, called for by the nature of the child's symptoms.

As noted above, in addition to the presence of a severe stressor, *DSM-III-R* (APA, 1987) criteria for PTSD fall into three symptom categories: "avoidance or numbing," "reexperiencing," and "autonomic hyperarousal" (the *DSM-IV* will be similar). Josh had symptoms of each type, but multiple manifestations of each category can occur, and very different clinical pictures can be found among traumatized children.

Examples of *avoidance or numbing* include: (a) avoidance of people, places, and/or things that stimulate memories of the traumatic event; (b) unwillingness or difficulty talking about the event; (c) lapses of attention ("spacing out") and/or trying not to think; (d) no or limited memory of the event; (e) decreased interest in previous activities; (f) loss of recently developed skills (e.g., toilet training); (g) return of previously mastered childhood fears (e.g., fear of the dark); (h) withdrawal and unusual shyness; and (i) unremitting sadness or depression (see McNally, 1993).

Expressions of *reexperiencing* common in childhood include: (a) repetitive talking about the traumatic event; (b) preoccupying, intrusive recollections, thoughts, or images of the event, which children might experience as daydreams; (c) recurrent nightmares about the event; (d) flashbacks in which the victim suddenly feels as if the event were recurring; and (e) intense psychological distress or intensification of symptoms when exposed to places, people, and/or things that are symbolically reminiscent of the event (e.g., see Benedek, 1985; Kiser et al., 1988; McLeer, Deblinger, Atkins, Foa, & Ralphe, 1988; McNally, 1993). Post-traumatic play (Terr, 1981, 1983, 1990) and other repetitive, symbolic representations of the traumatic events, including drawing (Pynoos & Eth, 1986), are ways children repeat the fragmented impressions of trauma. Unlike ordinary symbolic play, post-traumatic play is compulsive and generally does not result in anxiety reduction.

Finally childhood symptoms of *autonomic hyperarousal* include: (a) difficulty falling asleep and staying asleep, night terrors, and somnambulism (Benedek, 1985); (b) irritability, argumentativeness, impulsivity, temper outbursts, and aggression (McLeer et al., 1988); (c) distractibility and decreased concentration; (d) hypervigilance and hyperalertness to signs of danger; (e) worry and nervousness; (f) exaggerated startle response and jumpiness; (g) somatic complaints such as headaches, nausea, stomachaches, and vision problems (Davidson & Baum, 1990); and (h) loss of appetite.

As suggested earlier, dissociation may explain many of the manifest symptoms, such as lapses in attention and flashbacks (Putnam, 1993). Therefore, indications of cognitive fragmentation, confusion, or derealization, especially regarding the violent events, may in themselves be indications of traumatization (Silvern et al., 1990).

Considerable variation is found among traumatized children in which of the many symptoms actually dominate the clinical picture. For instance, traumatic nightmares were reported by 100% of children who witnessed parental homicide and 80% who witnessed sexual assaults against their mothers, while much lower proportions of children exposed to natural disasters had such dreams (McNally, 1993). No data are available about the frequency of specific PTSD symptoms among children of abused mothers.

Children may differ from one another in specific symptoms and yet be diagnosed with PTSD because *DSM-III-R* (APA, 1987) criteria stipulate only that children must manifest at least one type of the reexperiencing symptoms, at least three avoidance/numbing symptoms, and at least two symptoms that reflect autonomic hyperarousal. This stipulation allows for substantial variation in clinical pictures among children who meet the criteria.

Moreover, partial PTSD is common in children (Blank, 1993). When trauma-related symptoms are important but the full *DSM-III-R* criteria for PTSD are not met, trauma-specific therapy still might be suggested. The goal would be to target post-traumatic *aspects* of a child's problems, not to classify children as if they fell into non-overlapping groups.

Although post-traumatic symptoms should be distinguished from others, there is inevitably room for debate. Josh's strange fire-setting behavior raised a typical problem. There was no manifest, obvious similarity between this behavior and the abuse that Josh witnessed. Should the behavior be interpreted as trauma related? Repetitive behavior that persists despite punishment and self-criticism *might* entail the symbolic reenactment of an aspect of a trauma (post-traumatic play), but a decision is based on interpretation. Even if the fire setting is viewed as post-traumatic play, the aspects of the trauma that are enacted would initially be obscure. Throughout treatment, therapists must reassess whether and in what way such problems are trauma related.

## Step 2: Facilitating Disclosure With "Straight Talk"

The second step on the treatment hierarchy is to provide an opportunity to disclose the violence. This step is proposed for all children identified (at Step 1) as having post-traumatic symptoms, and so it is the most inclusive strategy for those children of abused women who are identified as psychologically traumatized. All models of PTSD point to the value of disclosing a detailed account of the traumatic event, together with its personal and affective meaning (Frederick, 1985; Pynoos & Eth, 1986; Silvern & Kaersvang, 1989). The violence must be "put on the table" between the therapist and a traumatized child.

Disclosure can alleviate painful emotional reactions to reminders of a traumatic event. Disclosure includes talking and thinking about the trauma and the surrounding details in a calm setting, without the recurrence of danger. In learning theory terms, disclosure provides for cognitive reexposure to the distressing, conditioned, aversive stimuli, allowing extinction of the link between these stimuli and trauma. Although desensitization (described below) was developed to promote such extinction, prior disclosure is required to use that strategy, and many children dislike such formalized techniques. Thus, if possible, it is advisable to rely on informal verbal conversation.

For disclosure or any form of reexposure to be helpful, the conditioned stimuli must be presented without intense distress, which otherwise could backfire and reinforce, rather than extinguish, avoidant defenses (Dutton, 1992; Lipovsky, 1992). For example, because of his severe distress when he returned home and first saw the parking lot, Josh probably felt relieved when he "escaped," and this relief reinforced his determination to avoid the lot. Although exposure to the lot was presented in the absence of danger, Josh probably did not notice, and extinction did not occur in the midst of his fright. Similarly, if disclosure evokes a storm of traumatic distress, then children will only again learn that the thoughts and events associated with the trauma are unbearable. Relaxation techniques can be employed (see below) to modulate distress, but a comforting relationship with the therapist is more often suggested to soothe children (Lipovsky, 1992). Psychodynamic views similarly call for a supportive "holding environment" within the therapy relationship to contain the affect elicited by reviewing the trauma (Pynoos & Eth, 1986; Rose, 1991; Schwartz, 1984).

Given a soothing relationship, cognitive and psychodynamic models suggest that disclosure further reduces distress through cognitive integration. Disclosure can clarify the source of cues that trigger symptomatic distress and defense. Reviewing fragmented impressions of trauma allows them to be integrated into a coherent event that can be consciously mastered (e.g., Dye & Roth, 1991; Rose, 1986, 1991).

From all perspectives, disclosure should be complete and detailed, including even incidental impressions and associations. Extinction of classical conditioning requires presenting *all* stimuli initially associated with the trauma (Foa et al., 1989; Keane et al., 1985). Trauma is encoded initially in terms of fragmented, dissociated details (Hartman & Burgess, 1993; Horowitz, 1986; Putnam, 1993), and the details are expressed in the unconscious cues that can arouse anxiety and be reenacted in post-traumatic play (Silvern & Kaers-vang, 1989; Terr, 1981).

Disclosure also must include the *personal* meaning and affect associated with the trauma. It is personal meaning that leads certain details to be preoccupying (Pynoos & Eth, 1984) and to form the kernel of symptom formation (Foa et al., 1989). Without affect, disclosure is too removed from the meaning of traumatic experience to provide relief (Dutton, 1992).

Finally disclosures should include the ways in which the child is coming to understand the dilemmas induced by traumatic violence: the meaning of the violence for the child's sense of safety or danger (Foa & Kozak, 1986), helplessness, or mastery (Donovan & McIntyre, 1990), and for attributions of self-blame and guilt (Pynoos & Eth, 1986). These issues are interwoven in the disclosures of children of abused women. Landis (1989) administered a semistructured interview about the spousal violence the children had witnessed. A review of the transcripts suggested that 15 of the 20 children *spontaneously* expressed distress and humiliation associated with their help-lessness, accompanied by a damaged sense of self-worth and fear, for instance: "I just sat there shaking; I couldn't do anything"; "He's only about ten times bigger" (than I am); "I couldn't do anything, so I just stayed there" (as his mother was beaten); and "Any day he (the batterer) could kill me. . . . I just sat there 'cause I didn't want to get hurt." Several children expressed the wish to turn the tables by assaulting the batterer. Two children told incredible stories about their heroism, suggesting defense against unbearable powerlessness.

The preceding review about the characteristics of useful disclosures sug-gests guidelines for therapists' communication style, which we refer to as "straight talk." It is necessary to ask specific questions and to draw explicit conclusions about the traumatic event. Directness is necessary to provide cognitive structure, to interrupt avoidance about the details of the trauma, especially details that are most personally salient, and to explore and reframe beliefs about guilt, helplessness, and compensatory "plans of action." It is often useful to tell children that we "need a little straight talk," and they usually respond to the clear invitation, in contrast to adults' more usual "polite" inquiries about violence.

Therapists must balance the need to soothe children's distress *versus* the danger of colluding with defenses. A balance is needed also between asking specific questions *versus* permitting children to organize disclosures spon-taneously in terms that are most personally salient to them.

Symbolic expression, including fantasy play and drawings, can help maintain the balance. Pynoos and Eth (1986) and the authors of Chapter 3 in this volume recommend that interviews begin with drawing. They trust that intrusive thoughts about the trauma will appear in the art and provide a bridge to direct, verbal disclosure. We have not found this step necessary, although some children do disclose symbolically before tolerating straight talk (Silvern & Kaersvang, 1989). Symbolic expression alone, however, allows too much room to misunderstand and avoid painful details, so it is necessary to work toward a direct, verbal disclosure (Coppollilo, 1987; Pynoos & Eth, 1986).

Systematic observations from Landis's (1989) sample confirmed the importance of straight talk. Only one child acknowledged witnessing violence in response to open-ended questions similar to those often used in shelters, such as: "Do you know why your mom came to the shelter?" Virtually all children, however, acknowledged that their mothers were abused, and they disclosed far more detail when asked specific questions, such as: "Did your parents have a fight shortly before coming to the shelter?" "Where were you during the fight?" (Silvern et al., 1990).

At this point in the proposed treatment hierarchy, children's fear and their concerns about guilt, helplessness, and self-worth should be taken as conscious sources of distress. These concerns should be reframed and normalized, and direct comfort should be offered when needed. For example, if a child laments his or her failure to take action, the therapist might assert that staying out of the batterer's way was smart. Praise for doing a "good job" at the difficult task of talking about the violence can also counter helplessness (Pynoos & Eth, 1986). Interpreting defenses, however, is not useful as part of straight talk.

Straight talk may strike some therapists as overly directive. On the one hand, however, a good deal of detail can be elicited without engendering resentment or distress (Pynoos & Eth, 1986; Silvern et al., 1990). On the other hand, if therapists are too tentative, many children who have witnessed violence against their mothers, like those who have been abused themselves, will be isolated. Most children have learned that family violence is taboo, and without very explicit invitations they readily believe that adults do not really want to hear their story. Then the children's reticence can be misunderstood as ingrained resistance.

For some children, straight talk will effectively elicit coherent disclosures, and this will be sufficient to resolve post-traumatic symptoms. Such disclosure may occur during the first weeks of therapy or even more rapidly. Perhaps if this opportunity was provided soon after trauma, it could sometimes prevent chronic post-traumatic pathology.

Children whose symptoms are resolved with straight talk are relatively able to integrate a traumatizing experience, given an opportunity. They have an "undefended" quality once they begin to disclose. When asked, one child answered tearfully that during an assault on his mother, he thought she would "get hurt," and he explained by recounting a previous assault. He said, "I'm really feeling mad because my dad won't leave my mom alone." Further specialized strategies were not needed. In contrast, for Josh, straight talk was useful but not sufficient to resolve his symptoms.

*Case Illustration:*
*Facilitating Disclosure.* Josh's first evaluation session was a conjoint meeting with his mother. The excerpt presented here is from the first evaluation interview, an individual meeting held in a playroom a few days later. Josh was aware that the therapist had access to some information about the violence. A period of spontaneous exploration of the playroom preceded this excerpt. However, Josh had not become engaged in focused fantasy or other play.

| | |
|---|---|
| **Therapist** | Please tell me a little more about the day you and your mother went to the shelter. |
| **Child** | I told you. They fought. |
| **Therapist** | Yes, you did. Do you remember if it was a bad fight? |
| **Child** | They fought sometimes. All parents fight sometimes. No big deal. . . . Maybe . . . I don't know (trying to sound indifferent). |
| **Therapist** | Do you know what they fought about that day? |
| **Child** | He didn't want her to take the car. They were just fooling around . . . probably . . . (sounds very uncertain). |
| **Therapist** | You'd like it, if they were just fooling around, but you're not too sure? Was Mom upset? |
| **Child** | Probably. Well, she was, just wanted the car . . . (long pause). She almost drove over Gary's toes. |
| **Therapist** | She almost drove into him? When they were fooling around? |
| **Child** | No. He was just in the way . . . she . . . I wasn't looking. . . . She wanted the car to leave . . . to leave him. |
| **Therapist** | It must have been all very confusing. . . . Anyone would be confused. Did she (Mom) say anything? |
| **Child** | Yeah, she said she hated him and we won't ever be back. He was real mad, and maybe that's when he . . . I don't know what next . . . (sounds scared and confused). |
| **Therapist** | He was real mad, and that would scare anyone. What did you do? |
| **Child** | I plugged up my ears. They were yelling and all (sounds very pained). I just sat there with my hands on my ears. I couldn't do anything about him. The car was in his face. |

| | |
|---|---|
| **Therapist** | Nobody would want to hear the yelling. So you plugged up your ears. Where were you then? |
| **Child** | In the car. Mom was driving, and we almost ran into him. |
| **Therapist** | Did you wish you could do something besides listen? |
| **Child** | (Nods) I wish I could get him. . . . I just sat there. |
| **Therapist** | There wasn't anything you could do. No one could do anything but get away. It was smart for you to keep out of it, but I bet it was hard. Let me see if I've got this. They were yelling at each other about Mom and you going away in the car, and you didn't want to hear it, and Gary was real mad. The car was real close to him? |
| **Child** | (Nods) |
| **Therapist** | Gary was acting real scary. Did he hurt you or Mom too? |
| **Child** | He didn't really hurt her. He just hit her. He was always doing that (sounds bitter). |
| **Therapist** | Did he hit her in the car? Or before? |
| **Child** | Before, I think (sounds confused) . . . in the apartment. But he was really mad in the car. |
| **Therapist** | What did you think might happen? |
| **Child** | He might really hurt her this time. . . . He was talking (obscenity) about the car, and . . . (long pause). |
| **Therapist** | You thought this time she might really get hurt because he was so mad? And your mom said you and she were leaving forever. Did Gary say anything? |
| **Child** | I forget (very pained). |
| **Therapist** | You forget what he said when you left? |
| **Child** | Yeah, he makes up (obscenity). . . . We left in the car. Gary was real (furious) then. |
| **Therapist** | It's scary to think of how mad he was when you left in the car. |
| **Child** | He made faces. The car pulled right out, almost over him. |
| **Therapist** | Something about that bugs you, I think. Did he say something? |
| **Child** | I don't care. Do I have to talk about this anymore? |
| **Therapist** | Bad memories like these are hard and scary to talk about, and you have been brave. We don't need to talk about them more now, but other times we'll need to do some more straight talk about what you've been through. I want you to remember that it wasn't your fault that any of this happened; kids can't stop parents from being violent. Just one more question for now. Do you worry that Gary might come back or that he could find you or Mom? |

**Child**          Nope. He lives in X (another state) now.

The interplay of cognitive and affective processes in disclosure is evident in the above transcript. There was a slight increase in tolerance for the affect associated with the trauma. The child moved from feigned indifference to some acknowledgment of his affect. He provided little detail but was clearer about the existence of a violent event. He apparently was preoccupied with the detail that his mother had swerved near Gary. Its significance, however, was obscure. As he began to disclose, the therapist could begin to reframe Josh's helplessness.

During the next weeks, the therapist provided frequent reassurance about Josh's self-worth and attempted to challenge his sense of helplessness. Josh became less depressed and sullen, and his self-denigration in school lessened. He also reported fewer nightmares. However, Josh's avoidance of extracurricular activities remained stubbornly intact; his disclosures continued to be confusing and to deny the batterer's threats; and there were continued, sporadic episodes of fire setting.

## Step 3: Desensitization and Cognitive Restructuring

Despite a chance for straight talk, the disclosures of some children, like Josh, remain hesitant and incomplete. Other children who do not fully benefit from straight talk are more talkative, but their disclosures are fragmented and dissociated. In either case it is likely that the children cannot tolerate disclosure because of well-established defenses and/or severe distress associated with interrupting those defenses. Disclosure threatens to evoke distress associated with remembering and discussing the trauma, and avoidance and other defenses then can be engaged to cope with this distress.

In the vicious cycle described earlier, defenses obstruct the disclosure, so distress is maintained and the need to defend is strengthened. Failure to fully disclose because of the arousal of such emotional pain and defense entails genuine "resistance" to therapy, which should be contrasted with failures because of an absence of opportunities for straight talk and the children's beliefs that adults do not want to hear them.

If opportunities for straight talk do not allow disclosure, the proposed hierarchy of interventions suggests that more specialized strategies can ameliorate distress and interrupt defenses. Because both affective and cognitive processes contribute to distress following trauma, in this section we include both desensitization, which emphasizes ameliorating the affect, and cognitive restructuring.

*Desensitization.* In learning theory terms, straight talk might fail if the child rapidly and completely avoids psychological exposure to the conditioned cues of trauma so that extinction of the link between these cues and the trauma is not accomplished. Desensitization is an "exposure" strategy intended to interrupt defensive escape or avoidance and allow adequate exposure to the aversive conditioned stimuli in the absence of the traumatic danger (Deblinger et al., 1990; Lipovsky, 1992).[5] In desensitization, the child and the therapist construct, from the child's viewpoint, a hierarchy of the least to the most feared stimuli. These conditioned stimuli are presented sequentially, for instance, by imagining relevant scenarios. Relaxation or other techniques can be used to minimize distress so that avoidance is not elicited.

Desensitization is widely recommended for treating PTSD, but caution is necessary even for adults (Dutton, 1992; Koss & Harvey, 1991). The rationale must be fully explained, and clients should be treated as collaborators. Communicating the rationale to children, however, is more difficult than to adults. Moreover, we have noted that many traumatized children resist formalized "techniques," which they fear will render them helpless or passive (see Lipovsky, 1992).

Even formulating the hierarchy of fears requires cooperation and disclosure from the child. Children, however, are less likely than adults to be motivated to overcome avoidance. Many children appear unbothered by avoidant symptoms, in contrast to painful hyperarousal and reexperiencing of traumatic affect. For example, Josh claimed indifference about quitting his activities.

In the light of the obstacles to standard desensitization, adaptations can often be accomplished with individually tailored fantasy or game formats that circumvent the child's sense of threat and lack of motivation. Although relaxation usually is suggested to counteract anxiety during desensitization, playfulness has a similar function for children. Moreover, with traumatized children it is best to support skills for mastering anxiety, along with employing exposure strategies. Children are unlikely to tolerate a passive review of traumatic memories unless the therapist is clearly allied with their wish for active mastery.

*Case Illustration:*
*An Adaptation of Desensitization.* Adapting desensitization for children requires capitalizing on their spontaneous self-expressions in fantasy, play, art, and conversation. Although Josh previously had ignored the question, during the sixth session the therapist asked again why Josh had quit his

after-school activities. Josh responded by picking up the puppet of a ferocious wolf.

| | |
|---|---|
| **Therapist** | Do *you* miss going to soccer? (speaking to the wolf). |
| **Child** | I'm tough—I go where I want (speaking as the wolf). |
| **Therapist** | So you can go to soccer or anywhere you want? |
| **Child** | Yep! (as wolf). |
| **Therapist** | Do you like soccer? |
| **Child** | (Wolf kicks, as in soccer, with accompanying sounds, obviously expressing enthusiasm for the sport.) |

The therapist and the "wolf" agreed that soccer was fun if you are not scared. Then they made up a "game."[6] In each session the wolf would tell the therapist whether Josh missed out on a "fun" activity. They would try to figure out a plan for Josh to resume the activity without getting scared. The wolf began with soccer, saying that Josh had quit because he felt scared while walking back and forth from home, but not at the field. They decided that Josh would try walking with a friend. Without explaining, he planned a route that carefully avoided the parking lot. The wolf was provided with some rudimentary breathing techniques to "help Josh" relax if necessary. Josh resumed soccer with little undue anxiety.

During the next weeks, additional activities were addressed in the spirit of the "wolf game." Then the therapist took the initiative to address Josh's avoidance of the parking lot. Josh hesitantly developed a plan to retrieve his bike, which had long been parked there.

Thus desensitization was approximated by discussion of (psychological exposure to) progressively more frightening activities (stimuli) while a playful, supportive atmosphere inhibited anxiety and protected Josh from the need to acknowledge helplessness and shame. Meanwhile cognitive rehearsal and skills for coping with anxiety were introduced (breathing techniques, planning a route to soccer).

*Cognitive Restructuring.* If post-traumatic symptoms are not resolved by straight talk, models that emphasize the cognitive aspects of PTSD call for more sustained attempts to alter cognitions about the trauma. Cognitive restructuring goes further than straight talk to articulate implicit beliefs that aggravate distress following trauma and that, therefore, interfere with tolerating disclosure and integration (Carroll & Foy, 1992; Lipovsky, 1992). Such beliefs are to be challenged by new information. Cognitive restructuring generally concerns beliefs that have societal support—for example, beliefs that induce self-blame among rape victims.

Clinical impressions suggest that many children of abused women adopt cognitions that have implications for sex roles and their place in the children's futures (Ragg, 1991). For example, a 9-year-old girl said she did not want to marry "because she wanted to be a gymnast." She explained, "Gymnasts can't be getting hurt all the time." An 11-year-old boy asked whether he could avoid marrying; he would "never want to hurt anyone like that." These children believed that violence was inevitable if they adopted otherwise valuable adult gender roles.

As another example, many children believe that their abused mothers are inadequate because the women lost their partners' love or did not protect themselves and their children. Such beliefs often exist in conflict with a fierce loyalty toward their mothers.

As indicated above, other problematic cognitions concern learned helplessness and self-blame. Here the goal of cognitive restructuring is to challenge children's beliefs that they are incapable of controlling pervasive life outcomes because of their real inability to control the batterer. Traumatized children may be helped to overcome helplessness by experiencing autonomy in the therapy playroom (Donovan & McIntyre, 1990) or by actively disclosing (Pynoos & Eth, 1986). For children whose symptoms have not been resolved by straight talk, however, more specific assistance appears warranted. Josh's teacher agreed to put him in charge of his peers on a major project, and she made sure he received substantial recognition for his efforts, which, indeed, increased.

After children's maladaptive beliefs about sex roles, violence, or their own helplessness and responsibility are identified, they should be challenged with information about woman abuse. For example, (a) violence in relationships is frequent (you and your mother are not alone), but it is not universal (you can hope for more); and (b) abuse is cyclical, aggravated by alcohol (Leonard & Blane, 1992), and punctuated by the batterer's contrition (Walker, 1984) (just because he is nice sometimes does not mean that you or your mother can stop him from being violent again).

*Case Illustration:*
*Further Disclosure and Progress at Four Months.* With progress in overcoming avoidance and facilitating cognitive integration, further disclosures are expected. They should be elaborated and supported by returns to straight talk. During the wolf game, Josh acknowledged that he had frequently witnessed violence against his mother before the day they left for the shelter. In contrast with his initial disclosure, his description of

the scene in the parking lot now included that Gary had made "threats." When asked about their content, however, Josh became anxious, appearing confused or dissociated, and he claimed that he "forgot." Josh still emphasized how close his mother had swerved to Gary, but the significance of this detail remained obscure.

Josh resumed soccer and visits to friends. He and his teacher agreed that he was less sullen and preoccupied. Even after he retrieved his bike, however, he otherwise continued to avoid the parking lot, and he still became distraught when his mother urged him to accompany her out of the apartment for optional activities. He sometimes had intrusive impulses to light fires and had done so twice. Discussing these impulses evoked acute anxiety and avoidance. Although improvement occurred, Josh remained somewhat hypervigilant. Thus the methods so far introduced were helpful, but they had not been sufficient.

### Step 4: Interpretation and Symbolic Symptoms

The proposed intervention hierarchy suggests adding interpretation at this point. If previous strategies are inadequate, it is often because the child's impressions of the trauma are extremely fragmented and/or symptom formation is heavily symbolized. Thus it is difficult for the child and the therapist to understand the trauma and its relationship to symptoms. Such understanding is necessary to use the strategies introduced above. For example, because desensitization requires exposure to all stimuli associated with the trauma (Keane et al., 1985), it is crucial to be aware of the important components of the trauma.

It is when therapists and children cannot make sense of the child's experience or behavior in ordinary, consensually shared ways, that they must consider interpreting it in terms of idiosyncratic or symbolized meanings (Silvern, 1990). Interpretation restores meaning to experience and behavior that otherwise appears to lack sense. One of the most troubling aspects of PTSD is that victims often fear they can no longer understand their own reactions and behaviors.

The symbolic aspect of symptom formation varies as a matter of degree. When cues or reminders of trauma are distant from the manifest content of the event, and when the connection is mediated by idiosyncratic or personal meanings, symptom formation can be viewed as *relatively* more "symbolic."

Post-traumatic play is inherently symbolic. It entails a repetitive reenactment of unintegrated aspects of a traumatic event (Terr, 1981, 1983). The play repeats the trauma and yet defends by symbolically disguising it. The child's role often is changed from "passive to active," transforming a traumatic event that was endured passively into fantasies about being in the powerful role (Terr, 1990; Wälder, 1976). The content of the event is also symbolically disguised (to varying degrees). If Josh's fires prove to be interpretable as post-traumatic play, it would be highly symbolized because of the substantial distance between the content of the play and that of the manifest or obvious traumatic event.

Because post-traumatic play is symbolized, its resolution is especially likely to require interpretation. Other symptoms, however, also can involve symbolization and, thus, require interpretation. For example, trauma-related cues that elicit avoidance or distress can be heavily symbolized and require interpretation. Conversely, post-traumatic play may be addressed with alternative strategies. Theoretically the defensive expression of unintegrated aspects of trauma through post-traumatic play could be ameliorated by any strategy that overcomes defense or that facilitates cognitive integration. Without interpretation, however, success is likely to be limited to post-traumatic play that involves relatively little symbolization. Terr (1983) warned that without interpretation, post-traumatic play can continue indefinitely and even be retraumatizing. Interpretation is often needed when post-traumatic play or trauma-related cues are highly symbolic.

*Interpretation.* In trauma-specific psychotherapy, the point of interpretation is to construct the fragmented sensory impressions of the trauma into a coherent event that has personal and affective meaning (Dye & Roth, 1991). Thus the intention is different from the traditional psychodynamic interest in interpreting taboo impulses and conflicts (Rose, 1986, 1991).

Interpretation should address the connections between the traumatizing event and symptoms. Insofar as symptom formation entails symbolization of the traumatic event, symptoms contain "clues" to the personal significance of the trauma (Rose, 1991). By the time therapy begins, the symptoms themselves often have undermined children's sense of coherence and mastery. Conscious awareness of the source of these symptoms can help victims regain a sense of self-understanding and mastery.

Compared with the strategies previously introduced, interpretation places relatively more emphasis on making specific connections between the content of the trauma, as well as on articulating the function of defenses and symptoms and on identifying idiosyncratic meanings (rather than societal beliefs) that contribute to distress and that fuel defense.

In child therapy generally, interpretation begins by identifying defenses before the content against which the defense is directed (Coppollilo, 1987; Freud, 1946). In trauma-specific therapy the initial focus is on defenses that obstruct the disclosure and integration of trauma.

*Case Illustration:*
*Interpretation.* At the end of the fourth month of Josh's therapy, interpretation gradually was introduced. Initial steps were taken toward labeling the presence of defenses when the therapist pointed out that neither of them completely understood what Gary had done in the parking lot. The therapist "guessed" it must have been very scary because Josh "forgot." The therapist explained that people "forget" things that are frightening.

Soon thereafter, the therapist commented that Josh's route to soccer avoided the parking lot and that this was like "forgetting" what Gary had said; both behaviors showed that Josh did not want to be reminded about what had happened in the parking lot. Josh's sad tone belied his words, which were intended to be defiant: "I don't care if he kills us. Gary's in X (another state) anyway—probably died getting there." Josh's response to labeling the defense captured its function. Josh "forgot" so that he would not "care" (be overwhelmed with anxiety) about being killed. Adding to Josh's confusion, the adults in his life had told him not to worry, but he was unconvinced. If he "remembered," the only remaining defense was the equally unconvincing fantasy that Gary was dead.

This response was the first time Josh revealed that he thought his and his mother's lives were endangered. His defense was erected against the terror entailed in this perceived danger. Moreover, on overcoming avoidance enough to allow this revelation, further disclosures quickly emerged. Now when the therapist asked, Josh also disclosed the details of Gary's threats.

Focusing on defense regularly leads to disclosures about the content that has been avoided. When identifying defenses, therapists should be ready to provide immediate emotional support and cognitive clarification, in the vein of straight talk, as well as desensitization and cognitive restructuring. This active approach violates the principles associated with viewing insight as the primary therapeutic goal. However, trauma-specific therapy with children requires continuous attention to modulating aversive affect and countering cognitive fragmentation. With Josh, considerable attention was paid to normalizing his fear and to providing additional, reassuring information about Gary's whereabouts.

With the details of Gary's threats on the table, it was possible to explore the meaning of the trauma and the symptoms. When he ventured outside the apartment, Josh was overcome with the experience of being hunted down. He (re)experienced the terror of the traumatic event, but as if it were attributable only to a present, rather than a past, danger. A connection between the traumatic event and his avoidance was explicitly interpreted.

After further exploration, Josh linked his particularly intense fears of accompanying his mother on activities with his perception that Gary had specifically threatened to find *them* (plural). As an association, he shared that in his "bad" dreams someone was chasing *two* people, not just one. The wolf game was employed briefly to help Josh go on walks with his mother. Traveling in the car with her, however, was too frightening.

During the sixth month of therapy, Josh and the therapist agreed that they still had a "mystery"—namely, his continued attraction to burning the paper-and-wire objects. Josh finally brought one of the objects to a therapy session. As the teacher had said, it looked like a round wad of paper encircled by wire. Josh was extremely hypervigilant in the session. He apparently had exceeded his tolerance for the fear that was evoked by revealing the object, and therapeutic attempts to soothe Josh's anxiety were unsuccessful. As he left, he said flatly, "I'll see you next week, if I'm still around," implying great danger.

The next week, Josh refused to come to therapy, and he "tantrumed" when his mother tried to force him. He was, however, willing to talk by phone. Noting Josh's comment at the end of the previous session, the therapist focused interpretation on his fear of retaliation for revealing his secret object. The therapist was explicitly reassuring about not being angry or seeking retaliation. Victims' fears of retaliation for their aggression complicate post-traumatic symptoms and require interpretation (Rose, 1991). The transference apparent in Josh's sudden fear of the therapist should be interpreted in terms of the child's feelings about the batterer (Rose, 1986, 1991), and children may require that distinctions between the therapist and the batterer be made explicit.

A review of breathing techniques and desensitization was employed to secure Josh's attendance the next week. This was one of several times when specialized techniques were employed to help Josh continue exploration and interpretation. Efforts to "dose" anxiety do not always succeed. Specialized strategies to ameliorate distress remain necessary.

For the next two sessions, the therapist and Josh speculated about the "mystery." What could be done with Josh's object? What would it do when it burned? Finally the therapist asked what Gary would do with the object. The ensuing dialogue is excerpted below.

| | |
|---|---|
| **Therapist** | What would Gary do with it if it were burning? |
| **Child** | (Makes loud, banging, exploding noises, waving arms) |
| **Therapist** | Is it a firecracker? A bomb? |
| **Child** | Bang! |
| **Therapist** | If this thing were on fire, Gary would bang things? Blow them up? |
| **Child** | Yeah. He blows things up! |

| Therapist | He does? |
|-----------|----------|
| **Child** | He was in the Marines. |
| **Therapist** | He was? When was he in the Marines? |
| **Child** | During the war, I think. |
| **Therapist** | I wonder what he did in the Marines. |
| **Child** | He blew things up. |
| **Therapist** | Like with bombs or guns? What do you think? |
| **Child** | I know. Bombs and guns (becoming excited). He hunted people down, and he blew them up if they were a target. |
| **Therapist** | He hunted people down? |
| **Child** | Yes, in the war. . . . He told me he snuck around and planted bombs and blew up (obscenity) when they weren't looking. Search and destroy mission. |
| **Therapist** | Pretty scary. |
| **Child** | (Barely nods) |
| **Therapist** | Was he telling you the truth when he told you this? |
| **Child** | I think so. |
| **Therapist** | When he threatened to search out you and Mom anywhere, maybe you thought that he could use his special training. |
| **Child** | He will. |

A discussion of this issue continued for a few minutes, with Josh making some halfhearted attempts to deny the level of fear he experienced.

| Therapist | I don't think anybody could stand just hanging out, waiting for Gary to find and blow them up. |
|-----------|----------|
| **Child** | (Obscenity) him. (He is touching the paper and wire object without realizing it.) |
| **Therapist** | If you could do anything with that thing that you wanted, what would you do? |
| **Child** | I'd blow his (obscenity) face off (very agitated or excited). (Gestures wildly with the object as if it's on fire) |
| **Therapist** | You'd light that on fire and see how he likes it? |
| **Child** | Yeah! (makes loud sounds of explosion). |
| **Therapist** | Would you light it and then search him out and blow him up? Search and destroy? |
| **Child** | Search and destroy. |

By the end of this exchange, Josh and the therapist shared the knowledge that the paper-and-wire wad symbolized a bomb. Josh was determined to arm himself and his mother against the terror of being helplessly hunted down by Gary. "Testing" his bombs (by lighting them) was more compelling to Josh than avoiding trouble at school.

After the above dialogue, further exploration clarified that Josh set the fires outside because he believed that Gary's search would focus outside; it was obvious they could be found in the apartment, and a search would not be needed there. Post-traumatic symptoms reflect victims' idiosyncratic beliefs about the implications of the traumatic event for their safety (Foa et al., 1989). More generally, victims' understanding of the severity of violence determines the severity of symptoms (Foa et al., 1989). The ongoing violence that Josh had witnessed and Gary's stories of his military exploits contributed to Josh's terror about the incident in the parking lot.

Again interpretation elicited disclosure of details that were pivotal to the meaning of the traumatic event and to symptom formation (Josh's beliefs about Gary's military experience). Yet a therapist could not have known to inquire a priori about these particular details. There is no way to know when all relevant information has been disclosed or which details that a child mentions are crucial. When symptoms remain, therapists should be ready to use straight talk to elaborate even seemingly irrelevant comments.

After disclosing the significance of Gary's special search-and-destroy skills, Josh again emphasized the fact that, as they drove out of the parking lot, Monica had swerved close to Gary. The significance of this detail could finally be clarified. From Josh's perspective, Monica had almost driven into a murderous man-hunter. When the car swerved toward Gary, Josh now revealed that he had briefly hoped Mom would run him down. When she did not, Josh was horrified—she "just got him madder at her," while driving so close that "he could kill us—he almost came through the window—he could have got her." This was Josh's "worst moment" (Pynoos & Eth, 1986), encapsulating his terror and rage at Gary, as he believed that he and his mother were about to be killed, as well as his protectiveness toward and disappointment in her.

Josh's symptoms represented not only his terror of Gary but also his conflicted feelings about his mother. Symptom formation reflects the concerns typical of a victim's developmental phase (Ragg, 1991; Schwartz, 1984). Because of developmentally appropriate preoccupations, many children of abused women are devastated by subjectively experiencing themselves to be abandoned by a mother whose own safety is uncertain. Although his mother rescued Josh and herself, he felt disappointed. Josh's conflicted feelings contributed to the overwhelming, traumatic affect. A most painful aspect of woman abuse is that the women and their children are robbed of experiencing a safe attachment.

Josh's most persistent avoidance symptom concerned leaving their apartment with Monica, as if he were angrily declaring that she was no protection (and only a danger) in the "war" he was forced to wage. Yet Josh designated the apartment as safe. Beyond his explanation that Gary would not need to search there, Josh's (conflicted) dependence on Monica unconsciously contributed to his sense of safety at home. Before Josh could travel comfortably by car or engage in activities with Monica, it was necessary to interpret his fear that Gary would kill them together, his fear of retaliation for his aggressive fantasies, *and* his angry wish to "do without" Monica. Only then were Josh's post-traumatic symptoms resolved, and he could end therapy without further incidents.

## WORKING WITH CHILDREN FROM DIVERSE SOCIAL GROUPS

The treatment hierarchy described above was offered as a tentative proposal to be tested clinically and empirically. One necessary aspect of this exploration should be to consider the appropriateness of the proposed approach to groups that are diverse in race, ethnicity, economic privilege, family structure, and caretakers' sexual orientation. Although there has been some recognition of the importance of cultural diversity among battered women (e.g., Coley & Beckett, 1988; Leeder, 1988), such attention has not yet been extended to their children. The general literature on childhood trauma also has ignored group differences.

The most fundamental practical issue is that all of the proposed treatment steps will be futile if mothers and children perceive service providers as inaccessible or unsafe. Many individuals from minority groups understandably eschew traditional psychological services because discriminatory biases have been institutionalized in both theory and practice (Brown, 1990; Coley & Beckett, 1988). Services for traumatized children must be embedded in treatment contexts tailored to their particular needs (e.g., language, physical access to buildings, location) and value systems (e.g., cultural beliefs about healing, beliefs about family closeness, violence). For example, intensive therapy for children of abused women typically is offered in more traditional "clinical" settings, which are isolated from the more accessible outreach centers and women's shelters where crisis services are offered. The need is for greater integration of long-term children's services with women's outreach and crisis agencies. It is also important that the staff include diverse members.

Moreover, therapists must be able to acknowledge openly how oppression affects the daily lives of minority individuals. For example, lesbian mothers who have remained "closeted" because of fears about matters of child custody may be appropriately frightened to seek assistance about relationship violence. As another example, minority-culture mothers and children may be vigilant to signs of disapproval or denigration by majority-culture mental health workers (Boyd-Franklin, 1989). It is crucial for therapists to validate the legitimacy of such concerns and to discuss openly their own or the agency's attitudes and values (Boyd-Franklin, 1989).

In addition to the general therapy context, issues about group diversity pertain to each step of the proposed treatment hierarchy. In terms of assessment at Step 1, it is unclear whether the expression of post-traumatic symptoms differs across ethnic and racial groups (Arroyo & Eth, 1985), but the possibility should be considered (Root, 1992). If clinicians are not intimately familiar with a child's culture, they should seek consultation to avoid missing or misunderstanding culture-specific symptoms that vary from the *DSM-III-R* symptom picture.

The prevalence of trauma-related symptoms among children of abused women might vary across groups with different experiences. For example, on the one hand, manifestly similar acts of violence might be more terrifying and more traumatizing if the child's mother is physically disabled or otherwise perceived as more helpless. On the other hand, if the perpetrator is another woman, a child might perceive that physical harm is less likely, but preconceptions about safety and sex roles might be profoundly (or differently) violated.

At Step 2, facilitating disclosure with straight talk requires that children divulge sensitive family business to a professional. Important group differences are found in the acceptability of revealing such information (Boyd-Franklin, 1989; Koss-Chioino & Vargas, 1992). The approach proposed here may be less appropriate or require additional culture-sensitive supports for certain groups. For instance, mothers may be integrated into the child's sessions (see Silvern & Kaersvang, 1989).

Moreover, the readiness to directly disclose details about family violence is influenced by the issues of more general trust that were discussed above. Children's fears about therapists' reactions to their disclosures are sure to be aggravated among children who are devalued on a daily basis and whose experience is ignored by the general culture.

Straight talk attends to the personal meaning of the abuse that the child has witnessed. The meaning includes the implications for the child's sense of danger, helplessness, and self-blame. Children from minority groups often experience an ongoing sense of vulnerability associated with chronic discrimination, threats, and violence directly related to their minority status (Root, 1992). Witnessing abuse against their mothers may intensify this sense of danger and helplessness, so that disclosure is especially likely to be blocked by the intensity of these painful emotions and by the associated need for defenses.

If a sense of danger, helplessness, and self-blame is heightened among minority group children, not only would straight talk be difficult, but at Step 3 of the proposed hierarchy, cognitive restructuring concerning these issues would also be complicated. The child's maladaptive beliefs about abused women may combine with beliefs about powerlessness that are realistically associated with the family's minority status. It would be harmful for therapists to deny the impact of group disparities in privilege and social power. Instead the goal is to support realistic attributions about the causes and "cures" of these disparities.

Step 4 involves interpreting symbolized aspects of dissociated, fragmented impressions of the traumatic event. Symbols are formed in terms of familiar linguistic expressions, images, stories, and myths that can be specific to specific subgroups within the general culture. For instance, the form of Josh's post-traumatic play depended on his images of bombs or grenades derived from movies and television. Therapists' ability to interpret symptoms depends on familiarity with the context of the child's experience.

Although the approach to intervention proposed in this chapter focused on individual therapy, support from the extended family and community may be an especially important resource to children in some minority groups, including African American communities (Coley & Beckett, 1988; Root, 1992). By the same token, an absence of such support can be harmful. Children of abused lesbian mothers face special challenges, in view of a relative lack of acknowledgment about intimate violence in some lesbian communities (Hammond, 1988).

Finally it should be noted that, widely quoted beliefs to the contrary, there is no evidence of ethnic or racial differences in the prevalence of woman abuse (Coley & Beckett, 1988). Early reports by Straus, Gelles, and Steinmetz (1980) indicated a 400% greater rate of woman abuse among blacks than whites. The difference, however, occurred among economically impoverished subjects, and subsequent research demonstrated that race alone is an inadequate predictor of the prevalence of woman abuse (Coley & Beckett, 1988). Attempts to tailor therapy to diverse groups should not focus on false or stereotyped ideas about prevalence. Instead such attempts should be conceptualized in terms of factors that theoretically are relevant to the effects of witnessing violence and to treatment needs. The approach to understanding children of abused women presented in this chapter provides a place to begin.

## CONCLUSION

The tentativeness of the specific approach we have proposed should not obscure the clear and urgent need to develop and test treatments for children of abused women. Including a trauma-specific therapy among the alternatives serves as an important reminder. Unless they are identified initially in women's shelters, if children of abused women receive therapy at all, it is usually because of troublesome, manifest symptoms, not because of the abuse itself. Yet a trauma model insists that if manifest symptoms are addressed outside the context of the violence, therapy can be ineffective or even harmful. Clinicians in all settings should ask children and parents about exposure to woman abuse. Similarly, throughout therapy, therapists should be alert to details of children's verbal and nonverbal expressions so that dissociated expressions of violence that children have witnessed will not be overlooked.

## NOTES

1. To protect the confidentiality and safety of the clients, the case material has been altered substantially. Every attempt has been made, however, to accurately reflect clinical process and issues.

2. Although this chapter uses *DSM-III-R* diagnostic criteria for PTSD, essentially the same criteria appear in the recently released *DSM-IV*. Children who meet the *DSM-IV* criteria can differ in their manifest symptoms.

3. The attempted integration does not include psychobiological models of PTSD, although there are diverse autonomic and neuroendocrine correlates of trauma (e.g., Pitman, 1989; van der Kolk et al., 1985). As yet, such research has been conducted almost entirely with adults, and related interventions with children have not been developed or accepted. Therapists should be aware, however, that there is undoubtedly a biological substrate to the reexperiencing and avoidant symptoms of traumatized children.

4. Although attempts have been made to conceptualize reexperiencing symptoms in terms of the two-factor model (Keane et al., 1985), it more adequately describes avoidance; cognitive and psychodynamic models of PTSD address reexperiencing more readily than does the learning model (Foa et al., 1989). This distinction, however, cannot be elaborated for the present purpose.

5. Exposure strategies include flooding, as well as desensitization. However, because flooding is stressful and risks retraumatization, it is not advised with battered women (Dutton, 1992). Its use with children of battered women would be even more questionable, and therefore this strategy is not reviewed here.

6. Children in psychotherapy often introduce fantasy figures that can be developed into representatives of important ego functions such as reality testing and anxiety modulation. The characteristics of these figures often indicate caretaker characteristics for which the child unconsciously wishes (e.g., the fierce protectiveness of Josh's wolf).

# REFERENCES

Alessi, J. J., & Hearn, K. (1984). Group treatment of children in shelters for battered women. In A. A. Roberts (Ed.), *Battered women and their families* (pp. 49-61). New York: Springer.

American Psychiatric Association (APA). (1987). *Diagnostic and statistical manual of mental disorders* (3rd ed. rev.). Washington DC: Author.

American Psychiatric Association (APA). (1994). *Diagnostic and statistical manual of mental disorders* (4th ed. rev.). Washington DC: Author.

Arroyo, W., & Eth, S. (1985). Children traumatized by Central American warfare. In S. Eth & R. S. Pynoos (Eds.), *Posttraumatic stress disorder in children* (pp. 103-120). Washington, DC: American Psychiatric Press.

Benedek, E. (1985). Children and psychic trauma: A brief review of contemporary thinking. In S. Eth & R. S. Pynoos (Eds.), *Post-traumatic stress disorder in children* (pp. 3-16). Washington, DC: American Psychiatric Press.

Blank, A. S. (1993). The longitudinal course of posttraumatic stress disorder. In J.R.T. Davidson & E. B. Foa (Eds.), *Posttraumatic stress disorder: DSM-IV and beyond* (pp. 3-22). Washington, DC: American Psychiatric Press.

Boggiano, A., Barrett, M., Silvern, L., & Gallo, S. (1991). Predicting emotional concomitants of learned helplessness: The role of motivational orientation. *Sex Roles, 25,* 577-593.

Boyd-Franklin, N. (1989). *Black families in therapy: A multisystems approach.* New York: Guilford.

Brown, L. S. (1990). The meaning of a multicultural perspective for theory-building in feminist therapy. In L. S. Brown & M.P.P. Root (Eds.), *Diversity and complexity in feminist therapy* (pp. 1-21). New York: Harrington Park.

Cappell, C., & Heiner, R. B. (1990). The intergenerational transmission of family aggression. *Journal of Family Violence, 5,* 135-152.

Carlson, B. E. (1990). Adolescent observers of marital violence. *Journal of Family Violence, 5,* 285-299.

Carroll, E. M., & Foy, D. W. (1992). Assessment and treatment of combat-related post-traumatic stress disorder in a medical center setting. In D. W. Foy (Ed.), *Treating PTSD: Cognitive-behavioral strategies* (pp. 39-68). New York: Guilford.

Coley, S. M., & Beckett, J. O. (1988). Black battered women: A review of the empirical literature. *Journal of Counseling and Development, 66,* 266-270.

Coppollilo, H. (1987). *Psychodynamic psychotherapy of children: An introduction to the art and techniques.* Madison, WI: International Universities Press.

Davidson, L. M., & Baum, A. (1990). Posttraumatic stress disorder in children following natural and human-made trauma. In M. Lewis & F. M. Miller (Eds.), *Handbook of developmental psychopathology* (pp. 215-251). New York: Plenum.

Davis, L. V., & Carlson, B. (1987). Observation of spouse abuse: What happens to the children? *Journal of Interpersonal Violence, 3,* 278-291.

Deblinger, E., McLeer, S. V., & Henry, D. (1990). Cognitive behavioral treatment for sexually abused children suffering post-traumatic stress: Preliminary findings. *Journal of the American Academy of Child and Adolescent Psychiatry, 29,* 747-752.

Donovan, D. M., & McIntyre, D. (1990). *Healing the hurt child: A developmental contextual approach.* New York: Norton.

Dutton, M. A. (1992). Assessment and treatment of PTSD among battered women. In D. Foy (Ed.), *Treating PTSD: Cognitive-behavioral strategies* (pp. 69-98). New York: Guilford.

Dye, E., & Roth, S. (1991). Psychotherapy with Vietnam veterans and rape and incest survivors. *Psychotherapy, 28,* 103-120.

Figley, C. R. (1985). From victim to survivor. In C. R. Figley (Ed.), *Trauma and its wake* (pp. 398-415). New York: Brunner/Mazel.

Foa, E. B., & Kozak, M. J. (1986). Emotional processing of fear: Exposure to corrective information. *Psychological Bulletin, 99,* 20-35.

Foa, E. B., Steketee, G., & Rothbaum, B. O. (1989). Behavioral/cognitive conceptualizations of post-traumatic stress disorder. *Behavioral Therapy, 20,* 155-176.

Frederick, C. J. (1985). Children traumatized by catastrophic situations. In S. Eth & R. S. Pynoos (Eds.), *Post-traumatic stress disorder in children* (pp. 71-100). Washington, DC: American Psychiatric Press.

Frederick, C. J. (1988). *The Reaction Index.* West Los Angeles, CA: Veterans Administration Medical Center.

Freud, A. (1946). *The ego and the mechanisms of defense.* New York: International Universities Press.

Hammond, N. (1988). Lesbian victims of relationship violence. *Women and Therapy, 8,* 89-105.

Hartman, C. R., & Burgess, A. W. (1993). Information processing of trauma. *Child Abuse and Neglect, 17*(1), 47-59.

Herman, J. L. (1992). *Trauma and recovery.* New York: Basic Books.

Horowitz, M. J. (1986). *Stress response syndromes.* Northvale, NH: Jason Aronson.

Hurley, D. J., & Jaffe, P. (1990). Children's observations of violence: II. Clinical implications for mental health professionals. *Canadian Journal of Psychiatry, 35,* 471-176.

Jaffe, P. G., Wilson, S. K., & Wolfe, D. (1988). Specific assessment and intervention strategies for children exposed to wife battering: Preliminary empirical investigations. *Canadian Journal of Community Mental Health, 7*(2), 157-163.

Jaffe, P. G., Wolfe, D., & Wilson, S. (1990). *Children of battered women: Issues in child development and intervention planning.* Newbury Park, CA: Sage.

Jaffe, P. G., Wolfe, D., Wilson, S., & Zak, L. (1986). Similarities in behavioral and social maladjustment among child victims and witnesses to family violence. *American Journal of Orthopsychiatry, 56,* 142-146.

Janoff-Bulman, R. (1985). The aftermath of victimization: Rebuilding shattered assumptions. In R. C. Figley (Ed.), *Trauma and its wake* (pp. 15-35). New York: Brunner/Mazel.

Keane, T. M., Zimmerling, R. T., & Caddell, J. M. (1985). A behavioral formulation of post-traumatic stress disorder in Vietnam veterans. *Behavior Therapist, 8,* 9-12.

Kemp, A., Rawlings, E. I., & Green, B. L. (1991). Post-traumatic stress disorder (PTSD) in battered women: A shelter example. *Journal of Traumatic Stress Studies, 4*(1), 134-148.

Kilpatrick, D. G., Veronen, L. J., & Best, C. L. (1985). Factors predicting psychological distress among rape victims. In C. L. Figley (Ed.), *Trauma and its wake* (pp. 113-141). New York: Brunner/Mazel.

Kiser, L. J., Ackerman, B. J., Brown, E., Edwards, N. B., McColgan, E. B., Pugh, R., & Pruitt, C. (1988). Post-traumatic stress disorder in young children: A reaction to purported sexual abuse. *Journal of the American Academy of Child and Adolescent Psychiatry, 27,* 645-659.

Koss, M. P., & Harvey, M. (1991). *The rape victim: Clinical and community interventions.* Newbury Park, CA: Sage.

Koss-Chioino, J. D., & Vargas, L. (1992). Through the cultural looking glass: A model for understanding culturally responsive psychotherapies. In L. Vargas & J. D. Koss-Chioino (Eds.), *Working with culture* (pp. 1-22). San Francisco: Jossey-Bass.

Landis, T. (1989). *Children in shelters: An exploration of dissociative processes and traumatization in some children.* Unpublished doctoral dissertation, University of Colorado, Boulder.

Leeder, E. (1988). Enmeshed in pain: Counseling the lesbian battering couple. *Women and Therapy, 7,* 81-99.

Leonard, K. E., & Blane, H. T. (1992). Alcohol and marital aggression in a national sample of young men. *Journal of Interpersonal Violence, 7,* 19-30.

Lipovsky, J. A. (1992). Assessment and treatment of post-traumatic stress disorder in child survivors of sexual assault. In D. W. Foy (Ed.), *Treating PTSD: Cognitive-behavioral strategies* (pp. 127-164). New York: Guilford.

Malmquist, C. P. (1986). Children who witness parental murder: Posttraumatic subjects. *Journal of the American Academy of Child Psychiatry, 25,* 320-325.

Marmar, C. R., Weiss, D. S., Schlenger, W. E., Fairbank, J. A., Jordan, B. K., & Kulka, R. A. (1994). Peri-traumatic dissociation and post-traumatic stress in male theater Vietnam veterans. Unpublished manuscript.

McLeer, S. V., Deblinger, E., Atkins, M. S., Foa, E. B., & Ralphe, D. L. (1988). Post-traumatic stress disorder in sexually abused children. *Journal of the American Academy of Child and Adolescent Psychiatry, 27,* 650-654.

McNally, R. J. (1993). Stressors that produce posttraumatic stress disorder in children. In J.R.T. Davidson & E. B. Foa (Eds.), *Posttraumatic stress disorder: DSM-IV and beyond* (pp. 57-74). Washington, DC: American Psychiatric Press.

Mowrer, O. H. (1960). *Learning theory and behavior.* New York: John Wiley.

Peterson, C., & Seligman, M.E.P. (1983). Learned helplessness and victimization. *Journal of Social Issues, 2,* 103-116.

Pitman, R. K. (1989). Posttraumatic stress disorder, hormones, and memory. *Biological Psychiatry, 26,* 221-223.

Putnam, F. W. (1993). Dissociative disorder in children: Behavioral profiles and problems. *Child Abuse and Neglect, 17*(1), 39-46.

Pynoos, R. S., & Eth, S. (1984). The child as a witness to homicide. *Journal of Social Issues, 40,* 87-108.

Pynoos, R. S., & Eth, S. (1986). Witness to violence: The child interview. *Journal of the American Academy of Child Psychiatry, 25,* 306-319.

Pynoos, R. S., & Nader, K. (1988). Children who witness the sexual assaults of their mothers. *Journal of the American Academy of Child and Adolescent Psychiatry, 27,* 567-572.

Ragg, D. M. (1991). Differential group programming for children exposed to spouse abuse. *Journal of Child and Youth Care, 5,* 59-75.

Root, M.P.P. (1992). Reconstructing the impact of trauma on personality. In L. S. Brown & M. Ballou (Eds.), *Personality and psychopathology: Feminist reappraisals* (pp. 169-184). New York: Guilford.

Rose, D. (1986). Worse than death: Psychodynamics of rape victims. *American Journal of Psychiatry, 143,* 817-824.

Rose, D. S. (1991). A model of psychodynamic psychotherapy with the rape victim. *Psychotherapy, 28,* 85-95.

Schwartz, H. J. (1984). An overview of the psychoanalytic approach to the war neuroses. In H. J. Schwartz (Ed.), *Psychotherapy of the combat veteran.* New York: Spectrum.

Silvern, L. (1990). A hermeneutic account of clinical psychology: Strengths and limits. *Philosophical Psychology, 3,* 5-27.

Silvern, L., & Kaersvang, L. (1989). The traumatized children of violent marriages. *Child Welfare, 68*(4), 421-436.

Silvern, L., Karyl, J., Waelde, L., Hodges, W. F., Starek, J., & Heidt, E. (in press). Retrospective reports of parental partner abuse: Relationships to depression, trauma symptoms, and self-esteem among college students. *Journal of Family Violence.*

Silvern, L., Landis, T., & Karyl, J. (1990). *Identifying trauma in children of violent marriages.* Paper presented at the 1990 National Symposium on Child Victimization, Atlanta, GA.

Straus, M. A., Gelles, R. J., & Steinmetz, S. K. (1980). *Behind closed doors: Violence in the American family.* Garden City, NY: Doubleday.

Terr, L. (1981). Forbidden games: Post-traumatic child's play. *Journal of the American Academy of Child Psychiatry, 20,* 741-760.

Terr, L. (1983). Chowchilla revisited: The effects of psychic trauma four years after a school-bus kidnapping. *American Journal of Psychiatry, 140,* 1543-1550.

Terr, L. (1990). *Too scared to cry: Psychic trauma in childhood.* New York: Harper & Row.

van der Kolk, B., Greenberg, M., Boyd, H., & Krystal, J. (1985). Inescapable shock, neurotransmitters, and addiction to trauma: Toward a psychobiology of post-traumatic stress. *Biological Psychiatry, 20,* 314-325.

Wälder, R. (1976). Psychoanalytic theory of play. In C. Schaefer (Ed.), *Therapeutic use of child's play* (pp. 79-93). New York: Jason Aronson.

Walker, L. E. (1984). *The battered woman syndrome.* New York: Springer.

Walker, L. E. (1991). Post-traumatic stress disorder in women: Diagnosis and treatment of battered woman syndrome. *Psychotherapy, 28,* 21-29.

# 5

# Process and Outcome in Small Groups for Children of Battered Women

EINAT PELED
JEFFREY L. EDLESON

Battered women seeking safe shelter and other services seldom arrive alone. They often are followed through the shelter or agency door by their children. In fact, it is the safety and well-being of their children that many times acts as a catalyst for women's decisions to leave their violent partners and seek help (Henderson, 1990; Hilton, 1992; Syers-McNairy, 1990).

Advocates, clinicians, and researchers who worked with and studied battered women were the first to report on the children (e.g., Dobash & Dobash, 1979; Hilberman & Munson, 1977; Martin, 1976; Stacy & Shupe, 1983; Walker, 1979). These authors described emotional and physical difficulties experienced mostly by children residing in shelters (e.g., Elbow, 1982; Hilberman & Munson, 1977; Layzer, Goodson, & Delange, 1986; Levine, 1975; Moore, 1975). It was suggested that these children suffer health problems (Kerouac, Taggart, Lescop, & Fortin, 1986; Layzer et al., 1986) and acute feelings of loss, anger, fear, sadness, confusion, and guilt as a result of the following conditions: (a) recent crisis following the witnessing of violence at home; (b) disruption of normal coping patterns and support systems following separation from father, friends, school, home, and the like; (c) rapid adjustment to a new living situation, including new living quarters, unfamiliar people, new schools, and new rules; (d) difficult living conditions, including lack of privacy and high emotional intensity displayed by other residents; and (e) emotional and/or physical unavailability of their mothers because of their own emotional turmoil and the practical demands imposed by the need to rearrange family life (see Alessi & Hearn, 1984; Carlson, 1984; Cassady, Allen, Lyon, & McGeehan, 1987; Layzer et al., 1986).

Women's concerns for their children and the growing awareness of the effects of violence on children have led to a variety of new services for children. Early in the history of battered women's shelters, child counseling often was delivered on a one-to-one, informal basis. As shelters and other nonresidential domestic violence programs have grown, many have developed formal programs to address children's needs. These services often include the provision of small support and education groups in which children "break the secret" of family violence. A survey of federally funded demonstration projects for children in battered women's shelters found that "the service most commonly recommended for the children was counseling, most often group counseling and play therapy" (Layzer et al., 1986, p. 4).

## GROUP PROGRAMS FOR CHILDREN

There is a small but growing literature on group work with the children of battered women (see Alessi & Hearn, 1984; Cassady et al., 1987; Frey-Angel, 1989; Gentry & Eaddy, 1980; Gibson & Gutierrez, 1991; Grusznski, Brink, & Edleson, 1988; Hughes, 1982; Johnson & Montgomery, 1990; Peled & Davis, 1994; Ragg & Webb, 1992; Wilson, Cameron, Jaffe, & Wolfe, 1986). A review of this literature finds groups offered in shelters, safe-homes, family court clinics, and outpatient social service agencies (some of which focus exclusively on domestic violence). These programs most often reported 60- to 90-minute group sessions that met weekly for 6 to 10 weeks, with the number of sessions sometimes depending on the child's length of stay in a shelter. The ages of child participants varied from 1 to 16 years, but most groups focused on 4- to 13-year-olds who were divided into groups according to developmental abilities. Reported groups also appeared to be small; membership in most cases ranged from 3 to 6 children.

The great majority of these programs reported highly structured sessions with specific goals and educational activities designed to achieve these goals. The stated goals included helping child participants: (a) define violence and responsibility for violence; (b) express feelings, including anger; (c) improve communication, problem-solving, and cognitive coping skills; (d) increase self-esteem; (e) develop social support networks; (f) develop safety plans; and (g) feel safety and trust during group sessions that are positive experiences. These goals were achieved through a variety of structured educational and play activities that included presentations, discussions, modeling, role playing, art projects, homework assignments, and, in one program (Gentry & Eaddy, 1980), a Family Night during which children's activities would take place either concurrent with a parent program or with parent participation.

Only a few evaluations of group programs have been reported in the professional literature. Jaffe, Wilson, and Wolfe (1986) reported a small pilot study that showed intervention to have some success in changing children's self-esteem, attitudes about violence, and practical skills in emergency situations. Cassady et al. (1987) failed to find a clear pattern of results in an analysis of an initial data set.

Our qualitative study (Peled & Edleson, 1992) of the Domestic Abuse Project's (Minneapolis) Children's Program suggested that a 10-session group could mostly achieve the major goals of (a) allowing participant children to break the secret of violence, (b) enhancing children's ability to protect themselves, (c) strengthening participants' self-esteem, and (d) providing a safe and fun environment in which the children can have positive experiences. We also found, however, a number of unintended outcomes—both positive and negative—that resulted from group participation. For example, many mothers hoped their children would more openly discuss past violence and resulting family turmoil once they had attended group sessions. Some children decided, however, that the group rule stating "everything we say here is confidential" required they not talk to their mothers about the group. This unintended result frustrated some mothers' efforts to communicate with their children.

In this chapter we present an overview of the processes and outcomes of children groups, as well as their unintended results. We focus on the program of the Domestic Abuse Project (DAP). During the past 15 years, DAP's Children's Program has provided services to hundreds of children whose parents also have sought help at the agency. The Children's Program provides intake, group orientation, and closing family sessions, a 10-session program for groups of children in differing age groups, and a concurrent parenting group. The program has been documented extensively (see Grusznski et al., 1988; Peled & Davis, 1994) and is the subject of a multiyear evaluation (Peled & Edleson, 1992).

Below we present common outcome goals for children's programs and illustrate the processes that DAP staff have developed to achieve them. We also identify potential unintended outcomes and offer strategies to prevent or overcome resulting problems. Although our focus is on DAP's program, we also occasionally provide examples from the work of others.

## PROCESSES AND OUTCOMES

At DAP we have combined some of the goals reviewed above and focused on helping child participants achieve the following outcomes: (a) "break the secret" of abuse in their families, (b) learn to protect themselves, (c) experience the group as a positive and safe environment, and (d) strengthen their self-esteem. Each of these larger goals is most likely achieved through group processes designed to attain specific, expected changes among child participants. In Figure 5.1 we identify the group processes and the outcomes they are expected to achieve.

A variety of group activities take place in any one session. Each of these activities reflects a process goal—for example, feeling education, assertive conflict resolution training, or maintaining group rules (see ovals in Figure 5.1). These activities should lead to specific emotional or attitudinal changes among the children attending the sessions (see boxes in Figure 5.1). These hoped-for outcomes, when taken together, should reflect achievement of the four major outcome goals (see bold boxes in Figure 5.1). The processes and outcomes shown in Figure 5.1 are relevant and appropriate for all age groups, though the specific group activities used to achieve them may differ, depending on the developmental levels of group members.

Our research (Peled & Edleson, 1992) indicates that changes among child participants seem to be an enhancement of already existing patterns of behavior, emotion, and thought. For some children, positive changes appear to come relatively easily and are more noticeable to parents and others in the child's environment. For others, the group is a first and crucial step in a longer journey of healing, and behavioral changes appear more slowly and are harder to identify. Individual differences in achieving goals are likely to arise from a multiplicity of factors such as the children's personalities and histories, the group leaders' personalities and training, and the group composition. Group processes also may produce new tensions within children and among family members. These mostly unintended results are an essential component of the change process.

We have organized the remainder of this chapter into sections focused on the four major goals above and shown in Figure 5.1 (bold boxes). In each section, we address both the processes and the outcomes derived from these larger goals, as well as likely unintended outcomes that may result.

### Breaking the Secret

"Breaking the secret" is a widely used metaphor for a common goal of intervention with victims of family violence (Saunders & Azar, 1989). The

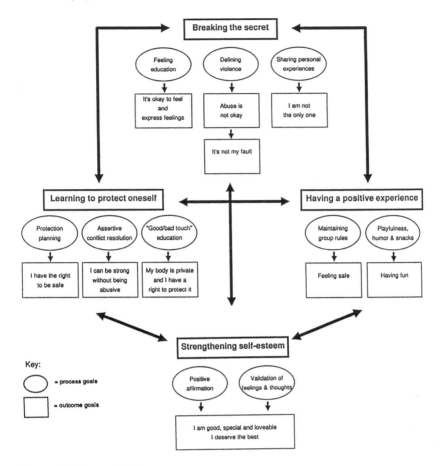

**Figure 5.1.** Group Goals

phrase alludes to the tangible, solid nature of the emotional isolation that many children of battered women appear to experience (Roy, 1988) and to the work required in dealing with it. This goal is complex in terms of group processes and outcomes. It includes three group processes, each with a complementary outcome. They are (a) defining violence → abuse is not okay and it's not my fault, (b) feeling education → it's okay to feel and express feelings, and (c) sharing personal experiences → I'm not the only one.

*Defining Violence → Abuse Is Not Okay and It's Not My Fault.* Starting with the first group session, children learn to define violence and to distinguish among different kinds of abuse. The members discuss types of abuse, and the leaders use a flip-chart or magnetic tiles with clear and simple drawings of abuse and a label, such as "hitting" or "kicking." Group leaders actively help child participants gradually acquire "violence vocabulary," which allows them to talk about abuse, share abusive experiences, and assign responsibility for abusive behavior. These processes also enable children to learn that abuse is not okay and that it is not their fault when someone is abusive to them or when other people abuse one another.

Our research suggested that most, if not all, children could define abuse, distinguish among forms of abuse, and state that "abuse is not okay" at the end of the group or later. For example, one child told us:

> I learned that . . . if you like, had had that happen that the dad was hitting the mom, that just because you're stronger and stronger doesn't mean that you're allowed to hit somebody else. . . . I also learned some kinds of violence that I didn't know about. They were physical, and threats. (child age 10, 5 months after group)

One possible unintended result occurs when children use new information gained in group sessions to reevaluate their parents' behavior and parenting style. This evaluation can put parents in an uncomfortable and even stressful position. For example, a mother recalled the following:

> I guess she got into the aspects of the idea, of the abuse. The whole idea about abuse, and how people couldn't be abusive any more. . . . And in another sense she kind of used it, too, to her advantage, by making statements. . . . She would say things like, "Well, if you touch me, I'll turn you in for child abuse!" . . . I felt like there were times when she has gotten, when she used it a lot. . . . I sometimes, I don't know if it was good or bad. (mother of a 9-year-old, 4 months after group)

Parents who have not gone through groups themselves may find "anti-abusive" responses of their child to be threatening, even to the point of leading to further violence.

Learning to define, judge, and attribute responsibility for the abuse not only influences children's present and future but also may change their past recollections through a process of retrospective interpretation, the process by which a child may redefine past events as new information is gained (Schur, 1971). After the acquisition of information on violence and abuse, children may go through a reevaluation of the extent of abuse contained in their past and the roles of the actors involved in it. In this context, attribution of responsibility for the violence is a highly charged emotional issue for children. They do not always have the skills to identify and express these emotions and, thus, the groups often engage in a process of feeling education.

*Feeling Education → It's Okay to Feel and Express Feelings.* Breaking the family secret often involves children opening up and expressing the full range of emotions triggered by their exposure to violence. Through "feeling education," group leaders work with children on awareness of different feelings, labeling of feelings, and alternative ways of expressing feelings such as pain and anger. The legitimacy of all feelings and of their appropriate expression is continually reaffirmed through group sessions. One example of a feeling education activity is the group "check-in" in which each child is asked to share how he or she felt during the week. This check-in often is conducted as a "weather report" in which a child chooses the kind of weather, shown on a poster, that best represents how he or she feels (e.g., sunny, cloudy, stormy) and then tells the group why he or she feels this way. In a different program, Wilson et al. (1986) used prepared sheets to elicit stories and situations focused on anger. One sheet was headed "I get mad when . . ." and had a drawing of an angry child covering part of the page and empty lines where a child completed the sentence with several examples.

Even when legitimate and supported, expressing feelings tied to traumatic experiences is often a hard and stressful experience that creates unintended tensions. The following field notes from our study illustrate one step in a painful process of dealing with emotions related to the violence:

[Group Leader A asks the children to draw the most violent event they either saw or heard in their family.]

| | |
|---|---|
| **Sharon** | Well, there was no violence in my family, nothing really happened. |
| **GL A** | Was there any yelling or threatening? |
| **Sharon** | Yeah. |
| **GL A** | Well, you know, that's what you should draw. |

[Sharon is getting agitated. She plays with her juice and makes all kinds of grimaces.]

| | |
|---|---|
| **Sharon** | (After a short while) Can I draw myself as an animal again? |
| **GL A** | Sure. |

[Sharon starts drawing an animal and, while drawing, she groans and moans.]

**Sharon**          I can't! I can't draw it. I can't do yelling.

[Sharon talks with GL A about drawing yelling and other alternatives. She keeps drawing for a while and then stops and puts her face on the floor. Then she raises her head again and continues to draw. She says she is frustrated because she can't draw a lion the way she would like. Then she turns her paper to the other side and starts a new picture.]

**GL B**            You know, sometimes when we do things like that it brings back all
                    the feelings we felt when these things happened. That's fine. We
                    know it's hard, but it's all right.

**GL A**            Sometimes we feel sad or mad about the things that happened.

[The children continue to draw for a while. Amy tells GL A she doesn't feel very well and goes out to drink water. Then Sharon says she doesn't feel very well, stops drawing, hugs her stuffed giraffe, and lies down on the floor, curled like a baby with her giraffe. She is saying again that she doesn't feel very well, that she wasn't feeling well all the time, but that now she really doesn't feel well.] (group observation, children aged 8 to 9)

Changes in the emotional expressiveness of children following the group experience may be a bittersweet experience for parents, as suggested by this mother:

I could probably remember one time, and I think it happened in the group, during the group, that he was just really sad, and I said "What's wrong? Do you want to talk about it?" And he just really opened up, and the tears, you know, tearful, and he told me how bad he was feeling about his dad being gone . . . and I am sure that was good for him . . . I mean, it was sad for me to see him so upset, but it was good because he was opening up. (mother of a 9-year-old, 4 months after group)

*Sharing Personal Experiences → I Am Not the Only One.* After discussion of violence and related emotions, children are encouraged to share their own personal violent experiences in their homes. At DAP, group leaders often use stories, such as *A Family That Fights* (Bernstein, 1991) or *Something Is Wrong at My House* (Davis, 1984), or videos, such as *It's Not Always Happy at My House* (Tri-State Coalition, 1986), to elicit a discussion of the children's own experiences. The use of drawings, piecing together magazine clippings, or enactments are other ways to facilitate telling personal stories.

Similar to expressing feelings, this process simultaneously reduces and increases stress for the children. Talking about violence that occurred in their homes requires children to remember what happened, to peel away layers of defenses they constructed with time.

Listening to their friends' stories, group members discover that they are not the only ones whose family experienced violence. This revelation is especially meaningful for children who never before have spoken openly about the violence in their homes and who feel ashamed, guilty, and confused about it. It is often a great relief to discover that what was thought of as an extremely deviant family situation is actually shared with other families. For example, one group member, in a response to a question about the group, stated:

> [We] talked about what was going on in my family and that other people have the same problems . . . and that people can help. . . . They've had these problems before, and they can help . . . and other people, you know, don't want to talk about it just as much as I don't . . . like, you know, if I had kids like me, I'd probably send them to a group like this too . . . so they know that other people have had the exact same experiences. Well, maybe not the exact same, but almost the same. (child age 9, 1 month after group)

Although children seem to have the ability to maintain safe boundaries in the group by controlling the amount and type of information they disclose, one unintended outcome is that some children might find themselves in pain after sharing their stories. Such pain was eloquently described by this 8-year-old girl:

> [I] sort of, get, I get this picture in my head, and it just all goes black. And then I get teary eyes, but I don't cry. That is pretty new. And then my stomach starts to hurt . . . I think like from talking about it all the time I just, I just get one thing in my head, and then another thing and then another thing. And so my mind, my mind isn't all that big, you know. It can only fit so many things and then, so, it just gets all black. And then it just, some of it goes to my eyes and gets all teary. But I don't cry for some reason. And then my stomach hurts, probably cause I'm nervous. . . . Cause it's from talking about this stuff so much from DAP, probably . . . I don't really know what to think of it. It's just, it's definitely not normal . . . cause I wouldn't think that would happen to any other kid. (child age 8, 1 month after group)

Children appear to note not only the mere existence of violence in other homes but also its form, severity, and victims. They compare the violence they experienced with the violence experienced by others in their group.

Ironically, by realizing that "it can be worse," children may feel better about themselves and their families. This may be especially true when children who have witnessed violence between their parents compare their circumstances with those of children who were also physically and sexually abused. Such comparison may produce burdensome consequences for the abused child who may come to a conclusion that, even in an environment where the secret of family violence is shared, he or she is nonetheless different, still having a shameful secret that is hard to share. Other differences that group members might note are race, ethnicity, or that their mom or dad was beaten by a same-sex partner.

The potential negative impact of feeling apart from other group members can be lessened through planning when groups are formed. We suggest that groups be composed in a way that allows every member to have at least one other member with similar dominant attributes. This is true when considering members who have been physically or sexually abused, who are children of color, or who are children of gay men or lesbians. Attempts to further lessen any potential feelings of difference include materials, videos, and stories depicting a variety of families, and leaders' use of broad definitions of families in examples used.

## Learning to Protect Oneself

The emphasis of DAP's relatively short program is on emotional and attitudinal changes. Our ability to achieve behavioral effects is rather limited. Still the children's reality, a potentially life-threatening one, at a minimum requires self-protection training. Such training includes three processes, each with a complementary outcome: (a) Protection planning → I have the right to be safe, (b) "Good/bad touch" education → My body is private, and I have a right to protect it, and (c) Assertive conflict resolution → I can be strong without being abusive. These aspects of self-protection are discussed below.

*Protection Planning → I Have the Right to Be Safe.* We hold parents and other adults in a child's life to be responsible for his or her safety and well-being. However, under the circumstances of family violence and dangerous situations in which the child's safety is at risk, we want the children to know that they also need to take care of themselves.

Children need to be able to protect themselves from risks both inside and outside their homes. The aim of personal protection planning is to equip children with some practical and realistic skills to be used in cases of emergency.

Protection planning activities take place later in the life of the group, after the children have had an opportunity to define abuse, enhance their ability to talk about their own situations, and gain a better understanding of the violence in their homes. Each child develops a protection plan card that identifies safe places to go to or to hide in in case of danger or when feeling threatened. Group members list, on their protection plan cards, names and phone numbers of trusted relatives, friends, teachers, or neighbors who live or work in proximity to them. Group time is devoted to role plays of telephone calls to police or of talking with others when an emergency arises. Wilson et al. (1986) supplemented these processes by bringing a police officer into their groups to talk to children about safety issues.

The focus of protection planning is concrete action, and not the psychological aspects of children's circumstances. However, some discussion of past unsafe events and potential risks in the child's life may be required. One mother recalled her children's responses concerning their protection plans:

> We went over it when we had our family session, and they asked them, "What would you do if, ya know, if there were violence in your home?" . . . [They] said they'd call 911 or they would go get a neighbor or something like it. So they could do something, I hope. You know, I don't know if they would actually do it, but at least it's in their head. (mother of 7- and 10-year-olds, 2 months after group)

The work on protection planning can be uncomfortable for children who, at the time of group participation, do not live with the abusive parent and do not have to deal with current violence. The concreteness of protection planning may have the unintended consequence of forcing the possibility of future violence into the consciousness of child participants while many seem to deny such possibilities (see Cottle, 1980). Some discussion of potential risks in the child's life may be required if the child denies this possibility and refuses to do protection planning. Further, activities such as role-playing a call to the police may evoke strong feelings in the children. This may be especially the case for children who have had a previous experience of calling the police or of having the police visit their homes.

*"Good/Bad Touch" Education → My Body Is Private, and I Have a Right to Protect It.* Group members are provided basic definitions and an understanding of sexual abuse and are taught basic protective skills. This information is introduced through stories, such as *No More Secrets for Me* (Wachter, 1983) and *No-No, The Little Seal* (Patterson, 1986), and films, such as *What Tadoo With Fear* (Mitchell Film Company, 1984) and *Touch* (Media Ventures, 1983), and then is followed by discussions among group members. In addition, the issue of sexual harassment may be addressed

with older children, especially if they already have encountered the term in school, the media, or elsewhere. The information provided on sexual abuse is aimed at prevention and is not sufficient as the sole intervention with children who were sexually abused.

One possible unintended outcome is that children in the group may feel discomfort when topics with sexual connotations are discussed. The group norm of confidentiality may create difficulties in cases of children who disclose information about sexual, physical, or other forms of severe abuse in the group. On the one hand, the norm of confidentiality is established because we want the children to feel safe to disclose in the group any family secret they may have. On the other hand, group leaders have the legal responsibility to report suspected cases of abuse. Such reports may be perceived by the child as a violation of the confidentiality norm and of his or her trust in the group leaders and the group. This potential problem can be prevented by qualifying the rule of confidentiality in intake, orientation, and early group sessions.

*Assertive Conflict Resolution → I Can Be Strong Without Being Abusive.* It is important that children be aware of conflict resolution strategies as an alternative to violent ones they have witnessed in their homes. Assertiveness also allows children to protect themselves and their rights in an appropriate manner. Assertiveness is modeled and encouraged by group leaders throughout the group. It also is taught directly through stories, such as *The Mouse, The Monster, and Me* (Palmer, 1977), and role-play exercises. Assertiveness training role plays with younger children may be enacted by using puppets. The group leader first might model specific techniques, followed by the children, who then repeat the role play with their own puppets.

Although only modest behavioral change should be expected in the light of group time constraints, we found that some children used this new information in their everyday life to prevent or respond to behavior that was perceived by them as abusive:

Before I went here, my brother would say: "Hey! You want to fight?" and I'd say: "Sure!" But that was like in the middle of the night, he would be keeping me up . . . and then we'd be up all the rest of the night, and then I'd get to school and I'd go ehhhh (yawning sound). Now my brother still says: "Hey! You want to fight?" right in the middle of the night, and I just ignore him and try to get to sleep, but he doesn't give up very easily. . . . I say, "No, I want to go to sleep," and now mostly I get to sleep now . . . and it improved on my report card. (child age 9, 4 months after group)

Increased assertiveness in children probably is desired and mostly welcomed by parents. Such behavioral change, however, may contain other, unintended consequences. Consider the following situation:

> She stands up more to [her father] if he's been drinking or something and might come and tell her to get to her room, and she gets upset. She'll go and hide in her room or go run to her room, and he'll come in and try, and she'll be like against the door, and he'll push the door, and she'll say, "You hurt me." And she'll tell him if he pushed the door too hard, you know. And she'll remind him of it the next day. . . . She's always been a person to be very blunt, and I think getting the idea that it's okay not to put up with that, I think is really instilled in her head. . . . She is really comfortable speaking out when she feels like she should. (mother of a 9-year-old, 4 months after group)

Although this mother viewed her daughter's behavior positively, other parents might not. A discrepancy between family and group norms regarding children's appropriate roles and behavior in the family may exacerbate already dangerous conditions for the child.

## Having a Positive Experience

Often taken for granted, this goal is very important for the success of groups for children of battered women. A positive experience is achieved through two processes and their corresponding outcomes: (a) maintaining group rules → feeling safe, and (2) playfulness, humor, and snacks → having fun. The children's feelings of trust and safety in the group are a precondition for "breaking the secret"; fun activities provide children with an immediate gratification that balances the "heavier," violence-related aspects of the group. In this way, group processes involved in providing a positive experience may contribute to the achievement of other group goals.

*Maintaining Group Rules → Feeling Safe.* Rules allow clarity and predictability, which are basic components of a safe environment. Such an environment is especially important for child witnesses who have experienced emotional and physical threats and abuse. Rules need not be overemphasized, however; as few rules as possible, and only realistic ones, should be established. Having members suggest the rules they would like to have in the group establishes some ownership by the children in the group and thus helps empower them. However, group leaders need to make sure that certain essential rules are established and that inappropriate rules are not. The following can be seen as "essential rules":

- Confidentiality (with the exception of suspicion of child abuse and "duty to warn" considerations)
- No physical or verbal abuse and coercion
- Respect for other's opinions, feelings, and personal space

Maintaining confidentiality seems to be an especially important rule for children:

> [A]nd they made rules and one of the rules that I think was the best was whatever said in the group, stays in the group. (child age 9, 4 months after group)

Although the norm of confidentiality contributes to the children's feeling of safety, it may have unintended influence on parents and on their relationship with their children. Consider the following comment:

> The hardest thing was that they told the kids that, you know, anything that was said there was to remain there. . . . That put me in a situation I've never been in before. Because if something's happened like say, between [my son] and his brother, and this one's saying this and this one's saying that . . . I need to know who started it or what actually is going on. And I couldn't do that with [my son]. I had no idea what he talked about . . . and that made me really uncomfortable. And I don't know if that's just being a mother or just that I know the information is real sensitive, what it was. But I didn't like that. (mother of an 8-year-old, 2 months after group)

Parents appear to understand the purpose and benefits of confidentiality. As we noted early in this chapter, however, at times they may find it hard to avoid feeling curious, uneasy, rejected, and a loss of control when their children choose not to share with them their group experience. In this way confidentiality may put a boundary between child and mother and, at times, influence the power balance between them by granting the child the advantage of control over desired information. Another difficulty with confidentiality may be experienced by children who feel compelled to process the group experience alone even though they would have liked to share it with friends or family members.

*Playfulness, Humor, and Snacks → Having Fun.* Initially many children perceive the group as a serious, threatening place, and some of them do not come of their own free will but are "strongly prompted" to do so by their mothers. Children do not like to come to groups because they may have to leave school early, may miss a favorite television show or club activity, may have to confront father's opposition to group, or may have to face the difficult issue of violence in their families.

Group leaders are challenged to transform these initial feelings of apprehension and resistance into an enjoyable and attractive experience. Although one part of this transformation depends on the development of trust and familiarity with the people in the group, it is crucial that the children also have fun in the group. As well as being educational and therapeutic, the group is a social setting in which children make new friends, play, and eat snacks. Positive experiences in the group provide immediate gratification to children and also may contribute to enhancing their self-esteem.

## Strengthening Self-Esteem

Like most children in our society, children of battered women are often disempowered. They also may feel different from other children and sometimes also are physically or sexually abused. It is hoped that participation in the group will empower the children and strengthen their self-esteem. Strengthening children's self-esteem is directly influenced by two processes that lead to one general outcome goal: (a) Positive Affirmation and (b) Validation of Feelings and Thoughts → I am good, special, and loveable, and I deserve the best. General supportive and validating interactions with group leaders occur throughout the group. For example, many group sessions end with an affirmation of a positive quality of each child. DAP groups often end with a game called Pass the Squeeze, in which all members stand in a circle holding hands, and one starts with a message—for example, "I am good, special, and loveable"—and squeezes the next child's hand; that child then makes the same affirmative statement, squeezes the next child's hand, and so on around the circle. Many other group processes, such as writing a positive statement about oneself on a card and having a child to the right or left read it to the entire group, offer additional opportunities for positive social reinforcement of the child. Children we interviewed appreciated these efforts:

I think that it was good that they have these, like, positive affirmations. . . . It's something you like about yourself or someone said nice to you or something like that. (child age 9, 4 months after group)

[A]nd also I remember when my teacher . . . turned out the light, and then we had our eyes closed, and . . . she was bringing us around, and we would get these things out of these baskets, and then, after everybody got one, we would turn on the light and then have us open our eyes. It was a star, and we were very special she told us. (child age 5, 4 months after group)

Children's self-esteem may be strengthened also through the achievement of other group goals. As shown in Figure 5.1, group goals and results are interdependent and depicted better as an interactive system, rather than as separate units. In this way the goal of strengthening a child's self-esteem also may be an outcome of the other three major goals and contribute to their achievement. First, the process of breaking the secret tends to reduce children's shame, guilt, and isolation associated with the violence. Second, through learning to protect themselves, children are empowered and their confidence in their own skills is strengthened. Third, a positive experience in group usually translates into a positive experience of themselves, of their capacities to be respected and cared for and to be part of a positive, enjoyable interaction.

## Family Involvement in Group

The influence of the group is not confined to the children, but rather reverberates in significant ways through their families. This is illustrated clearly in a number of the mothers' statements presented earlier in this chapter. The group can be both stressful and healing, not only for the participating child but also for his or her family, primarily for parents, but sometimes also for siblings and members of the extended family. Moreover, group processes and outcomes also influence interactions between family members. Finally, in their turn, family members and interactions between them have the power to influence group activities, processes, and outcomes.

Parents may be involved in the groups in four major ways: (a) an intake session, (b) a group orientation, (c) parenting groups, and (d) a closing family session. Each of these points of communication with parents is described briefly below.

*Intake Session.* The general goal of the intake process is to identify the needs of the child and the family and to connect them with resources inside or outside the agency that might meet their needs. The aim of the pregroup intake session is to determine whether the child can participate in a group and is in need of additional services during or after group and whether any special needs of the child can be met by the agency.

The intake is tailored to the developmental stage of the child and is divided into three parts. The first part consists of an interview with the parent (usually the child's mother) in the presence of the child. With this approach, the parent serves as a model for the child, thus giving the child permission to talk about violence, in addition to helping the child prepare for his or her interview. The second part consists of an interview with the child, without the presence of the parent. The third part is a discussion with the parent about the intake worker's recommendations for the child and the family.

*Group Orientation.* The orientation session follows intake but occurs before the first group session. It serves to introduce both children and parents to the agency, the group leaders, and the group program. Group structure, contents, and norms are reviewed to provide parents (usually only mothers) with initial information they may need in order to feel comfortable with their children's group participation. In this way the orientation can prevent potential misunderstandings and frustrations caused by insufficient information. Further and more detailed communication with parents regarding group activities and their potential effects on their children should be carried out during the entire 10-group sessions.

*Parenting Group.* A 10-week psychoeducational parenting group is offered as a voluntary option for parents of those in a children's group. The purpose of the group is (a) to provide information, to challenge attitudes, values, beliefs, and assumptions, and to create new insights and (b) to develop parents' child-rearing skills.

The first half of each session consists of an educational activity around the day's topic. In the second half, parents are given the opportunity to support each other by sharing child-related needs and concerns. In addition, the parenting group provides a convenient and safe setting for keeping parents informed of the weekly content of the children's groups and for discussing questions and concerns they may have about their children's group experiences.

*Closing Family Session.* A family session takes place soon after the last session of the children's group and is attended by the child and his or her parent(s). The purpose of this session is to review the group with the child, to discuss the influence of group on the child, and to provide parents with recommendations for future services (if needed). It also aims to further facilitate open communication about violence-related issues between parents and child and to provide both parents and child with the opportunity to give their feedback to the group leaders.

A careful design and implementation of parents' participation decreases the stress that a child's participation may create for parents. Maintaining communication channels with parents and keeping them well informed of their children's group should alleviate some of these stressors. For example, an early understanding of the reasons for maintaining group confidentiality, more information about group activities, and an opportunity to discuss concerns with group leaders may foster greater acceptance by parents of their children's privacy.

We also recommend that the (past) abusive parent's involvement in the group be encouraged as much as possible. While *always* considering the safety of the mother and the children a first priority, the participation of the other parent in the intake, orientation, parenting group, and closing processes is important if the child sees this parent on a regular basis. When the other parent cannot be involved in the group because of safety or other considerations, group leaders should help the woman and child by discussing with them related concerns.

Finally, making child participation contingent on a parent's involvement in a similar adult program is another way of preventing group-related stress among both parents and children. Children whose parents have not or are not currently involved in a structured domestic violence program may be better directed to a non-educational program. Parents who also have participated in groups for victims/survivors or abusers are better equipped to understand the group processes their children are experiencing.

## CONCLUSION

We have attempted to provide an overview of group processes and related outcomes in group work with children of battered women. Our earlier research (Peled & Edleson, 1992) found that 10 sessions using the processes we have described usually could achieve the four major goals.

Although the benefits of group participation to child and family may be many, such groups are not without unintended results. As we have shown throughout this chapter, many unintended results can be prevented or kept to a minimum, while others may be turned into useful motivation for further change within families.

Achievement of outcome goals and dealing with unintended stressors are often only the start of a longer process for the child and his or her family. As one group leader stated:

> They are not going to get it all in 10 weeks. Because the group is more of an educational focus . . . they are more apt to get content, and depending on where they are on their healing journey . . . some of the spiritual healing will take place for them. . . . But as far as "Do these kids get fixed in groups?" No, they don't. (Group Leader 01)

The healing process is most probably a very long one for children exposed to violence in their homes. Short-term group programs, as described in this chapter, probably best serve as a starting point of this healing journey.

## REFERENCES

Alessi, J. J., & Hearn, K. (1984). Group treatment of children in shelters for battered women. In A. R. Roberts (Ed.), *Battered women and their families* (pp. 49-61). New York: Springer.

Bernstein, S. C. (1991). *A family that fights.* Morton Grove, IL: Albert Whitman.

Carlson, B. E. (1984). Children's observations of interparental violence. In A. R. Roberts (Ed.), *Battered women and their families* (pp. 147-167). New York: Springer.

Cassady, L., Allen, B., Lyon, E., & McGeehan, C. (1987, July). *The Child-Focused Intervention Program: Program evaluation for children in a battered women's shelter.* Paper presented at the Third National Family Violence Researchers Conference, Durham, NH.

Cottle, T. J. (1980). *Children's secrets.* Garden City, NY: Doubleday.

Davis, D. (1984). *Something is wrong at my house: A book about parents' fighting.* Seattle, WA: Parenting Press.

Dobash, R. E., & Dobash, R. (1979). *Violence against wives.* New York: Free Press.

Elbow, M. (1982). Children of violent marriage: The forgotten victim. *Social Casework, 8,* 465-468.

Frey-Angel, J. (1989). Treating children of violent families: A sibling group approach. *Social Work with Groups, 12,* 95-107.

Gentry, C. E., & Eaddy, V. B. (1980). Treatment of children in spouse abusive families. *Victimology, 2-4,* 240-250.

Gibson, J. W., & Gutierrez, L. (1991). A service program for safe-home children. *Families in Society: A Journal of Contemporary Human Services, 72,* 554-562.

Grusznski, R. J., Brink, J. C., & Edleson, J. L. (1988). Support and education groups for children of battered women. *Child Welfare, 68,* 431-444.

Henderson, A. (1990). Children of abused wives: Their influence on their mothers' decisions. *Canada's Mental Health, 38,* 10-13.

Hilberman, E., & Munson, K. (1977). Sixty battered women. *Victimology, 2,* 460-471.

Hilton, N. Z. (1992). Battered women's concerns about their children witnessing wife assault. *Journal of Interpersonal Violence, 7,* 77-86.

Hughes, H. M. (1982). Brief interventions with children in a battered women's shelter: A model preventive program. *Family Relations, 31,* 495-502.

Jaffe, P., Wilson, S., & Wolfe, D. A. (1986). Promoting changes in attitudes and understanding of conflict among child witnesses of family violence. *Canadian Journal of Behavioral Science, 18,* 356-380.

Johnson, R. J., & Montgomery, M. (1990). Children at multiple risk: Treatment and prevention. In R. T. Potter-Efron & P. S. Potter-Efron (Eds.), *Aggression, family violence, and chemical dependency* (pp. 145-163). New York: Haworth.

Kerouac, S., Taggart, M. E., Lescop, J., & Fortin, M. F. (1986). Dimensions of health in violent families. *Health Care for Women International, 7,* 413-426.

Layzer, J. I., Goodson, B. D., & Delange, C. (1986). Children in shelters. *Response to Victimization of Women and Children, 9*(2), 2-5.

Levine, M. B. (1975). Interpersonal violence and its effect on children: A study of 50 families in general practice. *Medicine, Science and Law, 15,* 172-176.

Martin, D. (1976). *Battered wives.* New York: Simon & Schuster.

Media Ventures and Illusion Theatre. (1983). *Touch* [Film]. Deerfield, IL: Coronet/MTI Film & Video. (34 min.)

Mitchell Film Company. (1984). *What tadoo with fear* [Film]. Deerfield, IL: Coronet/MTI Film & Video. (18 min.)

Moore, J. G. (1975). Yo-yo children: Victims of matrimonial violence. *Child Welfare, 54,* 557-566.

Palmer, P. (1977). *The mouse, the monster, and me.* San Luis Obispo, CA: Impact.

Patterson, S. (1986). *No-no, the little seal.* New York: Random House.

Peled, E., & Davis, D. (1994). *Group work with child witnesses of domestic violence: A practitioner's manual.* Thousand Oaks, CA: Sage.

Peled, E., & Edleson, J. L. (1992). Multiple perspectives on group work with children of battered women. *Violence and Victims, 7,* 327-346.

Ragg, D. M., & Webb, C. (1992). Group treatment for the preschool child witness of spouse abuse. *Journal of Child and Youth Care, 7,* 1-19.

Roy, A. (1988). *Children in the crossfire: Violence in the home—How does it affect our children?* Deerfield Beach, FL: Health Communication.

Saunders, D. G., & Azar, S. T. (1989). Treatment programs for family violence. In L. Ohlin & M. Tonry (Eds.), *Family violence* (pp. 481-546). Chicago: University of Chicago Press.

Schur, E. M. (1971). *Labeling deviant behavior: Its sociological implications.* New York: Harper & Row.

Stacy, W., & Shupe, A. (1983). *The family secret: Domestic violence in America.* Boston: Beacon.

Syers-McNairy, M. (1990). *Women who leave violent relationships: Getting on with life.* Unpublished doctoral dissertation, University of Minnesota, Minneapolis.

Tri-State Coalition. (1986). *It's not always happy at my house* [Film]. Deerfield, IL: MTI Film & Video. (33 min)

Wachter, O. (1983). *No more secrets for me.* Boston: Little, Brown.

Walker, L. E. (1979). *The battered woman.* New York: Harper & Row.

Wilson, S. K., Cameron, S., Jaffe, P. G., & Wolfe, D. (1986). *Manual for a group program for children exposed to wife abuse.* London, Ontario: London Family Court Clinic.

# 6

# Empowering Battered Women as Mothers

JOAN BILINKOFF

Battered women consistently point to "the children" as a primary reason for staying in an abusive relationship (e.g., Henderson, 1990; Hilton, 1992). The cultural messages are powerful: "I don't want my children to come from a broken home," "The kids need a father," "I can't raise them alone," or "I want us to be a family" (Jordan, 1980).

The prohibition to discuss a strong, confident model of female parenting is so powerful in our patriarchal culture that most mothers have no frame of reference for seeing themselves capable of parenting alone. That social workers and other practitioners generally do not explore the association between staying in an abusive relationship and parenting children is a serious oversight.

Social norms define and social attitudes reflect the degree of respectability or stigma that single women and their children internalize. Therefore, if female-headed families are seen as "broken," "torn," "deficient," or "not normal," the members of these families are likely to internalize this message. Contrast this with an alternative set of social norms describing female-headed families as "positive" and "healthy," whereby the parent would feel more secure regarding her ability to parent.

---

AUTHOR'S NOTE: This chapter was inspired by Walters, Carter, Papp, and Silverstein's (1988) book *The Invisible Web*.

## BATTERED MOTHERS AS CLIENTS

Women are taught by our culture to invest their identities in their relationships or marriages. Women are taught also to take major responsibility for the success or failure of the relationships. They look toward their partner's and children's needs, not their own, to set life's goals.

As practitioners, our main task is to help our clients develop positive personal and emotional resources. Healing from the effects of violence can be facilitated by using the end of the relationship to help the client define herself first as a woman, and then as a mother.

In the case of battered women, it is likely that the woman's partner has drilled into her that both the failure of the relationship and his violence are her fault. Perpetrators generally accuse their victims by saying, "You make me do this," "You provoke me," or "I never did this with anyone else." When survivors come to see a therapist, they are often in a state of severe anxiety, guilt, and uncertainty.

## THERAPEUTIC GOALS
## FOR BATTERED WOMEN

When a battered mother is the client, several issues come up early in the therapeutic process: She asks why she was attracted to a violent man; she raises safety issues for herself and her children; she describes guilt about having raised the children in a violent home; she questions her legitimate temptation to enter into another relationship right away for economic assistance or to lessen her loneliness; and she expresses her generalized guilt for having left the relationship.

The woman's role in counseling is to mourn the end of her relationship and the hopes and dreams that ended. It is an important therapeutic stance to honor the positive and pleasurable aspects of her former relationship, for even the most violent families have moments of love and nurturance.

## PARENTING ISSUES

When you and your client both agree that she has gained insight into herself and the relationship, has mourned its end, and has started to heal from the effects of violence, it is the time to begin concentrating specifically on parenting issues. Four main issues need to be discussed and resolved before the victim/survivor is able to make proactive decisions about her parenting style: (a) using power and control, (b) making up for the absent father, (c) using the children as confidants or allies, and (d) dealing with her perception of her children's similarity to their father. Each is discussed below.

## Using Power and Control

Many victims/survivors are reluctant to take control of their children's behavior because they often associate control with the abuse they suffered by their partners. Family rules necessary for running the family in a respectful and efficient way are often seen by battered women as an imposition of their will and as abusive to their children. Assigning family chores is a good example of this issue. Mothers are reluctant to assign chores to older children and hesitant to enforce their completion. A mother may say, "I know how it feels to have to do something I don't want to do; my partner forced me to do stuff all the time."

It is crucial to help the client differentiate requests that are logical and fair from those that are not. Mothers need to reframe instructions in positive ways. For example, "This family needs to work together to have a clean living space to stay healthy and to find the things we need," instead of, "Do this because I said so." You can offer a positive reframing to the woman and help her believe and state to her children, "I am the mother, and I know how to take care of you."

## Making Up for the Absent Father

Women often feel so guilty for ending a relationship in a culture that clearly affixes the blame onto them that they indulge their children to make up for the father being gone. This tactic may be played out, for example, through new toys, games, or sports equipment a mother buys for her children whether or not she can afford it. One mother said, "I can't bear the thought that the children suffer because I kicked out their father, and these things will make us feel better." Another mother kept up an exhausting schedule of attending every one of her son's hockey games because "his father would have been there if we were still together." After careful questioning, it became clear that the father had rarely attended his son's games, and when he did, the son dreaded it because the father generally was loud and abusive to the coach.

As the mother gains more and more confidence in her ability to parent, she may be less likely to rush in and try to fill the father's space. The "hockey mom," for example, finally negotiated with her son while stating firmly that she would like to attend some, but not all, of his games and that together they would decide which ones.

## Using the Children
## as Confidants or Allies

One of the most prevalent means that perpetrators use to gain power is to isolate the victim and control access to her friends and family. It is within this context that the victim/survivor may start to inappropriately use the children to confide in and gain support. Mothers need to develop appropriate support systems that can offer help, parenting tips, recreational opportunities, and nurturance. It is confusing and damaging to the children to be privy to many adult fears and misgivings or to be forced to take sides with one parent against another parent. A phrase that women are encouraged to use with their children in this context is "This is grown-up stuff, and I can handle it without your help."

## Mother's Perception of
## Children's Similarity to Their Father

Battered women tend to weigh the misbehavior of their sons in a different way from that of their daughters. One clear example is when a client's 13-year-old daughter had two friends over to the house and was critical and disrespectful toward her mother in front of her friends. The mother defined it as "typical adolescent show-off behavior" and walked away. When her 14-year-old son did a very similar thing with his friends a short time later, the mother began to shout that she swore never to take criticism or abuse from anyone again and that he had better learn to control his mouth.

Former battered women may see the son as "exactly like his father," thus beginning a cycle of self-fulfilling prophecy for the child. Our cultural dictate "A boy needs a father to raise him" clearly brings the mother to feel more fearful and insecure about her ability to raise a strong and humane son. Victims/survivors may need a combination of developmental information, gender role information, and support in parenting their sons without overreacting emotionally. For example, one mother was quite relieved to hear that her 7-year-old son's description of girls as "yucky, boring, and weird" was quite typical for his age and not the result of living with an abusive father who constantly put down her and her friends in front of him.

With increasing insight into her own life, an understanding of the effects of violence on herself and her children, and a more balanced view of her family life, a client may be better prepared to begin looking at her vision of parenting.

## ROLE COMPLEMENTARITY
## AND A TRADITIONAL PARENTING MODEL

A male, authoritarian, hierarchical system of parenting is embedded so deeply into our culture that it is difficult even to conceptualize anything different. Basic to this structure is the concept of *role complementarity* (Walters, Carter, Papp, & Silverstein, 1988). This concept states that women take care of the emotional tasks of the family; they are supposed to be in charge of the "expressive or nurturing" tasks such as child rearing, development of family rituals, and tracking the social life of the family. Men are supposed to take care of the family's "managerial or executive" functions such as money, housing, and major decisions.

Simply stated, women do not parent like men. An isolated authority figure who manages the family executive functions without input from others is a style that women generally cannot relate to and, more often than not, fail to emulate. This prevailing patriarchal model of family is grounded in assumptions we as a society have long taken for granted. Consequently it is extremely difficult for women, and especially battered women, to conceptualize anything different or even to recognize a successful alternative parenting style.

One woman, for example, developed a lovely ritual for herself and her three children for Saturday night. Each of her children took a turn to plan and cook a Saturday night meal of his or her choice. Needless to say, the meals were "creative" in their nutritional content and scant in the four major food groups. When the grandparents found out about this, they were shocked that the children could eat "anything" they wanted, often left the kitchen a disaster, and were "in charge" instead of the mother. While being upset about the criticism, this woman was able to reframe the experiment as one of participatory democracy, a good way of teaching the children how to plan and execute a task, and a method of caring and nurturing the members of the family. The mother verbally countered her parents' criticisms and developed trust in her own intuition about what works in her family.

## ROLE SYMMETRY AND
## A FEMINIST PARENTING MODEL

The feminist model of parenting is based on the concept of *role symmetry* (Walters et al., 1988). The mother takes on both elements of work and nurture in the family. This is an egalitarian approach to power in which a democratic and consensual approach to managing children is recognized and valued. The opportunity for one parent to combine and integrate the nurturing and managerial roles in the family is invaluable for the children. Children witness firsthand an expansion of roles that are not limited to either gender or tradition.

For example, one mother volunteered to coach for her 11-year-old daughter's soccer team. She was the only mom out of five parents. Her daughter came home one day and told her that the team thought she was the best coach. She was thrilled and asked her daughter whether the team liked her style, thought she had more skill than the dads, or was more enthusiastic. Her daughter gave an exasperated sigh and said, "Mom, it's all that stuff, but you're the only coach that brings homemade cookies to practice." This woman had achieved the perfect mixture of executive and nurturing functions.

## DEVELOPING AN
## EMPOWERED VISION OF MOTHERING

When you ask a battered woman what her vision of parenting looks like, you are likely to get a blank, confused look and an answer like, "I want us to all get along." This answer is a logical consequence of living in a violent relationship in which she buried her thoughts and wishes and sacrificed herself in order to protect her children. Developing a vision of parenting intimately tied into what she believes her family needs and unencumbered by the patriarchy is a difficult and time-consuming task.

One possible exercise is to have a mother describe a typical day in the life of her family. She is asked to pretend that she is a movie camera and to describe in great detail what one would see looking at her family through the camera's lens. Then she is asked to describe, again in great detail, what one would see if her family would behave in a way she desires. Each scenario is dissected, and then the social worker and the client cooperatively create a plan to develop the desired family behaviors.

A mother I worked with had tremendous struggles getting her 4-year-old daughter to sleep. Before she divorced her partner, bedtime was tense and unpleasant because her partner was jealous of the time she spent with her daughter and degraded their bedtime rituals as "stupid and babyish." Even after the divorce, the mother, out of habit, rushed bedtime and wanted it over with, a stance the child sensed and exploited whenever possible.

The plan the client agreed on was to develop a mutually desirable bedtime ritual for herself and her daughter, balancing the daughter's need for closeness and security with the mother's need for relaxation and privacy. The mother firmly stated that mom-daughter time was from 7 p.m. to 8 p.m. and that the daughter could decide daily what she wanted to do: stories, television, a walk, a cuddle. The ritual then required that the daughter stay in her bed after that time and play quietly until she fell asleep. Although the 4-year-old tested her mom again and again, bedtime soon became a loving and nurturing time instead of an emotion-laden power struggle.

More importantly, the client was helped to use feminist language and concepts when developing a plan. We talked about empowering her daughter to ask for what she needed and mutually deciding what would work within this family. The client believed that both of their needs and rights were balanced and proudly said she felt like she was trail-blazing a new way to parent her child, based on love and respect, and not on power and control.

## DEVELOPING NEW FAMILY RITUALS

Another way to help a mother develop a new parenting vision is by assisting her to create a new set of family rituals and holiday celebrations. Many victims/survivors and their children have terrible memories of holidays and birthday celebrations because of violence associated with them. Older children especially become very enthusiastic and excited when asked their opinion on celebrating a holiday differently and come up with some creative ideas. One family decided to celebrate Christmas Eve by attending an afternoon movie, making a huge pizza at home, and driving around to see the holiday lights. Another family decided to remake Mother's Day into Mother's Week and planned a surprise for the mother every day for 7 days. Some families opt out of celebrating traditional holidays and make up their own milestones to celebrate. For example, a family of adopted children decided to celebrate the day they arrived at their new home, instead of their birthdays. Again it is important to stress to the children that this is not a deficit model of celebrating because their dad is not around. Rather, it is a free choice based on a vision that the family has developed for itself.

## HANDLING ECONOMIC CHANGES

Separating or divorcing a partner means for many women a dramatic shift in economic circumstances and, perhaps, necessitates a return to work after being home full-time with the children. Most women in our society struggle with guilt in balancing work and family, and formerly battered women are no different. It is crucial to help the woman explore and articulate to herself and her children what she is able to accomplish within a "working mother" lifestyle.

One mother admirably stood her ground in the following discussion with her 14-year-old son. He was complaining bitterly about the scarcity of his favorite home-cooked meals since his mother returned to work full-time. Instead of reacting defensively, the mother chose to discuss how difficult the change had been for them both since the divorce and how she wished sometimes that she could stay home and cook as she used to. She then wrote down in painstaking detail the recipes for some of her son's favorite meals and taught him how to cook them.

## DEVELOPING AN
## EXTENDED FAMILY NETWORK

One of the most important aspects of a new vision of single-mother parenting is the inclusion of friends and extended family members into the primary family. Both mother and children get to choose with whom they want to share their family life, but this is predicated on the mother's ability to be assertive and ask others for help. This task is extremely difficult for some women who see it as a point of pride to handle everything themselves.

One woman expressed doubt about her sister's generalized postdivorce stance—"If you ever need anything, call me." Learning that she had a mandatory out-of-town seminar, she role-played an assertive request of her sister's to take her children overnight. Her sister accepted without a moment's hesitation and now frequently takes the children overnight just for the fun of it. The sister later admitted that she wanted to help but had no idea what she could do.

## RECOGNIZING THE IMPACT OF OUR WORK

Our culture never fails to mention that a juvenile criminal is a product of a single-parent family. Yet mention is never made of the kind of family from which the local high school honor roll student comes. Blaming single mothers for the ills of society or for our troubled children remains popular without examination of other variables such as poverty, unsafe neighborhoods, impoverished school systems, and job discrimination that cripple our families.

It is imperative for a social worker or other helping professional to examine his or her own parenting vision before attempting to counsel others. Accepting a patriarchal model and identifying with authority, power, and dominance, rather than with consensual decision making, empowerment, and nurturance, are easy traps into which to fall.

It is crucial to develop a peer group of people working in the domestic violence field for supervision and support. This is a highly specific field, and a general supervision group ultimately will not be helpful. The goal for you and your agency is to develop a culture that both challenges the status quo in parenting styles and, in the meantime, nurtures the staff.

## REFERENCES

Henderson, A. (1990). Children of abused wives: Their influence on their mother's decisions. *Canada's Mental Health, 88,* 10-13.
Hilton, N. Z. (1992). Battered women's concerns about their children witnessing wife assault. *Journal of Interpersonal Violence, 7,* 77-86.
Jordan, J. K. (1980). Two minus one is one . . . plus a whole lot more: Coping with life as a single parent. *Issues in Health Care of Women, 2,* 49-57.
Walters, M. A., Carter, B., Papp, P., & Silverstein, O. (1988). *The invisible web.* New York: Guilford.

# 7

# Parenting Groups for Men Who Batter

## DAVID J. MATHEWS

An often missed opportunity for assisting children who witness violence in the home is working with the perpetrator. The statistics are clear and indicate that an overwhelming number of children witness their fathers' actions. In addition to working with the children and the mothers, challenging the men in these families to take ownership of the problems their behaviors have created is paramount to the process of establishing safety for children.

Parenting support groups have been available for many years throughout this country. Classes for parents are offered through local community education organizations, churches, and community-based agencies. Written materials have continued to increase in availability in bookstores and workshops. Parents' need-to-know or desire to understand their children has seemed to fuel this growing awareness about children's issues. Very little material, however, has been designed, developed, or available for the specific needs of men whose children have witnessed their violent behavior.

In this chapter I describe a model for conducting group counseling with fathers of children who have witnessed their violence toward a spouse or partner. This intervention model's usefulness is demonstrated in three ways. First, it contains a straightforward philosophy and approach to working with fathers who have perpetrated violence against their spouses or partners. It focuses heavily on the perpetrator taking responsibility for his actions. Second, this model possesses a built-in flexibility and potential for the therapist to enhance or mold the approach according to one's own style of facilitating groups. Third, the content of the model has appeared to fit for a variety of clients from diverse backgrounds.

In addition, in this chapter I identify some of the primary counseling issues for men whose children have witnessed their violence. Practical ideas and simple group interventions are suggested as ways to examine and confront the attitudes that many of these men seem to possess.

## MODELS OF PARENT TRAINING

Before describing the specific intervention model with men whose children have witnessed their violence, it is important to have some understanding of what is currently available for parents in general. Three parenting programs seem to stand out among others on the basis of popularity, amount of time on the market, and availability of relatively current research. The three programs are Parent Effectiveness Training (PET) (Gordon, 1975), Systematic Training for Effective Parenting (STEP) (Dinkmeyer & McKay, 1976), and Active Parenting (Popkin, 1993a, 1993b).

PET is a predominantly text-based program relying on manuals and books (Schofield, 1979). This approach focuses on parents identifying ways to act that will direct the family in positive directions (Chant & Nelson, 1982). STEP stresses the parents' need to identify the reasons for their child's "misbehavior" and then to develop strategic responses (or steps) that will promote learning for the child and strengthen the family unit (Sharpley & Poiner, 1980). Active Parenting is the newest program of the three. It is a video-based program designed to assist parents in dealing with a variety of family problems and situations. The videos act as discussion material in group sessions and encourage parents to role-play or practice ways to implement new parenting strategies within the family setting. More recently, a set of manuals and leader's guides has been developed to further assist in examining parenting issues (Popkin, 1993a, 1993b).

These three programs seem to share a number of characteristics. The contents of all of the programs appear to have roots based in an Adlerian educational-psychology approach (Cole, 1986). The emphasis is on conducting groups of parents, rather than working with individual parents or couples. Techniques suggested seem to be enhancements of each other, but the way these programs begin to address family problems seem to differ. For example, STEP appears to focus initially on the child, while PET directs its primary attention to the parents.

These programs appear to have had a major impact on participating parents' behaviors and attitudes. STEP has been studied extensively, including its use with parents who have experienced violence in their homes (e.g., Carney, 1985; Hitchcock, 1987; Jackson & Brown, 1986). Although these three programs show promise, there appears to be an incorrect assumption that they simply can be applied to working with men who are perpetrators of domestic violence and to any other identified group of parents without modification or specialized activities related to the specific needs of participating parents.

Increasing attention is being paid to programs for fathers, particularly teen fathers (Huey, 1987). In their book *Deadly Consequences,* Prothrow-Stith and Weissman (1991) describe a program designed to reduce violence by allowing young men in grade school through high school to provide nurturing and caring for babies who are either brought in by their parents to be observed or in an on-site day care program. It seems that as a result of this program, significant positive changes in attitude have occurred. Additionally some correctional facilities within the state of Minnesota have provided parenting support group opportunities for those living in these facilities. Early childhood family educators throughout the United States seem to be challenged to find new ways to draw fathers into parenting support groups. From a public health perspective, most of these programs are aimed at primary and secondary levels of prevention (Prothrow-Stith & Weissman, 1991). Few programs focus on fathers who have been abusive toward a partner or a child, and little has been written on such efforts.

## A MODEL PROGRAM FOR FATHERS

The Men's Parenting Program, developed by staff at the Amherst H. Wilder Foundation Community Assistance Program (CAP), was created with the intent of increasing fathers' understanding of their children, confronting the fathers' violent behaviors, increasing their understanding of how their violent behaviors have affected their children, and providing an opportunity for these men to learn, develop, and practice new parenting skills.

Wilder CAP is dedicated to preventing, reducing, and eliminating violence in families and communities by developing and delivering effective services to children, adolescents, and adults. It established the domestic abuse component of its programs in early 1982 with the encouragement and assistance of the Ramsey County Community Corrections Department. Wilder CAP provides counseling services for more than 600 clients a year—women, men, and children. Other services provided are crisis intervention counseling, information and referral, advocacy, and assessments in the area of family violence for women, men, and children who call for assistance.

Since its beginning, Wilder CAP has emphasized the strong need for collaborative efforts to address the problem of domestic violence. The long-standing relationship with Ramsey County Community Corrections continues. A unit of Ramsey County Probation Officers is housed in the same building and supervises the domestic assault cases from criminal court. Ramsey County Human Services also has joined our efforts in confronting the issues of child abuse and neglect by providing both funding and professional support to Wilder CAP.

The Men's Parenting Program began when men receiving domestic abuse services at Wilder CAP expressed an interest and a need to focus on their parenting. The first men's parenting group was started in February, 1987, with four group members attending.

Initially men volunteered or were referred to the group through a spouse or a court worker. As the program developed, men were court-ordered as part of their probationary agreement to attend the parenting group. This was true particularly when a man was found guilty of malicious punishment of his child. Throughout the group counseling process, the CAP staff work closely with the Ramsey County Community Corrections Department.

## Program Philosophy

The Wilder CAP intervention model is based on the following assumptions about violence:

- Violence is a personal, family, community, local, state, national, international, economic, societal, and cultural issue.
- Violence is learned behavior that has rewards and consequences.
- Violence is reinforced by our society.
- Violence can be passed on from one generation to another.
- Violence is a choice made to gain power and control.
- Violence can be unlearned; there are alternatives when expressing feelings.

The model also is founded on the following assumptions about individual responsibility with regard to violence and abuse:

- People are responsible for their behaviors.
- The "one hundred percent" rule: Each person is 100% responsible for his or her own behavior in any relationship.
- Provocation by another person does not justify violent responses.
- The only person one can control is oneself.
- Individuals have the capacity to change their behaviors.

These statements help clients create a framework in which to take responsibility for their behaviors and to build a foundation toward hope and change.

In addition to these statements, counselors are encouraged to create a non-shaming, respectful environment, accepting the man as a human being but still challenging his violent actions. Making connections between these points and being a father or a male role model in the family is related to the primary goals of the Men's Parenting Program.

## Program Structure

The structure for this model was created with flexibility in mind. The decision to provide a group setting for working with perpetrators came directly from the staff's experience with facilitating men's domestic abuse groups for 12 years. The staff also recognized that group work helped deal with the resistance of the men coming to the program. Additionally the group process appeared to be efficient and highly effective in dealing with violence issues and to increase men's opportunities to take responsibility for their actions.

Wilder CAP historically has conducted fathers' groups one session per week for 12 weeks, with each meeting lasting about $2\frac{1}{2}$ hours. Prior to the start of the group, each man meets with the group counselor for two individual sessions to gather background information, sign releases, and begin to examine the level of resistance he may exhibit. The intake interviews allow the counselor to assess how the man will fit into a group, not whether the man can be in the group. Another goal is to model acceptance of the man as an individual without giving him permission to be violent. Experience shows that the allocated time for individual and group sessions is not enough to cover all of the necessary issues and information. Men often request to extend the number of group sessions.

During the 12 sessions, the overall agenda is determined by the counselors, taking into account the needs and desired outcomes of the men. This information is gathered in individual sessions, as well as at the first group meeting. Some popular topics routinely addressed during the sessions are a father's role, what is violence, discipline versus punishment, changing children's behaviors, child development, logical and natural consequences, the effects of children witnessing violence, communication skills, assertiveness, and expressing feelings appropriately.

The first session usually begins with men getting to know each other and identifying similarities (rather than differences) among themselves. Then the group rules and expectations are established. A final goal for the session is to further motivate the members to invest in the group process. Subsequent sessions are focused on activities related to the subjects listed above.

## CRITICAL ISSUES IN FATHERS' GROUPS

The varied contents of the group often trigger a number of issues with which group leaders must deal. Six specific issues relevant to many men are (a) resistance in the group, (b) limited knowledge of child development, (c) shame and how they cope with it, (d) ability to have empathy for their children's experience of their violence, (e) stepparenting, and (f) willingness to make a commitment to nonviolent parenting. Each of these issues is discussed below.

### Men's Resistance

The vast majority of the clients attending the Men's Parenting Program tend to resist the program on one level or another. These men, most often fathers or stepfathers of the children who witnessed their violence, usually are court-ordered to complete the program or are referred by the criminal courts or county child protection services. Men's resistance seems to stem from having been pressured to be in the group, their minimization of the impact of their violence on others, or complete denial that their behavior is a problem.

The resistant attitudes these men present can be handled in a number of ways. Optimally, in initial intake sessions, the group leader not only can assess how this potential group member will fit into the group but also begins to build a relationship with the man. This relationship may be a strong tool in decreasing the defensive attitudes exhibited. Through this relationship the group leader may examine with the man his violent behaviors and insights regarding the effects his behaviors have had on children and others in his family. Avoiding power struggles between the leader and the client is highly advised. Delivering confrontational information as observations and concerns can be extremely effective for reaching these men when it is done within an established relationship.

Many men also seem to be resistant to changing their behaviors. Maintaining minimization or denial of the violence serves this resistance. It appears that men connect an acceptance of the need for behavioral change with being a bad person or a bad parent. This type of thinking feeds directly into feelings of shame and the perceived need to control those people who elicit these feelings. Allowing the men to share their opinions within the group often reveals this attitude. The group leader can address it with all group members by drawing out how others may feel and discussing this sequence of thinking. This process tends to disarm some men of their defensiveness and enables some to examine their denial.

Additionally men sustain their investment in the power and control dynamic they have established in their family by not changing their behavior. It seems that once a person experiences this position of control (or perceived control) over others, it is difficult to motivate him or her to relinquish it. Many of these men have been socialized for years into their role as "head of the household." Helping group members explore where they learned their roles as men and fathers helps them see the destructive path these traditional perceptions sometimes take.

## Knowledge of Child Development

A father's lack of knowledge about child development sometimes leads to violent interactions between child and father. The father/perpetrator may view his child's questions, particularly questions related to family functioning, as personal challenges or attacks. He may perceive such questions as "power moves" and react aggressively toward the child in order to maintain control. Children quickly learn not to voice questions in this environment.

When someone steps out of line in the home of a violent father, the father often makes it his job to aggressively reestablish the family balance (bring things under his control). An example behavior is demanding family members to "tow the line or else." These types of threats often have been carried out in previous situations. As a result the threats usually are followed by obedient behaviors on the part of other family members.

Misinformation about child development can be as damaging to the child and as frustrating for the parent as is no information at all. This is especially true regarding *discipline* and *punishment.* Although those words often are used interchangeably, the two actions produce entirely different results. For example, it seems that fathers often focus more on control aspects of punishment than on the teaching aspects of discipline. As the child becomes increasingly resistant and outwardly rebellious of the punishment, the father may increase the severity of the punishment to the point of abusing the child. Straus (1994) states that spanking over time becomes less effective and ultimately impossible to carry out as the child grows older.

Such dynamics occur between fathers and children of all ages. For example, one client believed that his son should be toilet trained by the age of 2. As the child continued to be unsuccessful in learning the task, the father became increasingly demanding that his son "be a man," giving the child frequent 10- to 15-minute talks about the issue. This behavior went on for several months, with the father gradually escalating his response. This father clearly did not have the correct information for helping his son master appropriate developmental skills. For all of these reasons, it is important to address issues of punishment, discipline, and normal child development. Having group members examine their current understanding of these issues and then providing accurate information to them are invaluable to the men's continued reshaping of their parenting values. One activity commonly used to help fathers refocus their parenting on constructive and developmentally appropriate change is to work closely with them in group on behavior change plans as described in Activity 7.1.

**Shame**

Another characteristic often shared by perpetrators is the feeling of shame regarding their violence. Fathers may feel shame as a result of their behavior and its impact on their children. They often feel responsible for any behavioral problems their children have. In fact, many of these parents seem unable to distinguish acting-out behavior from normal, developmentally appropriate behavior and, as a consequence, label all problem behaviors as results of the violence. This is especially true if the child is preadolescent, a universally difficult stage for all families and a particularly explosive time for families of child witnesses.

The father/perpetrator's shame seems to come from two sources. First, some perpetrators view themselves as bad parents because they cannot adequately control their families. Second, many perpetrators state that they do not want to repeat the same violent acts they witnessed as children, while at the same time they realize that they do. Recalling the intense feelings from their own experiences of witnessing violence raises shame and embarrassment for these men. The shame intensifies if the man believes that no one else has had these feelings or experiences. Such feelings also may lead to isolation, fearing to disclose these experiences, feelings, and thoughts to others. This tendency to be isolated and not trust the input of others makes it more difficult to accept alternatives or come up with new behavioral options.

The group process assists each man in lessening his isolation from others and gives him an opportunity to receive input from others having similar experiences. One activity that helps facilitate this process (see Activity 7.2) focuses men on their individual parenting styles by reflecting on how they have come to be the kind of parent they are and by sharing these insights with other group members.

As mentioned earlier, another shame-related issue is the perpetrators' need to maintain control over their families. At the same time, perpetrators often instruct their sons to be tough, to stick up for themselves, and to "never be beaten." In some families there comes a point when the young men assert

ACTIVITY 7.1

**Constructive Behavior Change**

This activity is aimed at all fathers in the group. The main purpose is for the father to experience success in nonviolent, noncoercive change of one specific unwanted behavior displayed by one of his children. Related goals are giving the father an opportunity (a) to put into practice some of the information he has learned about children's psychosocial development and the difference between discipline and punishment and (b) to practice the use of natural and logical consequences.

*Activity Format*

Group members are each asked to think of a behavior that one of their children does that is irritating to them and that they would like to see the child change. Fathers are encouraged to write down all of the behaviors that they would like their child to change and then to pick one of these behaviors to focus on in the subsequent weeks of the group.

The behavior they choose must meet three criteria. First, it must be a specific behavior. In other words, "mouthing off" is too general of a descriptor. Ask the father to state what exactly the child says when "mouthing off." Fathers can be assisted in selecting behaviors by having them envision someone coming over to their house with a video camera to take movies of their child and then asking what exactly the child did or said in the video that was the unwanted behavior needing to be changed. Second, the behavior cannot be whatever the father thinks is the child's worst behavior. Having the father initially identify simpler behaviors and work on these promotes success in changing the behavior, instead of trying to deal first with the most difficult one. Third, the behavior to be worked on must be chosen after the man consults with other group members to get their opinion about what might be the most manageable target for change.

During group sessions, after everyone has chosen a behavior to change, raise some of the following questions to assist participating fathers in devising a plan to change the behavior:

- What would you rather have the child do instead of the unwanted behavior? (This desired behavior needs to be as specific as the unwanted behavior and realistically attainable.)
- How will you communicate the desired outcome behavior to your child?
- How will you communicate your feelings to the child when you observe the unwanted behavior?

---

**ACTIVITY 7.1**

**Continued**

- What can you control when the child exhibits the unwanted behavior?
- What natural and logical consequences are or should be in place?
- How will you reward the child when you see the desired behavior?

Each of these questions must be dealt with by the group members in order for them to create their plans for changing unwanted behavior. During subsequent group sessions they will be sharing their successes and failures, looking for ways to fine-tune their approach in dealing with other unwanted behaviors.

During this exercise fathers are able to explore their ability to control or not control certain aspects of their children's behavior. They begin to learn how to lessen their focus on certain behaviors and issues that draw their attention away from the specific unwanted behaviors. Their gradual improvement at devising and carrying out their nonviolent and nonthreatening behavior-change plans sends a message to the child about change, risk, and the need to know one's own limits.

---

themselves against their fathers. Fathers may view such behavior as a direct challenge to their authority and try to control it. Fathers often fear that if their sons' behaviors are not "handled," they will be perceived as weak and unable to control their families, thus not being good parents.

A common reaction of fathers who experience shame in the ways described above is to deny or minimize the effects that witnessing violence has had on the children. As a result a perpetrator may explain his child's behavior problems as a lack of discipline, which—he may seem quick to point out—is the fault of the child's mother. Shame also may interfere with the perpetrator's capacity for empathy toward the child. Rationalizations such as, "It didn't hurt me none to see my dad take it to my mom, once in a while," or, "I got some whippings when I was young, but I deserved it, and besides, it made me a better person," are commonly expressed by men who experience this shame.

Many of these fathers seem unable to compare the effects of their experience of witnessing violence or being abused with that of their children's. They often do not understand the connection between childhood experiences of violence and use of violence as an adult. In the process of rationalizing their own use of violence, they may give credit to their parents' use of violence as a valid, reasonable, and useful solution for managing childhood

---

**ACTIVITY 7.2**

**Learning to Be Fathers**

This exercise assists fathers in understanding why they parent the way they do. This exercise focuses on fathers' ability to recognize and understand the positive and negative messages about parenting that they are passing on to their children. This exercise may also increase fathers' empathy toward their children.

*Activity Format*

This activity requires fathers in the group to respond, first on paper, and then verbally, to two questions: (a) What are three things you have learned from your parents about how to be a parent (negative or positive)? and (b) What are three things you have learned from others in your life about how to be a parent (positive or negative)? Allow the fathers enough time to think about and then write their responses. After they have shared verbally what they have written, ask them to identify any themes they heard in each person's accounts. Listen for some of the following issues being raised: family of origin, grief and loss, and abuse and abandonment. Some of the more positive themes raised may be meaningful relationships, significant times of their lives, and particular events connected with learning a new skill.

In subsequent sessions, time is taken to check whether the fathers have done any further thinking about these issues as part of their parent education process. Allowing them time to reflect on these events, situations, and learning gives fathers an opportunity to understand some nagging feelings and questions about why they react to their children the way they do.

---

behavior problems. Thus the use of violence as part of their parenting skills is reinforced. Assisting group members to understand how their violent actions affect others in the family, particularly their children, is an important priority within group processes. Steps toward a better understanding of the effects may include examining what violence and abuse are and the reasons for using them.

## Men's Empathy for Their Children

The vast majority of these fathers/perpetrators have a genuine concern for their children. This concern may be expressed in different ways, however, providing the therapist with critical diagnostic information. For example, on the one hand, if the perpetrator maintains that the children are unaware, asleep, or out of the house when the violence has occurred and that they generally are unaffected by his behavior, he may be denying the conse- quences of his violent actions. On the other hand, a perpetrator who articu- lates the effects of violence on his children in terms of gender roles, aggressive behavior, role modeling, and their fear may be in an advanced stage of taking responsibility for his behavior and acknowledging its consequences.

Usually fathers in the groups experience difficulty when taking on their children's view of life and attempting to see the family through their chil- dren's eyes. It seems that these fathers are at a loss for having empathy, due, in part, to shame as well as to the rewards they receive for maintaining coercive power and control. One way to deal with this issue is periodically to raise the questions: What is in the best interest of the child? How would your child view your behavior? If a video camera were set up in the corner of your home, what exactly would it show? Another way to generate empathy for their child's view is to use a group activity (see Activity 7.3) that focuses on their children's experiences, feelings, and behaviors resulting from wit- nessing violence at home.

## Stepparenting

Many of the fathers in these groups are either divorced or separated, and some families have a stepparent, usually a stepfather, living with them. Stepparenting is a complex issue in our society, and there is a great deal of confusion regarding the appropriate role of the stepparent (Tedder & Scherman, 1987). However, stepparenting can be particularly problematic for fathers whose children have witnessed their violent behaviors.

Men entering into a previously formed family are often seen by all family members, including their partners, as outsiders. This makes stepparenting extremely challenging for a man, particularly when he is the perpetrator of violence within that home. These fathers may enter the family system as a self-proclaimed power and authority over the family in general and the chil- dren's behavior in particular. This approach most often seems to be carried out in an aggressive and punishing manner. A perpetrator also may demand that the child refer to him as "father" or give the children negative messages about their birth father or mother. Another tendency is for some men to adopt a totally "hands-off" parenting approach with the child. This parenting style can become extremely frustrating for the man; the pressure and stress resulting from not being in control may lead him to violent "blowouts."

## A Commitment to Nonviolent Parenting

A final issue addressed with fathers/perpetrators is their desire to make a commitment to violence-free parenting. This issue can be an indicator of the

**ACTIVITY 7.3**

**A Framework of Resourcefulness**

This exercise is used, first, to assist group participants in gaining a better understanding of their children and how witnessing violence has affected them. Second, it provides fathers with a realistic outlook on their children's problematic behaviors and with practical ways to fulfill their children's needs. Third, the structure of this activity creates a framework that can be used in addressing children's experiences and other parenting issues—for example, experiencing loss or family transitions.

*Activity Format*

Divide a chalkboard or easel space into five columns. At the top of the first column write "EXPERIENCES." Ask group members to list all of the violent situations or experiences their children have witnessed or heard or knew about. Fill the column with the responses provided by the group members. Label the second column "FEELINGS." Ask the group members to develop a list of feelings the children may have had as a result of their experiences from Column 1. Label the third column "BEHAVIORS." This list should describe the types of behaviors that fathers observed in their children (e.g., talking back, acting out, physical abuse or aggression directed at others, absenteeism from school, using drugs, suicide attempts, isolation). Ask some of the following questions as the group members review the information before them:

- What are the themes in each of these lists?
- Can any connections and similarities be drawn between the lists?
- How does it feel to look at these lists?
- What can be done regarding these experiences, feelings, or behaviors?

Explain the continuity and logical progression of the three columns: When a child experiences those situations listed and the resulting feelings in the next column, it seems to make sense that the behaviors described in the third column might follow. Ask the group to discuss the similarity of experiences among participants and the behaviors their children exhibit.

Label the fourth column "NEED." This list includes all of the things fathers think their children need. After this list has been developed, ask the fathers to reflect on the four columns and to report on their reactions to these lists. Expect some fathers to report feeling overwhelmed and how so often the lists are negative in nature.

---

**ACTIVITY 7.3**

**Continued**

The fifth and final list is meant to address their feelings of hopelessness. First, ask the fathers what are some of the obstacles to getting the children's needs met? If necessary, start another list of these obstacles. Then ask the group to contribute concrete examples of how they currently meet the needs of their children or could do so in the future. List these responses in the last column, labeled "I DO/I CAN DO." This list provides the group participants with a better understanding of some of the large and small ways that they can fulfill their child's needs.

It is important to process this activity with the group members by asking further questions about how these lists now appear. Examine the differences in feelings at this point with when they first started the exercise. Many fathers recognize that they already have begun to assist in the healing process of their children who have witnessed their violence. At the very least, this exercise brings forth new options of satisfying and fulfilling the needs of their children. It also affirms the group members for having attained some parenting skills.

---

man's ability to focus on the best interests of his children. Such a commitment may demonstrate the man's taking responsibility for his actions and marks a potential ending of his violent behavior. Many men in group tend to avoid making such commitments. Exploring their attitudes about corporal punishment and having them develop specific alternatives to hitting their children needs to be a focus of the group. The group leader should state strongly how the use of spanking is inefficient and lacks long-lasting effects (Straus, 1994).

## CONCLUSION

There are many excellent programs and curricula for parents. Few, however, address the specific needs of fathers who are perpetrators of violence. This chapter has provided an overview of the philosophy, structure, and critical issues raised in the Men's Parenting Program at Wilder's CAP. Additional materials related to this program can be found in *Parenting Under Stress: Group Counseling Manual* (Mathews, Matter, & Montgomery, 1990).

It is important for the group leader who may consider facilitating a fathers' group for perpetrators to prepare for this work by grounding the program in a strong philosophical base. Approaching participating fathers in a respectful manner and allowing them to state their case will result in a long-lasting learning experience for these men. The adaptation of other parenting programs and materials to the needs of these fathers will further enhance this model.

Working with these men, whose children have witnessed their violence, very often contributes to the safety of their children. When a program is strategically developed and carried out, all members of the family benefit.


## REFERENCES

Carney, K. (1985). *Impact of participation in Systematic Training for Effective Parenting on current and former residents of a battered women's shelter.* Unpublished master's thesis, Southern Connecticut State University, New Haven.

Chant, C., & Nelson, G. (1982). The effects of mother's use of I-messages and active listening on a child's behavior in the home. *Family Therapy, 9,* 271-278.

Cole, E. S. (1986). Active parenting. *Techniques, 2,* 109-114.

Dinkmeyer, D., & McKay, G. (1976). *Systematic Training for Effective Parenting (STEP).* Circle Pines, MN: American Guidance Service.

Gordon, T. (1975). *Parent Effectiveness Training (PET).* New York: New American Library.

Hitchcock, R. A. (1987). Understanding physical abuse as a lifestyle. *Individual Psychology, 43,* 50-55.

Huey, W. C. (1987). Counseling teenage fathers: Maximizing a life experience group. *School Counselor, 35,* 40-47.

Jackson, M. D., & Brown, D. (1986). Use of Systematic Training for Effective Parenting (STEP) with elementary school parents. *School Counselor, 34,* 100-104.

Mathews, D., Matter, L., & Montgomery, M. (1990). *Parenting under stress: Group counseling manual.* Charlotte, NC: Kidsrights.

Popkin, M. H. (1993a). *Active parenting today: For parents of 2-12 year olds: Leader's guide.* Atlanta, GA: Active Parenting.

Popkin, M. H. (1993b). *Active parenting today: For parents of 2-12 year olds: Parent's guide.* Atlanta, GA: Active Parenting.

Prothrow-Stith, D., & Weissman, M. (1991). *Deadly consequences.* New York: HarperCollins.

Schofield, R. (1979). Parent group education and student self-esteem. *Social Work in Education, 1,* 26-33.

Sharpley, C. F., & Poiner, A. M. (1980). An exploratory evaluation of the Systematic Training for Effective Parenting program. *Australian Psychologist, 15,* 103-109.

Straus, M. A. (1978). Wife beating: How common and why? *Victimology: An International Journal, 2,* 443-458.

Straus, M. A. (1994). *Beating the devil out of them: Corporal punishment in American families and its effects on children.* Lexington, MA: Lexington.

Tedder, S., & Scherman, A. (1987). Counseling single fathers. In M. Scher, M. Stevens, G. Good, & G. Eichenfield (Eds.), *Handbook of counseling and psychotherapy with men* (pp. 265-277). Newbury Park, CA: Sage.

# 8

# Advocacy for Children of Battered Women

## HONORE M. HUGHES
## MICHELE MARSHALL

The writings on children of battered women often have reflected the authors' dual role as both researchers and advocates. Some of the earliest writers in this area described the negative consequences experienced by children who observed their mothers being beaten, and pointed out the need for services for these children (e.g., Haffner, 1979; Labell, 1979; Lystad, 1975; Moore, 1977). Within the past decade, researchers have noted again that children of battered women are indeed unintended (Rosenbaum & O'Leary, 1981) or forgotten (Elbow, 1982) victims and made a strong plea to intervene with their plight and needs.

At the present time, with the negative impact of observing woman battering better documented, little doubt remains that the consequences for children of battered women are indeed adverse. Adequate assistance for these children, however, is still a pressing need (e.g., Davis & Carlson, 1987; Hughes, in press; Jaffe, Hurley, & Wolfe, 1990; Moore et al., 1990). Although progress has been made, it is crucial that more people become aware of these youngsters' special requirements and advocate for them.

This chapter is focused on children's advocacy in shelters. Such focus is in line with the findings of a recent study indicating that the majority (62%) of advocacy services for battered women and their children are provided in shelters, rather than in other settings (Peled & Edleson, in press). We hope, however, that the material presented will be useful to practitioners working with children of battered women in other settings as well.

With that goal in mind, we first discuss the conceptual framework and definition of advocacy, the skills needed to be an advocate, and the function and role of children's advocates. Next we discuss important practice concerns of which children's advocates must be aware and some strategies for dealing with these issues. The processes of working within the shelter with individual families, as well as interfacing with the larger systems that impinge on the lives of families, are described. Within each section we include available literature and information based on our experiences working in children's programs in shelters for battered women.

To make this chapter as practical as possible, we have included two figures that make our work more concrete. For those programs establishing children's programs, we also recommend an on-site consultation with an experienced children's advocate.

As cited in Alessi and Hearn (1984), according to the 1981 edition of the *Programs Providing Services to Children,* 172 of the 325 shelters for battered women that allowed children had some form of children's program. Most were described as "child care," with only three programs listing "counseling" as available. In the ensuing decade, shelters grew to more than 1,200, with 800 children's programs listed (Roberts, 1981; National Coalition Against Domestic Violence, 1991).

That growth is very encouraging. However, it is not always possible to know what is included in a "children's program" in terms of assistance and advocacy. Programs range widely in sophistication and complexity. On one end of the continuum might be a program with staff who meet with the children occasionally in a child care role. At the other end might be a children's advocate with advanced training in child and family therapy who oversees a well-funded, secure program. The types of activities in which a child advocate may be engaged will depend both on her or his training and on the particular characteristics of the program within which she or he works. Advocates in both formal and informal types of children's programs can be very effective, and our comments are directed toward both.

## WHAT IS CHILDREN'S ADVOCACY?

In this section we offer a general framework for advocacy including both a conceptual discussion and a description of the behaviors associated with those ideas when put into action. Examples of how we have carried out the advocacy role also are presented.

### Conceptual Framework

The two principles guiding our conceptual framework for children's advocacy are (a) to follow an empowerment model and (b) to be sensitive to issues of cultural and individual diversity.

*Empowerment.* The empowerment of individuals and families is always an overarching goal. Regarding empowerment, Miller (1991) defined power as the "capacity to produce a change" (p. 198) and discussed how women have used their power to "empower" others by increasing the others' resources, capabilities, effectiveness, and ability to act. It is crucial that an advocate not only obtain the necessary services for the women and children but also teach the mothers themselves to navigate and mobilize systems to meet their needs. This focus on empowerment was supported by Peled and Edleson's (in press) national survey on battered women's advocacy. In defining their outcome goals, 32% of the responding advocates explicitly listed empowering women as a desired outcome.

Much of the work with children in shelters also consists of empowering them, thereby enhancing their self-esteem. One way this is done is by helping children understand what types of actions are their responsibility and which are not, as well as the difference between what they can control or change and what they cannot (see Rosenberg & Rossman, 1990, for more detail).

*Diversity.* Families in need are likely to vary in their characteristics, such as socioeconomic status, racial/ethnic group, sexual preference of members, and type of community (e.g., rural, urban). Hence, knowledge of and sensitivity to cultural and individual diversity issues are very important. For example, it is important to be aware that parenting styles may differ by ethnic group, as well as by socioeconomic status (e.g., McLoyd, 1990; Miller & Miller, 1990; Rutledge, 1990).

A requirement for a culturally sensitive service is to conduct any assessment or intervention, whether short- or long-term, with the ethnic background of the family members in mind (e.g., Vargas & Koss-Chioino, 1992; Webb-Watson, 1989). An example is employing Hispanic *cuentos* (folktales) or Native American fables with youngsters when appropriate. Sensitivity can be further reflected by having both white and black dolls among the selections of toys, as well as hair and skin care products suitable for different races.

Diversity among staff members is also significant, both to help other staff members learn about different lifestyles and points of view and to provide role models for the families residing in the shelter. In addition, the presence of a minority staff member can indicate to minority families that they are welcome. An African American advocate, for example, will not always be able to understand an African American family's issues better than a European American staff member can, but her presence probably will increase such understanding. If difficulties in communication arise because of race or culture, the African American advocate may be able to help clarify the misunderstandings. Still, it is not up to the minority advocate to educate all of the nonminority staff; it is the responsibility of staff members who are members of the majority culture to educate themselves and to seek out opportunities to learn more about the cultures of the families they serve.

Advocates also need to be comfortable confronting prejudices based on gender, racial or ethnic background, age, sexual preference, and disability. For example, some of the staff or residents may protest the need to make rooms and bathrooms wheelchair-accessible; or disagreements and conflicts among staff members or residents may arise over how to handle a certain situation involving racist or homophobic attitudes. Advocates need to help deal with these situations in a sensitive, understanding manner in order to sensitize and educate staff and residents about prejudice. Because these attitudes often are a reflection of the institutionalized prejudices prevalent in our society, communicating information in an educative manner is often effective. For example, discussions of racism within the shelter will make it clear to everyone that this issue is important and can be addressed. These are also good opportunities to educate the children about homophobia and racism and to help them learn how to combat the negative impact of different types of oppression.

### Definition of Advocacy

Although many researchers discuss the concept of *advocacy,* rarely do they provide a definition of the concept. One of the few articles defining advocacy (Herbert & Mould, 1992) characterized it as "actively working to meet the needs of the client," but also as "a frankly partisan intervention on behalf of an individual or group. . . Advocacy is not primarily concerned with providing a service, but rather assuring the availability and relevance of the service that is provided. It implies a proactive step beyond the mandated delivery of service" (p. 118). Thus the definition includes not only the services delivered but also the action taken to obtain additional relevant services if needed.

In their study of advocacy, Peled and Edleson (in press) asked practitioners who were providing services to battered women to define advocacy. Results show that advocates responded in terms of outcome goals for the women and process goals for their own work. Peled and Edleson noted that the majority of the respondents focused on immediate rather than long-term goals. The authors thought the priority given to short-term over long-term needs was based on legitimate concerns. However, they also observed a shift in the last two decades in the focus of advocacy from centering on social change to a primary concern with the individual battered woman.

Similarly, children's advocates often have three main functions. The first two are short-term ones: providing different services to children in the shelter and attempting to get additional needs met through contacting the appropriate systems. The third, long-term function is working with larger systems to effect social change. As stated above, the relative emphasis on these three types of efforts will vary according to the interests and skills of the individual advocate and program and to the resources available within a particular program and community.

### The Children's Advocate Role

Many advocates for children of battered women see their role as assessing and addressing the needs of children on an individual basis, within their families, at the shelter and in the greater community. This role may be pursued through varied activities, as diverse as completing a child's intake interview, assisting with a child's transfer to a new school, and educating other staff on the special needs of a sick child. Advocating for children residing in the shelter with shelter staff is an often overlooked but important aspect of the advocate's role. This task is accomplished by providing staff with information about issues such as normal child development and children's reactions under stress.

Generally children's advocates are involved with assessment, intervention, and prevention activities. These are discussed in greater detail in the "Practice Issues" section later in this chapter. Figure 8.1 illustrates the many facets of the child advocate role with an example of a typical workday. This outline demonstrates the demand for juggling numerous tasks and priorities and the flexibility required from the child advocate to successfully achieve his or her goals.

### Skills Needed by a Children's Advocate

As illustrated in Figure 8.1, a number of basic skills and attributes are required by a good advocate. Authors of one article on advocacy with battered women suggested that advocates need empathy and active listening skills, information on woman battering, and both knowledge of and proficiency in the strategies of generating, mobilizing, and accessing community resources (Sullivan, Tan, Basta, Rumptz, & Davidson, 1992).

8:30 a.m.
   Arrive at shelter. Review last night's events. Go through files for information, complete paperwork, and set tentative agenda for the day.
9:00
   Check in with all mothers to see who may need child care. Coordinate child
   care priorities with volunteers.
9:30
   Keep appointment with a woman to complete child intakes on her three
   children. During the intake process, the woman reveals that her 10-year-old
   daughter may have been sexually abused by the child's stepfather.
10:30
   On the basis of the woman's concerns and the evidence presented, assist the
   woman in making a hot line call to report the suspicion.
11:00
   Support the woman and provide her with information while she tries to
   explain to her daughter what might happen next.
12:15 p.m.
   Cancel lunch plans.
12:20
   Take call from CPS worker. Arrange for meeting in her office the next day.
12:30
   Meet with another woman to compile family goal plan. Try to explain to her
   the "no hitting rule" and provide her with as many options as possible.
1:30
   Think again about having lunch.
1:35
   Take call from a volunteer who is ill and needs to cancel for tonight. Try to
   contact another volunteer to fill in so there will be child care during parenting
   group tonight.

**Figure 8.1.** A Day in the Life of a Children's Advocate

In addition, advocates must be able to provide nonjudgmental support, stay
calm in emergency situations, help a woman view her options in an unbiased
manner, validate a woman's or a child's experiences, and introduce women
and children to new ways of thinking about situations while continuing to
provide them with support. These skills set the stage for interacting with
families in an empowering manner.

   Important personal characteristics for an advocate are flexibility and good
interpersonal skills. Flexibility is necessary for dealing with the many
unexpected situations that arise and juggling work on numerous tasks simultaneously. Good interpersonal abilities are essential not only for establishing

1:45
Take five children to the park to play.
3:00
Eat a graham cracker and some peanut butter.
3:15
Assist a mother with her intervention into a squabble between a brother and sister. Try to help them use some problem-solving skills. Remind them of no violence rule.
3:30
Confiscate a toy gun. Attempt to explain why no one plays with war toys here.
3:35
Meet with a woman to discuss safety issues related to upcoming court-ordered visitation.
4:15
Attend staff update and fill in staff on what is going on with the children in the shelter. Provide night staff with some suggestions on how to help with bedtime. Advocate for an ADHD child by helping the other staff members understand what additional obstacles he struggles with and that he feels distressed too. Help staff see acting-out behavior as reflecting distress.
5:00
Eat dinner with a new woman and her toddler. Help them feel welcomed.
5:30
Take a few minutes to collect thoughts and prepare for kid's group.
5:45
Facilitate kid's group on "Why are we here."
6:45
Chart day's events.
7:00
Go home and take care of self.

**Figure 8.1.** Continued

rapport with the children and women with whom an advocate interacts but also for establishing and maintaining good working relationships with key people in community agencies.

As previously mentioned, children's programs vary in the type of services provided, and additional skills needed by advocates would vary in accordance. The backgrounds and training of advocates range from simply liking children but having no formal training, to being preschool or elementary school teachers, to having a professional education in social work or psychology. Thus the capabilities of advocates and the focus of programming provided would vary as well. Highly trained advocates are likely to provide themselves more of the services needed by the family. Other advocates more often may refer families to other community agencies and programs.

## PRACTICE ISSUES AND STRATEGIES

Interventions provided by children's advocates are generally based on information acquired through the assessment process and vary depending on the particular needs of the child, skills of the advocate, sophistication of the overall program, and availability of community resources. Children's advocates may provide interventions in the form of dispensing appropriate information and referrals; conducting individual, group, and family therapy; and helping with unresponsive or challenging systems. These are in addition to creating and maintaining a shelter environment that is responsive to the emotional, physical, and developmental needs of children. Specifically, the latter task might include responsibilities such as safety-proofing the shelter, maintaining a "no hitting" rule, recruiting, training and coordinating volunteers, soliciting donations and funding, and bringing the needs of children to the attention of other staff.

In the following pages, we discuss in more detail critical practice issues for children's advocates and present strategies for providing services to the families. In keeping with the goal of working with both individuals and systems, we also discuss interactions with organizations having an impact on battered women and their children.

On the assumption that requirements for safety and shelter are addressed, the following practice issues are discussed in a rough order of priority, with the highest priority presented first: (a) providing mental health care, (b) providing physical health care, (c) working with the legal system, (d) interacting with the educational system, (e) taking part in the agency's operation and responsibilities, and (f) preventing burnout.

Although the issues are presented separately, it is important to remember that children's advocates rarely have the luxury of dealing with one issue at a time. Most typically, an advocate will balance several priority issues simultaneously. Moreover, priorities shift quickly, depending on the particular family. As one moves down the list, the issues seem to become less pressing and more to be taken on "as possible." Nonetheless, although we place professional and personal issues at the end of the section, we do not consider them a low priority. It is essential to attend to staff burnout when working in such high-stress positions with multi-need and multi-problem families, as well as with recalcitrant systems. More is said about this later.

## Mental Health Issues

Ongoing and long-term concerns about mental health care consume most of the child advocate's time because they involve every family that enters the shelter. Steps we discuss in this section that are taken by the advocate are intervention, assessment and goal planning, work on parenting issues, referrals, and prevention work (see other chapters in this volume for detailed description of individual and group work with children and parents).

*Crisis Intervention.* The first steps that children's advocates take when a family enters the shelter would likely be considered crisis work. These actions involve both an assessment of the children's immediate needs and a prompt intervention designed to assist with the crisis. The children are often upset when they enter the shelter because they may not have known they were going to leave home or where they were going. The advocate must reassure the children that they are safe. In addition, the children need to deal with issues related to (a) the separation from the mother's partner, (b) the trauma of the violence, and (c) the tremendous change in their lives. Intervention with all of the foregoing involves immediate reassurance and acknowledgment of feelings and more long-term work. For example, if the perpetrator of the violence against the mother is the children's father, the children are likely to have very mixed feelings about him, especially the boys (Hughes, 1982, 1986; Peled, 1993). It is important to acknowledge children's feelings of sadness, anger, and confusion and to let them know it is okay to love their father and that he could be a good person even though he did bad things. Children's sadness often includes feelings of loss related to their playmates, their possessions, or their pets, and these issues need to be addressed as well. The majority of children who reside in shelters are age 6 and younger, and their level of cognitive development must be taken into consideration when working with them, especially at the crisis stage. To provide structure and immediate intervention, some workers give children coloring books that serve as their introduction to the shelter (see Roberts & Roberts, 1990). This technique is especially helpful with younger children. For example, a coloring book helps children deal with feelings by providing concrete examples of feelings, such as sadness and missing father, that are felt by a child portrayed in the book.

*Assessment and Goal Planning.* An informal assessment of the children's needs and capabilities is an important part of goal planning. Generally an evaluation of a child's situation is necessary prior to providing long-term intervention or advocacy. One way to gather information on a child's

experiences, current level of functioning, and types of needs is to incorporate a child's intake form into the shelter intake process, along with the
mother's or family's intake form. Other assessment procedures are direct
observation of the family members' interactions and contacting other
agencies that have been in touch with the family.

The child's intake form is used during an interview with the mother to
obtain basic demographic data and information regarding custody and other
legal matters, day care arrangements, physical health and development,
stress responses and coping strategies, and family alliances. Pertinent educational information that may dictate a transfer of schools or in-house
tutoring (e.g., performance levels, special needs, level of safety required)
may also be gathered. Moreover, the intake can serve as a child abuse and
neglect screening, including an assessment of the frequency, duration, and
severity of abuse witnessed and the child's response to that trauma. The
child's intake form often is designed individually to meet the needs of the
particular children's advocate or shelter program.

We recommend that the advocate complete the child intake form with the
mother within the first 2 or 3 days that a family is in the shelter, in an effort
to expedite goal planning and service delivery. A second intake form may be
developed to obtain additional information from older, more verbal children
and to better grasp the children's perspectives on their situation.

Direct observations of the child alone, with family members, and with
others are also helpful in assessing the child's needs. Some areas to examine
are the child's development and sense of boundaries; the level and quality of
interaction between mother and child, child and siblings, and child and
others; and the way the child responds to limits, frustration, or praise.

Additional information regarding the child's needs may be obtained from
other agencies or systems involved with the family. With the appropriate
release of information documentation, the child's teacher, physician, protective service worker, or mental health professional may be very helpful in
adding to the overall evaluation.

Goal planning takes place on the basis of an assessment of the information
gathered; goals for the family and the children while in the shelter and a plan
for reaching those goals are developed. An example of a family goal plan
form used at St. Martha's Hall shelter in St. Louis, Missouri (P.O. Box 4950,
St. Louis, MO 63108), is presented in Figure 8.2 and is discussed in more
detail. This form may be used as is or altered to meet the specific requirements of an agency or a program.

The family goal plan is filled out, with the woman listing her goals for her
family for the next 2 weeks, along with a tentative time line for the accomplishment of the tasks listed and any pertinent referrals. For example, she

may want to improve her nighttime routine and make bedtime go more smoothly, and the children's advocate would provide her with some suggestions regarding this goal. At least once in the next week (likely more often) the advocate would meet with the mother to discuss her progress. At the end of the 2 weeks, her goals are reviewed and new ones are planned. A similar procedure can be followed with individual children who work on their own goals. In conjunction with this short-term assessment planning, children's advocates must be alert to signs indicating a child's need for additional, more formal assessment and treatment. Such intervention may be provided within the shelter or domestic violence program or by referring the child to another agency.

The issues that a child's advocate addresses most often are related to the impact of woman battering on family members. These concerns by children manifest themselves in many ways, including somatic problems, nightmares, bed-wetting, acting-out, and intense fears. Advocates must be prepared to deal with issues such as post-traumatic stress disorder (PTSD) and the resultant anxiety and depression. Although for many of the children their distress is relatively short-lived and not too intense, research indicates that as many as one in three children in shelters experiences emotional or behavioral problems to a degree severe enough to warrant intervention by a licensed professional (e.g., Hughes, in press).

*Parenting Issues.* One of the most crucial and difficult tasks of a children's advocate is to intervene in the area of parenting. Child rearing is a very sensitive issue for many battered women for a number of reasons. One of the few things a woman may perceive herself as having control over is how she parents her children. Much of her self-worth may be tied up in her mothering. Many of these women have already been told by their abusers that they are incompetent or bad mothers. They have been belittled and contradicted in front of their children, and they have had their authority undermined. Furthermore, recent data indicate that conflict between the adult partners over child rearing may precipitate episodes of wife beating (Edleson, Eisikovits, Guttmann, & Sela-Amit, 1991). Consequently, any suggestion or challenging of the woman's parenting methods, no matter how warranted or well-intended, may be viewed by her as another attack and likely will be met with resentment and resistance.

Therefore, the advocate must find a balance among meeting the emotional and physical needs of the children, enforcing shelter rules such as "no one gets hit," and supporting and encouraging the mothers. We have found that focusing on the woman's strengths as a mother, shedding light on the child's point of view, and acknowledging her struggle to be the kind of parent she

Family  Carla, Marcus, Krystie                          Date 11-15-94

Case Number  1924ab                            Intake Date 11-12-94

| Goal | Plan of Action | Referrals | Time Frame | Achieved |
|---|---|---|---|---|
| Get Krystie's immunizations caught up | 1. Go to Dr. Frank's office and get shot records | — People's Clinic 434-9122 | By 11-19 | 11-20 |
| | 2. Call new clinic and make appointment | —Lester Health Center 561-3003 | By 11-22 | 11-24 |
| Enroll Marcus in new school | 1. Call former school and inform of reason for transfer and need for confidentiality | | By 11-16 | 11-16 |
| | 2. Get backpack & school supplies from advocate | | By 11-16 | 11-16 |
| | 3. Talk to Marcus about transfer & his feelings about same | | | |
| | 4. Collect needed documents (shot records, residence letter, report card) | | By 11-16 | 11-17 |
| | 5. Enroll in new school | | By 11-17 | 11-17 |
| | 6. Inform new teacher of Marcus's special needs in reading | | By 11-17 | 11-17 |
| Practice alternatives to physical punishment | 1. Give praise when kids are behaving appropriately | | | |
| | 2. Give time-outs for aggressive behavior | —Handout on time-outs | Daily | |
| | 3. Be considerate, firm, & fair | | | |
| | 4. Ask staff for support when patience is running thin | | | |

**Figure 8.2.** Family Goal Plan

desires to be are all helpful in forming the type of rapport necessary to deal with this delicate topic.

| Goal | Plan of Action | Referrals | Time Frame | Achieved |
|---|---|---|---|---|
| Find day care | 1. Make list of questions to ask day care agencies | | By 11-20 | 11-19 |
| | 2. Apply for financial assistance | —Title XX Day Care Assistance 340-7100 | By 11-24 | 11-23 |
| | 3. Call places to set up interviews | —Latch Key Program 491-6060 | | |
| | | —A Child's Place 227-4108 | | |
| | | —Kid's World 921-9914 | | |
| Have kids in bed by 8:30 p.m. | 1. Limit naps to 12:30-1:30 | | Daily | |
| | 2. Start bedtime routine at 7:00 p.m. | | | |
| | 3. Give praise for cooperative behavior | —Handout on establishing a bedtime routine | | |

**Figure 8.2.** Continued

Common parenting issues that often require an advocate's assistance include alternatives to physical punishment and helping mothers enforce the rule of "no hitting" between their children (research indicates that the greatest amount of violence within a family occurs between siblings [Patterson, De Baryshe, & Ramsey, 1989]); communication skills; and realistic developmental expectations. These topics may be dealt with individually or in a group format. More specific information regarding parenting is covered by Mathews (Chap. 7) and Bilinkoff (Chap. 6) in this volume (see also Gibson & Gutierrez, 1991; Roberts & Roberts, 1990).

*Referrals.* An important part of the children's advocate's role is knowing when to refer a child to mental health professionals in the community for assessment or treatment. Such referrals may take place, for example, when a child needs a more complete assessment for appropriate school placement or suffers from PTSD-type symptoms requiring therapy. The frequency of and reasons for referrals will vary according to the advocate's skills, the resources available, and the severity of the problems. Regarding treatment, advocates must trust their own professional judgment and instincts when deciding whether or not she or he is able to handle a situation. A consultation with an "expert" in the community may be helpful when a child's (or a mother's) need for referral is difficult to determine. For example, on occasion a child may need to be hospitalized. Two situations in which hospitalization may be needed are when a child or teen is experiencing severe depression and suicidal feelings and when a youngster's out-of-control behavior problems threaten the safety of others in the shelter. Children's advocates need to be aware of referral sources in their communities. Especially important are names of clinicians knowledgeable about domestic violence and the special needs of children of battered women and about low-cost treatment and hospitalization programs (including insurance options). Keeping a file of such information in the agency will enable the advocate to show mothers pamphlets or other materials describing the different programs. We also recommend establishing, if possible, a connection with an interested, knowledgeable mental health professional in the community who is able to provide some free or low-cost consultation on behavioral problems and interventions for children. That person may also be able to assist with decisions regarding referrals for a child or family.

*Prevention.* An important goal of most domestic violence programs is to break the cycle of violence—to prevent the occurrence of this crime in the future. One effective method of prevention is to provide community education about the dynamics of woman battering and its effects on children. More is said about this topic later.

## Physical Health Issues

Some of the earliest reports on children of battered women noted their problematic physical health. Hilberman and Munson (1978), on the basis of chart surveys of 209 children of battered women, reported the prominence of headaches, abdominal complaints, asthma, insomnia, and enuresis among the children. Such somatic complaints often are cited as reactions to stress (Arnold & Carnahan, 1990; Johnson & Cohn, 1990; Pynoos & Eth, 1985). Furthermore, one study found that nearly 20% of the children served by a shelter were not fully immunized (Stagg, Wills, & Howell, 1989).

Children of battered women may not receive appropriate or timely medical attention because of the violent, controlling, and isolating behavior of the abuser. For example, a woman may be reluctant or unable to keep her child's medical appointment because of injury, fatigue, or fear. Lack of medical insurance coverage, transportation, or an available facility are all additional barriers to health care. Because children who come to shelters will often require medical attention for their immediate health needs, children's advocates should be familiar with the health care resources in the local area—for example, knowing where to go and how to apply for Medicaid and WIC and which clinics provide free immunizations or lead testing.

Other common health issues that arise include outbreaks of chicken pox, head lice, ringworm, and other communicable diseases. It is helpful to be familiar with the symptoms of these maladies and their treatment, to have educational materials available for the families, and to normalize the medical situation in the shelter as much as possible. Some women also may need assistance with reading a thermometer, bringing down a fever, administering medication, and deciding when to use the emergency room.

The number and types of health care resources available vary, depending on the community, and urban areas are likely to have a larger number of services available. If the shelter is in a rural area, the children's advocate might need to locate physicians who will volunteer to examine children free of charge or to donate samples of medications. Public health agencies and civic groups also may be willing to donate over-the-counter medicine and other first-aid supplies.

### Interface With the Legal System

Legal and child protective issues arise frequently in shelters, but we only briefly touch on them in this section because they are addressed at length in other chapters of this book.

Children's advocates need to be familiar with the processes required for obtaining both Adult and Child Orders of Protection in their states. A child's safety and emotional well-being must be considered when decisions are made related to custody and visitation. Although children's advocates cannot provide legal counsel, they can help a woman explore her options and the possible outcomes for her child. In addition, they can put her in touch with the community legal aid service. Often this agency can be a resource for contacting attorneys who are familiar with the legal and safety issues facing battered women and who will take cases pro bono or at a low fee.

Children of battered women are at a great risk for child abuse and neglect. One study of battered women's shelters found that approximately 70% of the children who came to the shelters had been abused or neglected (Layzer, Goodson, & Delange, 1986). Whether to engage child protective services in cases involving children of battered women is an area of controversy for some advocates (Jaffe, Wolfe, & Wilson, 1990; Schechter, 1982). An advocate may be hesitant to report incidents of child abuse and neglect because the allegations may further victimize the battered woman either by reinforcing the belief that she is a bad or incompetent mother or by actually having her child removed. However, children of battered women need protection as much as any other child. It is the responsibility of adults and the legal obligation of all mandatory reporters to relay to the proper authorities information regarding any suspected cases of child abuse or neglect. All shelter staff should be clear about the appropriate policy and procedures for reporting abuse and neglect. This is a difficult issue for all shelter staff, and specific suggestions for working with local child protection agencies are found in Echlin and Marshall's chapter (Chap. 10) in this volume.

We have found it necessary also to establish policy and procedures for cases of child abandonment. On rare occasions women have left their children at the shelter and disappeared. We suggest that children's advocates consult with the local child protection agency, juvenile court, and police department for suggestions and protocol when establishing a policy for child abandonment.

### Interactions With Education Systems

Children of battered women have been found to have a high rate of academic problems such as poor school performance, truancy, absenteeism, and difficulty concentrating (Hilberman & Munson, 1978; Wildin, Williamson, & Wilson, 1991; Wolfe, Zak, Wilson, & Jaffe, 1986). Possible contributing factors to such problems include having to miss school while the family is in hiding from the abuser and being unable to attend because of mother's injuries or isolation. Frequent moves and the need for confidentiality and anonymity may make it difficult for a battered woman to comply with transfer procedures, which prolongs the child's leave from school. A child who requires special education services may not be receiving them because of frequent moves, the lengthy evaluation process, transportation difficulties, and the demands placed on the parent. Also, as is common among adults under stress, a child at school may find it difficult to concentrate. Furthermore, he or she may have trouble completing homework assignments or studying amidst the violence at home and, consequently, fall behind.

School-age children who come to the shelter for services will, therefore, often require advocacy in getting their educational needs met. Advocacy in this area may include facilitating a transfer of schools, providing in-house tutoring, coordinating special school services, and arranging transportation or after-school care. Some assistance in this area was provided through recent federal legislation.

In 1990, Title VII-B, Education for Homeless Children and Youth, of the Stewart B. McKinney Homeless Assistance Act (PL 100-97) was amended substantially to further address the educational needs of homeless children. These provisions cover children who reside in shelters and those who are staying temporarily with friends or relatives for want of a permanent residence. In part, the act dictates that each state shall adopt a plan to "address problems with respect to the education of homeless children and homeless youths including problems caused by transportation issues and enrollment delays which are caused by immunization requirements, residency requirements, lack of birth certificates, school records, or other documentation or guardianship issues" (Section [e] State Plan, Stewart B. McKinney Act, 1990). Furthermore, each state is required to appoint a Coordinator of Education of Homeless Children and Youth, who is responsible for the development and coordination of services, data collection, and report submission. This person in each state is a good resource for advocates.

One common task of a children's advocate is coordinating school attendance. We have found that, if safety allows, placing a child back in school as soon as possible is beneficial on several grounds. One important reason is that it is in compliance with compulsory school attendance laws. Other benefits include providing the child with some sense of normalcy and stability and at the same time minimizing the child's isolation.

However, when deciding which school the child will attend, be it the previous school or a new one in the vicinity of the shelter, the child's safety is of utmost importance. The last-attended school may be one of the first places an abuser goes in an effort to locate his family. It is not uncommon for the abuser to wait at the school for the child or his partner, to call the school for information regarding the woman's or child's whereabouts, or attempt to take the child from the school premises.

If, after discussing safety issues, a mother decides to keep her child in the same school and transportation is available, the following safeguards are recommended:

- Inform the school of the situation and ask for cooperation with confidentiality and a safety plan.
- Provide the school with a copy of the Order of Protection if it includes the children, and establish a plan of action in case the abuser calls or comes to the school.
- Review a safety plan with the child regarding what to do if the abuser comes to school or follows him or her home.

It has been our experience that most women choose to transfer their children to a school in the vicinity of the shelter. Children's advocates can help facilitate this process by establishing a close working relationship with the school and school board in the area and by being familiar with the enrollment procedures. The school secretary, social worker, and principal are key people to know because they generally will have contact with each family from the shelter.

Even though a child will be attending a new school, safety remains an issue. The same safeguards recommended when keeping a child in the previous school also apply when a child is transferred. In addition, a children's advocate may be able to make arrangements with the school district to keep all identifying information about the shelter off the child's records as an added safety precaution. It is helpful for the woman if the children's advocate accompanies her and her child to the school and assists with the enrollment process. The advocate's familiarity with school personnel, procedures, and the building will help minimize any anxiety, concern, or confusion the woman or child may have. The advocate will be at hand also to answer any questions the school personnel might have regarding safety, confidentiality, or transportation.

In some cases it may be necessary to tutor the child at the shelter, either if the child is going to be in the shelter only for a few days or if it is not safe for the child to be away from the shelter. In addition, we have found that some adolescents prefer to receive tutoring at the shelter, rather than go to a new school for a (possibly) brief time and have to make new friends.

As an advocate for children of battered women, staff also can provide school personnel with information about woman battering, the impact it has on children, and the resources available in the community. Although school personnel are clearly in a position to identify and assist children of battered women, they often are unaware both of the significance of the problem in their school and of signs to look for in child witnesses (Davis & Carlson, 1986).

Jaffe, Hastings, and Reitzel (1992) proposed developing a protocol for school personnel, which is approved by the local school board, for responding to disclosure and identifying child witnesses to woman battering. Furthermore, Jaffe and his colleagues recommend that schools adjust their policies, procedures, and curriculum content to reflect a philosophy of support for a nonviolent society. Children's advocates can serve as both a catalyst and a resource for this type of transformation.

## Agency's Operation and Responsibilities

Other responsibilities of children's advocates include community education, volunteer training, and grant writing. Making educational talks to community groups is an excellent method for engaging in prevention, as well as for building financial and community support. When advocates give talks in the community, it is not unusual for people to approach the advocate afterward and reveal that they currently are being battered or have a friend who is. They may ask what they should do, and the advocate should be able to provide them with resources in the community. Handing out cards with important phone numbers is one approach that can be helpful.

Training volunteers is very important because no shelter or family violence program could operate without them. Children's advocates must make sure the volunteers are well trained in working with children, especially regarding appropriate discipline.

Grants are a source of funding for some children's programs. Woman battering and child abuse are areas that draw interest at the foundation and governmental levels. It is helpful to obtain consultation from an experienced grant writer. Some experts in this area will assist nonprofit agencies at no or a very low charge.

## Burnout

One of the most important professional/personal issues confronting children's advocates is feeling "burned out." Because of work circumstances, individuals employed in the helping professions seem to be especially susceptible to this syndrome. *Burnout* is a situation in which health care professionals frequently feel emotionally exhausted and even cynical about their work (Raquepaw & Miller, 1989) and is "the result of constant or repeated emotional pressure associated with an intense involvement with people over long periods of time" (Pines, Aronson, & Kafry, 1981, p. 15).

These feelings have important implications for staff working in shelters for battered women. Burnout often involves a loss of concern and a loss of positive feelings for one's clients, resulting in a declining quality of services. People who feel burned out may show various signs of the syndrome, including low morale, poor job performance, and absenteeism. Physiological symptoms are often present as well: constant fatigue, insomnia, frustration, and depression, as well as colds, headaches, and gastrointestinal disturbances (Raquepaw & Miller, 1989).

It is easy to become burned out as a children's advocate. Long work hours increase the risk for burnout (Raquepaw & Miller, 1989). A profile of the "emotionally exhausted clinician" as one who is young, is overinvolved, has feelings of low control, sees many clients with medical/health issues, and sees many clients who are victims of sexual abuse/rape has been described (Ackerley, Burnell, Holder, & Kurdek, 1988). Burnout also is associated with lower income, as well as with feeling isolated. All of the above symptoms are clearly relevant for advocates who work in shelters.

Although women's advocates also have to struggle with burnout, children's advocates may be at greater risk because of feeling especially isolated. When a program or a shelter has a children's advocate, there is almost always only one, while there are likely to be several advocates who work with the women. Over time, advocating for children's needs in the face of a number of people operating from the adult's perspective can be very tiring.

There are a number of ways to remedy and prevent burnout, at both the individual and system levels. At the individual level, actions likely to help with burnout consist of expressing one's feelings about one's job and establishing a social support system. Other ideas are engaging in physical exercise, taking breaks, separating one's work from one's private life, and having a proper diet (Raquepaw & Miller, 1989). Basically children's advocates need to take care of themselves—for example, by taking enough time off even though it feels as if one cannot possibly be away. That latter feeling may be a warning sign that a person is on the verge of burnout.

At the institutional level, suggestions include shortening work hours, allowing time-outs during the day, and changing the function of staff meetings to enable discussion of one's feelings and obtaining support from coworkers. Improving work relations between staff members can make a big difference (Raquepaw & Miller, 1989). One suggestion is to establish a weekly or bi-weekly get-together of all staff members to discuss how each person is coping with the stress and how staff members can support and help one another maintain a healthy level of involvement. When staff are exposed to the inevitable tragedies experienced by children of battered women, processing the situation with colleagues is crucial. We have found that it is as important to pay equal attention to the "process" aspects of the advocate's role as to its content and tasks.

## CONCLUSION

Children's advocates must know how to "prioritize" the tasks to which they must attend. It is essential that advocates be able to achieve and maintain a balance among competing demands. Children must be put first, with life-threatening safety needs addressed before anything else. Flexibility is very important because advocates will often need to leave in the middle of one task to attend to an urgent situation that has arisen, as well as to provide some attention to the children and women as needed. In addition, using an empowerment model that includes sensitivity to cultural and individual diversity is crucial to the effectiveness of the advocate's work.

One of the most important things a children's advocate can do in terms of networking effectively with community systems is to establish working alliances with key people in the different systems. Good interpersonal skills are essential in this process. It may feel as if establishing person-to-person contacts takes too much energy and time, but it will be a worthwhile investment in the end. Having a person with whom a work liaison has been established is essential when assistance is needed in a time of crisis.

When a family comes into the shelter, children's advocates need to be prepared to reassure the children about their safety, do an assessment of the family's short-term needs, and provide an evaluation of their long-term requirements. Advocates will need to create plans addressing the family's goals for their shelter stay and to make any referrals the family might require. With mothers, much of the intervention time will be devoted to working on such issues as bedtime, realistic developmental expectations, and alternatives to physical discipline. Much of the advocate's time with the children will be spent working with them either individually or in groups about their feelings and reactions to their mothers being beaten.

Knowledge of the legal system is essential, and children's advocates must be cognizant of the federal and state laws in the area. Establishing working relationships with knowledgeable attorneys to whom referrals can be made is very helpful. It is also essential that children's advocates establish a collegial relationship with some of the Department of Youth and Family Services or Child Protection Services workers in the area.

The safety of the children is the primary consideration in establishing priorities for their educational requirements. Children's advocates must know the educational system well and how best to get children's needs met within it. We recommend that advocates meet face-to-face with the school personnel at the schools where most of the shelter children will be attending. It is crucial to enlist the aid of the school and to establish working relationships there as well.

Children's advocates must pay attention to the signs of burnout, such as feeling as if they cannot take time off or feeling angry, resentful, and frustrated with the residents much of the time. Everyone needs to attend to feelings of burnout before it is too late. Prevention is the best approach. Taking care of oneself now is an investment in the future. We recommend instituting additional staff meetings at which advocates talk about process issues related to their work and give each other much needed emotional support.

We recommend that, to feel less isolated, children's advocates attend meetings with other people in the community who are interested in children's issues and avail themselves of opportunities for continuing education. This is especially important because in many battered women's programs, children's needs are secondary in importance after the women's needs.

Although the work of a children's advocate certainly can seem never-ending and highly stressful, the rewards of assisting children and their mothers improve their lives and of helping change society can be great. We have discussed what we see as critical practice issues in working with children of battered women, presented within an advocacy context. The primary focus of the chapter has been on children's advocates in shelters for battered women, but we hope that some of the points we made will be useful to clinicians and other professionals in different settings as well. Regardless of setting, it is essential that we provide services to individual family members and meet individual children's needs. At the same time, however, women and children will never be free from the fear of family violence unless we work to prevent that violence by advocating for major social changes.

## REFERENCES

Ackerley, G. D., Burnell, J., Holder, D. C., & Kurdek, L. A. (1988). Clinician profile. *Professional Psychology: Research and Practice, 19*, 624-631.

Alessi, J. J., & Hearn, K. (1984). Group treatment of children in shelters for battered women. In A. R. Roberts (Ed.), *Battered women and their families* (pp. 49-61). New York: Springer.

Arnold, L. E., & Carnahan, J. A. (1990). Child divorce stress. In E. Arnold (Ed.), *Childhood stress* (pp. 374-403). New York: John Wiley.

Davis, L. V., & Carlson, B. E. (1986). School personnel's awareness of spouse abuse among parents. *Social Work in Education, 8*, 175-186.

Davis, L. V., & Carlson, B. E. (1987). Observation of spouse abuse: What happens to the children? *Journal of Interpersonal Violence, 2*, 278-291.

Edleson, J. L., Eisikovits, Z. C., Guttmann, E., & Sela-Amit, M. (1991). Cognitive and interpersonal factors in woman abuse. *Journal of Family Violence, 6*, 167-182.

Elbow, M. (1982). Children of violent marriages: The forgotten victims. *Social Casework, 63*, 465-471.

Gibson, J. W., & Gutierrez, L. (1991). A service program for safe-home children. *Families in Society: The Journal of Contemporary Human Services, 72*, 554-562.

Haffner, S. (1979). Victimology interview: A refuge for battered women: A conversation with Erin Pizzey. *Victimology, 4*, 100-112.

Herbert, M. D., & Mould, J. W. (1992). The advocacy role in public child welfare. *Child Welfare, 71*, 115-130.

Hilberman, E., & Munson, K. (1978). Sixty battered women. *Victimology, 3*, 460-471.

Hughes, H. M. (1982). Brief interventions with children in a battered women's shelter: A model preventive program. *Family Relations, 31*, 495-502.

Hughes, H. M. (1986). Research with children in shelters: Implications for clinical services. *Children Today, 15,* 21-25. (DHHS Publication No. 86-30014)

Hughes, H. M. (in press). Research concerning children of battered women: Clinical and policy implications. In R. Geffner & P. Lundberg-Love (Eds.), *Research and treatment in family violence: Practical implications.* New York: Haworth.

Jaffe, P. G., Hastings, E., & Reitzel, D. (1992). Child witnesses of woman abuse: How can schools respond? *Response, 14,* 12-15.

Jaffe, P. G., Hurley, D. J., & Wolfe, D. (1990). Children's observations of violence: I. Critical issues in child development and intervention planning. *Canadian Journal of Psychiatry, 35,* 466-470.

Jaffe, P. G., Wolfe, D. A., & Wilson, S. K. (1990). *Children of battered women.* Newbury Park, CA: Sage.

Johnson, C., & Cohn, D. (1990). The stress of child abuse and other family violence. In E. Arnold (Ed.), *Childhood stress* (pp. 268-295). New York: John Wiley.

Labell, L. (1979). Wife abuse: A sociological study of battered women and their mates. *Victimology, 4,* 258-267.

Layzer, J., Goodson, B., & Delange, C. (1986). Children in shelters. *Children Today, 15,* 5-11.

Lystad, M. (1975). Violence at home: A review of the literature. *American Journal of Orthopsychiatry, 45,* 328-345.

McLoyd, V. C. (1990). The impact of economic hardship on black families and children: Psychological distress, parenting, and socioemotional development. *Child Development, 61,* 311-346.

Miller, J. B. (1991). Women and power. In J. V. Jordan, A. G. Kaplan, J. B. Miller, I. P. Stiver, & J. L. Surrey (Eds.), *Women's growth in connection* (pp. 197-205). New York: Guilford.

Miller, R. L., & Miller, B. (1990). Mothering the biracial child: Bridging the gaps between African-American and white parenting styles. In L. Brown & M.P.P. Root (Eds.), *Diversity and complexity in feminist therapy* (pp. 169-179). New York: Haworth.

Moore, J. (1977). Yo-yo children: A study of 23 violent matrimonial cases. In M. Roy (Ed.), *Battered women: A psychosociological study of domestic violence* (pp. 249-262). New York: Van Nostrand Reinhold.

Moore, T., Peplar, D., Weinberg, B., Hammond, L., Waddell, J., & Weiser, L. (1990). Research on children from violent families. *Canada's Mental Health Journal, 38,* 19-23.

National Coalition Against Domestic Violence. (1991). *1991 national directory of domestic violence programs: A guide to community shelter, safe home, and service programs.* Washington, DC: Author.

Patterson, G. R., De Baryshe, B. D., & Ramsey, E. (1989). A developmental perspective on antisocial behavior. *American Psychologist, 44,* 329-335.

Peled, E. (1993). *The experience of living with violence for preadolescent witnesses of woman abuse.* Unpublished doctoral dissertation, University of Minnesota.

Peled, E., & Edleson, J. L. (in press). Advocacy for battered women: A national survey. *Journal of Family Violence.*

Pines, A. M., Aronson, E., & Kafry, D. (1981). *Burnout: From tedium to personal growth.* New York: Free Press.

Pynoos, R. S., & Eth, S. (1985). Children traumatized by witnessing acts of personal violence: Homicide, rape, or suicide behavior. In S. Eth & R. S. Pynoos (Eds.), *Post-traumatic stress disorder in children* (pp. 19-43). Washington, DC: American Psychiatric Press.

Raquepaw, J. M., & Miller, R. S. (1989). Psychotherapist burnout: A componential analysis. *Professional Psychology: Research and Practice, 20,* 32-36.

Roberts, A. (1981). *Sheltering battered women: A national study and service guide.* New York: Springer.

Roberts, A. D., & Roberts, B. S. (1990). A comprehensive model for crisis intervention with battered women and their children. In A. R. Roberts (Ed.), *Crisis intervention handbook: Assessment, treatment, and research* (pp. 105-123). Belmont, CA: Wadsworth.

Rosenbaum, A., & O'Leary, K. D. (1981). Children: The unintended victims of marital violence. *American Journal of Orthopsychiatry, 51,* 692-699.

Rosenberg M. S., & Rossman, B. R. (1990). The child witness to marital violence. In R. T. Ammerman & M. Hersen (Eds.), *Treatment of family violence* (pp. 183-210). New York: John Wiley.

Rutledge, E. M. (1990). Black parent-child relations: Some correlates. *Journal of Comparative Family Studies, 21,* 369-378.

Schechter, S. (1982). *Women and male violence.* Boston: South End.

Stagg, V., Wills, G., & Howell, M. (1989). Psychopathology in early childhood witnesses of family violence. *Topics in Early Childhood Special Education, 9,* 73-87.

Sullivan, C. M., Tan, C., Basta, J., Rumptz, M., & Davidson, W. S., II. (1992). An advocacy intervention program for women with abusive partners: Initial evaluation. *American Journal of Community Psychology, 20,* 309-332.

Vargas, L. A., & Koss-Chioino, J. D. (Eds.). (1992). *Working with culture: Psychotherapeutic interventions with ethnic minority children and youth.* New York: Guilford.

Webb-Watson, L. (1989). Ethnicity: An epistemology of child rearing. In L. Combrinck-Graham (Ed.), *Children in family contexts* (pp. 463-481). New York: Guilford.

Wildin, S. R., Williamson, W. D., & Wilson, G. S. (1991). Children of battered women: Developmental and learning profiles. *Clinical Pediatrics, 30,* 299-304.

Wolfe, D. A., Zak, L., Wilson, S., & Jaffe, P. G. (1986). Child witnesses to violence between parents: Critical issues in behavioral and social adjustment. *Journal of Abnormal Child Psychology, 14,* 95-104.

# PART THREE

# Child Protection and the Criminal Justice System

# 9

# How Abused Women Can Use the Law to Help Protect Their Children

JOAN ZORZA

Men who abuse women seldom stop their abuse after the parties separate. Separation only increases the danger for battered women (Pagelow, 1984). In the United States, although only one tenth of all women are separated or divorced at any one time, three quarters of all women hospitalized because of domestic violence are separated or divorced. Separated battered women report being battered 14 times as often as women still living with their partners (Harlow, 1991).

Child witnesses of domestic violence need protection from the perpetrators to keep from being revictimized. Even if abuse prior to separation has been directed only against the child's mother, an abusive man is likely to shift his focus to control of the child as a way to continue the terror and violence against the mother. Abusive fathers are far more likely to fight for custody and not pay child or spousal support than are nonabusive fathers (Liss & Stahly, 1993). Furthermore, over half of men who abuse women, deliberately abuse their children (Zorza, 1991). Even men who do not deliberately abuse their children, often inadvertently injure their children as a result of reckless violence—for example, when they throw furniture or hit the mother while she is holding her child (Jaffe, Wolfe, & Wilson, 1990; Roy, 1988). Moreover, even when children are not injured, they are damaged emotionally by hearing and seeing the violence or its aftermath (Jaffe et al., 1990).

In Chapter 10 of this volume, the authors explore how the state intervenes to protect a child who has witnessed violence. But a protective parent need not wait until the state becomes involved. A protective parent can protect a child witness to domestic violence from the perpetrator by obtaining the following legal measures: (a) an order for custody of the child, (b) an order for protection to exclude the abuser from the home or otherwise restrain him, and/or (c) conditions of bail, probation, incarceration, or parole imposed on the abuser through a criminal action. Orders for protection, which exclude and/or restrain the abuser, and custody orders usually can be granted in a variety of family law proceedings, with divorce and domestic violence (or abuse prevention) cases being the most common.

In this chapter I explore how children can be protected through custody, protective orders, criminal proceedings, and tort suits. I also explain why such protection may not be easy to obtain or be completely effective. To understand some of these legal proceedings, it is helpful to know something about how the courts work.

Unless a federal law or the United States Constitution dictates otherwise, each state is allowed to determine how its courts should make family law decisions. Every state has its own laws (or statutes) and court decisions that guide its courts in how they should determine custody and domestic violence disputes. Some court decisions interpret statutes or prior court decisions. Other opinions may decide a novel issue, one for which there is no statute or prior judicial decision. In addition, the federal government has placed jurisdiction for hearing some custody disputes in the tribal courts and has other laws that state courts must use in considering the custody of some Native American children.

Every decision of an appellate court is binding on trial judges in that district unless it is overturned by an even higher state court or, in some instances, unless a new law is passed concerning the same issue.

Courts consider family law cases to be notoriously problematic mostly because one or more of the parties act difficult, rather than because the legal issues are particularly complex. Men who batter women are especially likely to continue their abusiveness in the litigation process. Other problems arise for battered women and their children because courts often are unwilling to recognize the abuse, its seriousness, or that it profoundly affects the children.

## CUSTODY ORDERS

The vast majority of child custody cases arise in the context of divorcing or separating parents. If the parents were married, the custody dispute usually is a part of a legal separation, divorce, or, very occasionally, annulment case. In many states a parent can bring a custody case in which custody and visitation are the only matters to be decided by the court. If the parents were never married to each other, custody is likely to be litigated in the context of a custody case or, in some states, paternity case. The advantage of custody being decided in a divorce or paternity case, rather than in a custody case, is that other issues affecting the parties, such as paternity, child support, alimony, and property disputes, can be decided at the same time.

Custody disputes can arise also in other contexts. Any two or more people could be fighting for custody of a child in guardianship or adoption proceedings. In virtually every state, custody can be awarded by a court in a domestic violence case in which one parent alleges that the other parent abuses the first parent or one or more of the children. In addition, the state can move to take away custody from parents who are abusing, neglecting, or abandoning a child (see Chap. 10). Although it is not unusual for someone to report an abusive parent to the child protective service agency, it is also not unusual for an abusive partner or his family to falsely accuse the abused parent of child abuse as part of his control over her (Adams, 1989).

## What Is Custody?

Custody of a child includes both legal and physical custody. *Physical custody* is the right to physically possess the child (to have the child live with you). It also encompasses who has visitation with the child. *Legal custody* is the right to make major decisions about the child's upbringing: the child's education, medical care, religious practices, and discipline. Because courts do not want to get involved with frequent day-to-day decisions made by the child's primary caretaker (e.g., what the child should eat, wear, watch on TV), courts generally ignore them unless they involve health, education, or religious issues.

Either or both physical and legal custody can be sole (had by only one individual) or joint (sometimes called "shared," because two or more individuals share it). *Joint physical custody* means that the child physically lives with both parents. *Joint legal custody* means that both parents have the right to make the major decisions about the child. Joint custody works best when both parents respect each other and can cooperate about decisions concerning the child. When one parent abuses or tries to control the other parent or child, however, joint custody, whether physical or legal, is unlikely to work and may endanger the abused parent and any children in the family (Polikoff, 1987). Most children need the security of having one home. They are especially likely to become unhappy and depressed when they are traded frequently between hostile parents (Furstenberg & Cherlin, 1991). In addition, many abusive fathers physically or emotionally abuse the mother when the children are picked up or dropped off (Adams, 1989).

Joint physical custody gives the father the legal right to question and oppose any decision the mother makes that affects their child. When a court gives an abusive man any legal custody (joint or sole) over his children, it effectively sanctions his right to continue controlling the mother and undermining her authority. When an abusive father does this, he not only demoralizes the mother and saps her of her emotional reserves but also makes her a less effective parent. He may also be able to drive her further into poverty by forcing her to pay for more expensive options (e.g., private or parochial schooling, music lessons for the children) than she can afford or by forcing their disagreement back to court for the judge to resolve it at a further expense.

## Which Parent Gets Custody?

When a child is born during a marriage, the husband is presumed to be the father. Usually this means that any child who was born after the parties wed or who was conceived before the marriage ended by divorce or annulment is deemed to be a child of that marriage. In cases in which paternity of a child born of a marriage is disputed or in cases in which the parties have never been married, paternity is established if both parents acknowledge the child in writing or a court declares that the man is the father of the child. If more than one man could be the child's father, it may be necessary to notify these other men to have a valid paternity determination, and blood for testing may be taken from the child, the mother, and any possible father to help determine paternity. Once paternity is established, however, courts usually consider custody disputes between unwed parents much as they do between married parents, especially if the parents lived together with the child or the father was fairly involved with raising the child.

The standard used in almost every American state and Canadian province for determining custody is the best interest of the child (Canadian Department of Justice, 1993; Crean, 1989). Almost everything in each parent's life is considered relevant to determining what is in the child's best interest: his or her reputation, lifestyle, moral fitness, values, education, employment, credit record, economic ability, criminal record, health, ability to care for the child, stability of the environment, and ability to foster a good relationship between the child and the other parent. In addition, the wishes of the parents and the child; the child's adjustment to the home, school, and community; and any special problems the child or a parent has may all be considered relevant. Although none of these factors are considered to favor one parent over the other, virtually every factor favors fathers over mothers, if not in actuality, then in the way the courts apply them. Many states have conducted studies finding that courts treat women's custody claims far less favorably than men's (Abrams & Greaney, 1989). For example, a mother's new boy-friend usually is viewed suspiciously, with him being perceived as a possible danger to the children or at least deflecting the mother's time and energy from the children. In contrast, the father's new girlfriend is seen as bringing stability to his life, with her being able to care for the children.

Women often are penalized for having less stability, although if they lack stability, it is often because society has long discriminated against women by making it harder for them to find decent jobs, receive adequate pay, receive adequate child support, and not be penalized for having given up employment opportunities to raise their children (e.g., *Porter v. Porter,* 1979). Battered women are particularly likely to appear less stable. Many will have had to move frequently to avoid the abuse or will have been or are homeless because of the abuse (Zorza, 1991). Many batterers refuse to let their partners work, thus undermining the mothers' self-confidence and leaving them disadvantaged in the workplace. It is not uncommon for a batterer to refuse to share any responsibility as either a homemaker or a breadwinner, but then take virtually all of his partner's earnings, leaving her exhausted and even hungry as she struggles to work and run the household without adequate assistance (Kirkwood, 1993). Furthermore, one fifth of working battered women are so harassed at work either in person or on the phone by their batterers that they lose their jobs (Zorza, 1993). Batterers cost their victims enormous amounts financially: One 1992 study found that the average battered victim going to criminal court had spent $6,900 just in medical, legal, and counseling fees for herself in the year before the batterer first appeared in court (Goodman, 1992). This amount did not include all of the money needed for household repairs, replacing damaged furniture or clothing, new locks or moving, getting an unlisted telephone, or any medical or counseling fees for the children.

A few appellate courts have reversed trial courts that have penalized mothers for economic inferiority on the theory that the court can always equalize the discrepancy by awarding more child support, alimony, or a greater share of the marital assets (e.g., *Dempsey v. Dempsey,* 1980).

One of the main ways that courts penalize women is by failing to recognize the role of the child's primary caretaker. Many courts do not even consider a mother's past child caretaking as relevant in future custody decisions. In West Virginia, however, the Supreme Court of Appeals reversed a custody award to the better educated, brighter, wealthier father because those factors paled in comparison to the mother's love, affection, concern, tolerance, and willingness to sacrifice that she displayed as the child's primary caretaker. The court held that a primary caretaker parent must be awarded custody when that parent is even minimally fit (*Garska v. McCoy,* 1981).

Another way that courts discriminate against mothers is by trivializing or denying the seriousness of domestic abuse that fathers frequently perpetrate on women. In recent years the vast majority of states—at least 38 and the District of Columbia—have enacted statutes that make domestic violence at least relevant in custody decision. Canadian provinces have as yet to enact such statutes, although some Canadian court cases have held that the violence is relevant to the custody decision (Canadian Department of Justice, 1993).

Some of these enacted statutes, however, limit relief to numerous victims of domestic violence. For example, some statutes condition the use of the provision on the abuser having been convicted in a criminal trial or on the victim's ability to prove a pattern of abuse by clear and convincing evidence. Others state that the provision may be used only in a case filed under the domestic violence statute, not in any other custody case (Zorza, 1993). Battered women who do not carry through with obtaining orders of protection may have a much harder time proving later in a custody dispute that the violence occurred. In cases in which her batterer was arrested but charges were either never brought, dismissed, or continued without any final conviction, the custody judge may be unwilling, without further proof, to believe that she was battered. Other judges assume incorrectly that domestic violence ends when the parties divorce or that the woman is greatly exaggerating the abuse because she would have left long before if the abuse was severe. Judges may also conclude that the abuse was mutual when only one party was abusive or when the other parent was acting to defend herself in self-protection.

Mothers are judged particularly harshly in custody cases when allegations of child sexual abuse are made. The widely believed myth is that women frequently and falsely raise such allegations in custody cases to win tactical advantage. Such allegations, however, are raised in only 2% of all custody cases and are as likely to be true in custody cases as at other times. Even when the accusations cannot be substantiated, they usually are made in good faith. Still, this myth is so widely believed that some child protective service agencies even fail to investigate sexual abuse allegations when custody is being litigated (Liss & Stahly, 1993; McGraw & Smith, 1992; Pennington & Woods, 1990). A survey of more than 100,000 women who used California domestic violence program services found that when the court knew of allegations that a father was physically or sexually abusing his children, the court was actually more likely to award him full custody than when it knew he was not abusing any children (Liss & Stahly, 1993).

## Custody Mediation

Mediation generally favors men and hurts women. It particularly hurts a woman when she must mediate with the man who abuses her. Mediators seldom ask the woman whether she is afraid of her partner or whether her partner has ever been abusive to her. When the abuser manipulates the woman or uses intimidating tactics, there can be no equal bargaining power between the two parties. Even if the abuser does not use unfair tactics in the mediation session, the woman will remember how he has used threats and violence to get his way in the past. This memory may make her so afraid that she cannot stand up for her demands. Or she may appear so emotional that the mediator encourages the husband to get custody. Although mediators have an ethical obligation to end any negotiation when the parties do not have equal bargaining power, they almost never do so.

Mediated agreements are far more likely to result in joint custody awards, lower or no child support payments, and worse property and alimony arrangements for the women. Mothers are often so eager to keep custody that they give up more child support, alimony, or marital assets than they should have to not lose the children. Furthermore, most mediators assume that joint custody is best for children and strongly encourage joint custody or at least frequent visitation (or access) arrangements. In addition, few mediators encourage the use of supervised visitation or of a safe, responsible, impartial person picking up and dropping off the children; this happens partly because such arrangements seem to blame one party and partly because mediators tend to assume that all prior bad behavior will automatically stop because the parties have come to a mutually agreed upon arrangement.

Mediation is a process that looks only to the future in trying to resolve disputes. As a result, most mediators refuse to place blame on either party for past misconduct. Until batterers acknowledge and accept responsibility for their abuse, however, they cannot change their behavior. Thus mediation has the effect of actually encouraging the batterer in his abusive behavior.

Mediators do not explain the law to the parties. They measure their success by striking a mutually agreed upon solution. Because men have more money than women, they usually have better access to lawyers and knowledge of the law. This gives them a huge advantage in mediation. Women are far more likely to be reasonable and understanding (and be expected to act in these ways), giving in to most men's requests in mediation. Mediators take women's requests much less seriously than men's, further advantaging the men.

Mediation does not speed up court cases appreciably and is almost as costly as litigating a case. This is especially true when the man is abusive. Batterers fight unfairly and continue manipulating and being abusive both during and after the mediation process. Many batterers enter agreements with no intention of honoring them. When the agreement fails, the case goes back to the judge, who sends the parties back to mediation. Because few mediators are willing to admit that the abuser fights unfairly, they facilitate another agreement, probably more favorable to the abuser, that the abuser still may violate.

Given all of the ways that mediation hurts women and children, it is not surprising that men are far more satisfied and women far less satisfied with mediation, compared with couples whose cases went directly to the judge to decide (Bryan, 1992; Sun & Woods, 1989; Treuthart & Woods, 1990).

Some mediators who are truly knowledgeable about domestic violence and committed to protecting any victim and her children believe they can mediate abusive cases safely. They either meet in teams (generally a female mediator with the mother and a male mediator with the father), or one mediator does shuttle mediation, meeting separately with each party. The first meeting is with the mother to explore any power and control issues, what the safety concerns are for her and the children, and how they can be met with restraining and visitation orders. Is a supervised visitation program available that will carry out long-term visitation at no cost to the victim? Can a protective friend or relative realistically and safely supervise visitation or pick up and drop off the children? Or would it be safe to exchange the children in a public place? What substance abuse problems exist, and how should they be addressed? Should any weapons be surrendered? After making referrals to any desired counseling for the woman and the children, a session is held with the father. He is allowed to explore his abusive behavior and any substance abuse problems that he may have, his feelings of loss as a result of the estrangement, and the need for addressing safety and other concerns. Usually an agreement is worked out successfully between the parents, one that addresses the safety issues. However, no studies have shown whether such mediation helps reduce future violence (Landau & Charbonneau, 1993; Magana & Taylor, 1993).

## Domestic Violence Affecting Custody Decisions

The overall trend in American courts is to recognize the seriousness of domestic violence, including the detrimental effect it has on any children in the home. Some Canadian courts have recognized it too (e.g., *M.[B.P.] v. M.[B.L.D.E.]*, 1992; *Young v. Young*, 1989). Despite this trend, however, men still are winning 70% of contested custody disputes in America, getting at least joint physical and legal custody or sole custody. Men win so often largely because so many cases are mediated, few women raise the domestic violence issues, and mothers still are held to a much higher standard than are fathers (Abrams & Greaney, 1989). As the statistics show, mothers should not assume that they are favored to win in custody cases. A battered woman may need an expert witness who is knowledgeable about domestic violence (or wife abuse) to best present her case. She will also want the court to know the many ways her abuser has disadvantaged her and the children and how the court can help fashion a decision that will realistically protect her and the children. Battered women's shelters (or refuges) often can make referrals to good, sympathetic lawyers and expert witnesses who understand the seriousness of domestic violence and how it affects children.

## Which Court Decides the Custody Case?

Two laws determine which state must hear and decide the custody determination when families move to different states. By 1984 every state had adopted its own version of the Uniform Child Custody Jurisdiction Act (UCCJA), and in 1980 the federal government enacted the Parental Kidnapping Prevention Act (PKPA), which supersedes a state's UCCJA whenever they are incompatible. These complex laws require that if child custody has never been determined in any court, it must be decided, except in an emergency, in the child's home state, the state where the child lived for the past 6 months preceding the filing of the custody case. When there is no home state, the state with the most significant connections to the child should make the determination. In addition, once custody has been decided properly according to these laws, all other states should recognize and enforce the custody decree. In general, unless all of the parties have moved from the state, courts in other states may not modify another court's custody decree. There are limited situations, however, in which an out-of-state court can issue a temporary modification to protect a particular child who has been seriously abused, neglected, or abandoned. But even such a temporary order probably will require that the child be returned to the original state for final resolution of the case.

Unfortunately the UCCJA was written in 1968, before this country had any awareness of domestic violence and that it affects children. The UCCJA makes some effort to protect a child who is abused by a parent. But the UCCJA does not even assume that a parent who abuses one child is likely to abuse the other children or that abuse of the mother or abuse of one child almost certainly causes all of the children emotional abuse. The PKPA, although written in the early 1980s, copied the minimal protection provision of the UCCJA. Under the UCCJA and the PKPA, however, a judge knowledgeable about domestic violence can sometimes issue protective measures to try to ensure the safety of any children and their protective caretaker. The court may issue a temporary order to protect any child once the court understands how the abuse of the mother affects this child or how the abuse of another child affects this child as well.

One goal of the UCCJA and the PKPA is to encourage courts to communicate with each other. This communication gives the judge who knows about the abuse an opportunity to persuade the other judge how great the danger is and what steps may be necessary to ensure safety. Sometimes a sympathetic judge even can persuade the other judge to decline jurisdiction (refuse to hear the case) so that the sympathetic judge can continue to decide the custody case. Sometimes it is at least possible to have part of the case heard in the new state where experts who know about the abuse can testify about it (Zorza, 1992).

## VISITATION

Regardless of which court hears a custody case, the court will decide not only which parent gets custody but also whether and under what terms the other parent will get visitation. "Reasonable visitation" is never appropriate for an abusive parent. *Reasonable visitation* is an open-ended visitation arrangement that effectively requires the parties to confer continually to decide when the noncustodial parent may see his children. This requirement means that the abuser can repeatedly call or even come by to set up and change visitation. Reasonable visitation orders hold the mother captive. She can never make plans for herself and the children without risking a visitation request. Many batterers abuse these orders to snoop constantly on the mother and the children or even to continue to beat her up. Reasonable visitation orders also encourage the father to keep litigating each unmet visitation demand and even may reward him for bringing a false complaint that she denied visitation (Adams, 1989; Edleson & Tolman, 1992). The custodial mother who refuses any reasonable visitation request does so at her peril, as she has almost no defenses and will bear all responsibility for proving that her denial was reasonable. Unfortunately, few judges treat her protecting herself from even threatened physical abuse as a legitimate reason for her to refuse him visitation. In contrast, when the abusive father has custody and refuses to let the noncustodial parent have her reasonable visitation, a court is less likely to enforce her right to see the children.

Although few courts will deny visitation to even the most abusive parents, courts can order supervised visitation, preferably done at a supervised visitation center where staff understand domestic violence, child abuse, and child development (see Chap. 11, this volume). Visitation can be supervised also by family members or friends. However, because so many parents of abusive spouses are also abusive, feel overly guilty about their child's abusive behavior, or feel afraid of their abusive child, it is generally unwise for the grandparents or other family members to supervise visitation. Friends and family seldom are willing to recognize the potential for abuse to the child or to protect the child.

In cases in which even supervised visitation is too dangerous or emotionally abusive, courts sometimes allow the abusers to have telephone or letter visitations or require that photographs of the children be sent periodically to the fathers.

## THE RIGHT TO RELOCATE

Even when a parent has both sole legal and sole physical custody of a child, the parent may not be free to move the child to wherever she or he chooses. Short-distance moves that do not involve crossing state lines are seldom a problem. But in most states either the noncustodial parent must consent to the move (probably in writing) or a court must give its consent if the move is of any distance, particularly if it involves relocating to another state. Court cases to decide whether a parent can relocate a child or to require a child to return to the original state are becoming more frequent. These are among the most gender biased decisions that courts make. Only rarely are courts unwilling to let a father move his child to accept a new job or to remarry: Courts view men's concerns as very legitimate.[1] Yet courts have been very reluctant to let a mother move her child, particularly when the father has visitation. Women's concerns are seen as unimportant, and her desire to move is frequently attacked as being selfish or vindictive (Abrams & Greaney, 1989). The court may be unwilling to see that the continued battering demoralizes the mother and hence hurts the children. Or it may believe that her desired move is purely vindictive or that she exaggerates or even fabricates the abuse to give her a reason to leave.

Frequently an abused parent or the protective parent of an abused child wishes to move with the child to a place where regular visitation would be difficult or impossible. Although the standard for relocation varies from state to state, trial courts generally have been upheld in prohibiting either the custodial or the noncustodial parent from removing the children to another state (see *Halliday v. Halliday,* 1991; *Trudeau v. Trudeau,* 1991). Indeed, the laws of many states prohibit such moves.

Courts are least sympathetic to permitting a relocation when the reason is to deny visitation to the other parent, particularly in states that have "friendly parent" provisions directing the court to consider which parent will most foster a good relationship with the other parent. Because battered women often want to move to escape the violence, courts see their relocation as a purely vindictive attempt to deny visitation. They do not view the women's moving as protective of themselves and their children and, hence, something that should be encouraged.

Every state punishes parental kidnapping. Some do so only when the nonkidnapping parent has custody or visitation rights. But frequently the law of the state assumes that the rights of parents are equal unless a court has ordered otherwise. States punish by giving custody to the other parent, and/or by jailing or fining the parent who left, and/or by requiring the kidnapping parent to give extra or makeup visitation time to the other parent (e.g., see *Pearson v. Caudle,* 1992). Courts often punish a parent who even temporarily seeks refuge in another state because of domestic violence. These practices of punishing protective parents show that most courts consider the children's best interests and even safety to be less important than the right of the noncustodial parent to have access to the children even when the noncustodial parent abuses visitation as a means of abusing the custodial parent or the child. The gender bias studies of various state courts have found courts to be particularly hostile to mothers in these relocation issues (Abrams & Greaney, 1989). A few states, however, protect mothers who go to battered women's shelters and/or call the police quickly to report that they are fleeing from abuse.

Courts are most likely to be sympathetic to requests to relocate in which the custodial parent can demonstrate that the move will have real advantages both for the custodial parent and the children, while providing the noncustodial parent with some kind of new visitation (e.g., see *D'Onofrio v. D'Onofrio,* 1976). This condition means that any plan to move should be thought out carefully, with all possibilities explored, including (a) where the custodial parent will work and get emotional support, and the comparative financial situations; (b) where the children will go to school, get medical care, and be able to continue any religious education; and (c) what reasonable alternative visitation arrangements are proposed.

In cases in which the major argument for the move is to protect the parent or the child, the custodial parent is expected to show that no other reasonable alternative enables the family to continue the current situation without seriously jeopardizing the child's physical and emotional safety. Such arguments are more likely to be recognized in those states that have provisions in their statutes directing courts to protect an abused child or an abused parent from further harm when fashioning a custody or visitation award.[2] Even in states that have such provisions, the court is unlikely to grant permission for the move unless the court is assured that (a) the custodial parent will not leave without court permission, (b) prior court orders have been unable to protect the child and the parent, and (c) the abuse is frequent and intense, seriously affecting the family. Although there are few written cases in which safety is the reason for allowing a parent to relocate the children, the National Council of Juvenile and Family Court Judges recommends that

> credible evidence of family violence [should] create a rebuttable presumption that where relocation will serve the safety, community-support and/or employment interests of the abused party who is the custodial parent, it is in the best interest of the children to permit relocation of the custodial parent and the children. Any inconvenience caused to the abusing party by the relocation of the abused party and children should not weigh against the presumption. (Hart, 1992, p. 35)

## DOMESTIC VIOLENCE STATUTES AND CIVIL PROTECTION ORDERS

Effective police protection is needed for women and children to be safe from violence. Because state laws give police much latitude in how they respond to abusive situations, women and children generally need courts to issue protection orders before the police will protect them. Protection orders are a new phenomenon. They are called "restraining orders," "protective orders," or "injunctions," depending on the state or stage in the proceeding.

No state offered any meaningful protection to battered women and their children before 1976, when Pennsylvania enacted the first statute in the United States to protect victims of domestic violence. Those states that provided some protection through their divorce statutes or through peace bonds generally granted relief only to married persons in only rare instances and generally for short periods of time. Further, the likelihood that this relief would be enforced was low. What limited enforcement existed was slow, difficult, and frequently very expensive for the victim.

### Who Can Be Protected Now?

Domestic violence statutes now exist in every state to protect victims of domestic violence. They vary as to whom they cover, but in every state they protect married and formerly married persons, and in virtually every state they also protect persons who live together and close relatives. Approximately three quarters of state codes specifically include children as eligible for protection when they are abused by a family or household member. A few states allow children the right to seek relief on their own, particularly if they are married, over the age of 16, emancipated, or abused in a dating relationship. But in most states parents can seek protection in the courts on behalf of their abused child (Hart, 1992).

**What Protection Is Available?**

The most frequent protection available to a victim of domestic violence, including the protection available to child witnesses, is for the court to (a) exclude the abuser from the victim's household,[3] (b) order the abuser to not abuse the victim,[4] and (c) give custody of the victim's children to the victim.[5] Some statutes that are silent about custody awards effectively permit them under a general provision allowing the court to grant other relief to protect a victim (Finn & Colson, 1990). Indeed, the domestic violence acts of about one third of the states specifically direct the court to protect the abused parent or the child from further harm by making a custody and visitation award (Hart, 1992).

Most courts can grant child support to the victimized parent if the abusive parent has a legal obligation to pay such support. About one half of the states permit courts to award the victim attorney's fees and filing costs. The victim can receive monetary compensation for any expenses resulting from the abuse in one fourth of the states. Such expenses might include medical payments; the cost of household repairs or to replace damage, destroyed, or stolen items; and the cost to move, change locks, or get an unlisted telephone number.

**Defining Abuse**

Each state has its own definition of what constitutes abuse. Some states, such as Arizona, Georgia, New Jersey, and New York, define abusive behavior as conduct between protected individuals that violates certain sections of the state's criminal code. But most states define their own prohibited acts, which typically include attempting to cause or actually causing physical or sexual harm.[6] Unfortunately states do not protect women and children from emotional abuse in domestic violence statutes unless the abuser threatens physical abuse. However, virtually all states now protect victims against stalking, though usually in a separate, often criminal, statute.

A few states (California, Massachusetts, New Hampshire, Oregon, Rhode Island, and Vermont) charge no fees for protection orders. Although most domestic violence statutes require fees to obtain an order of protection or for serving the court papers on the defendant, all states except Hawaii allow the court to waive the fees if the victim is unable to pay them. A few states, such as Nevada and Arkansas, provide that the court can decide at the full hearing which party will pay the fees (Finn & Colson, 1990).

At least 30 states allow victims of domestic violence to file on their own for a protection order without an attorney (Finn & Colson, 1990). This allowance often requires that the court have special, simplified forms that a victim can fill out easily and without help. A few states, such as Florida and New Jersey, direct the clerks of court to assist unrepresented petitioners in filing for orders of protection. A number of states enable the victim to not disclose the address where she or her children are staying, particularly when the address is a shelter for battered women (Rauch, 1993).

In every state except Delaware and South Carolina, a victim can obtain an emergency temporary order of protection, usually on the same day that the victim submits her petition to the court. About one half of the states provide court access 24 hours a day for obtaining these emergency orders, though often the victim must return to court the next day during regular business hours for another order (Finn & Colson, 1990).

### Notice to the Abuser and the Hearing

In every state, once the papers are filed with the court, the abuser must be given a copy of the papers and notified when he is to appear in court for a hearing. Most states require that the alleged abuser be handed the papers in person, but a few allow service by mail, publication, or as otherwise directed by a court. Law enforcement officers often must serve the order to the alleged abuser, frequently without any fee. The full hearing must occur fairly quickly, typically within 10 to 30 days. At this hearing, the court decides whether the abuse was more likely than not and what relief to grant if it believes that the abuse happened.

Orders may remain in effect indefinitely in Colorado, Michigan, Nebraska, Nevada, North Dakota, and Oklahoma. California and Hawaii permit orders to remain in effect for 3 years, and Illinois and Wisconsin for 2 years. In Alaska, Connecticut, Idaho, Indiana, Louisiana, Missouri, New Mexico, and Utah, orders expire in fewer than 180 days. In the remaining 30 states, orders after hearing can last from 6 months to 1 year (Hart, 1992). In Massachusetts the initial order can last only 1 year, but if the victim returns to court to renew her order, the judge can extend the order indefinitely.

### Mutual Orders of Protection

*Mutual orders of protection* are orders directed at both parties to not abuse, to stay away from, or to not communicate with the other party. Usually they are part of the same order, but sometimes they are on separate orders that may have been issued in the same or in different courts, possibly at different times. Victims should avoid mutual orders of protection, as they greatly increase the danger to the victim and her children. Mutual orders of protection seldom give the police any guidance in how to enforce them, thereby resulting in either both parties being arrested or the police refusing to enforce the order. At least eight states prohibit mutual orders, but even in states that prohibit these orders, it is not unusual for some judges to issue them or for mediators or attorneys to urge parties or the court that mutual orders be entered by the court (National Center on Women and Family Law, 1993).

### Enforcement of Protection Orders

All protective orders are useless unless the police, prosecutor, judge, and entire criminal justice system enforce them. Not only must the judiciary and law enforcement cooperate with each other, but the cooperation of the social service system and women's advocacy groups is also needed (Finn, 1991), such as exists in Duluth, Minnesota; Quincy, Massachusetts; London, Ontario; and Portland, Maine. Without laws and policies requiring enforcement, public pressure, and adequate training, the criminal justice system has not taken domestic violence seriously, leaving offenders unarrested, unprosecuted, unsentenced, or their probation or parole unsupervised.

Where children are in danger, police must be willing to enforce custody, visitation, or no-contact provisions and to use common sense to document and temporarily prohibit visitation when a defendant shows up for visitation drunk or abusive.

To make abusers fully accountable for their violence, courts must order them to pay for all resulting damages. Monetary damage amounts are virtually never ordered, but they can be staggering for both the victim and the community.

For example, in the 1980s, New York City spent at least $500 million annually on domestic violence, half of that cost paid by New York City employers from reduced worker productivity, greater absenteeism, and higher turnover. Domestic violence also added at least $77.5 million to emergency room costs at hospitals in New York City alone (Goodman, 1992). Other studies have found that the average employed battered woman misses work 18 full days per year and is late for work 60 days per year because of the violence. Furthermore, she often must take time off from work during the day to call attorneys or counselors, whom she dare not call from home, or to go to court or appointments. Three quarters of employed battered women are so harassed by their partners in person or on the phone at work that 20% of the women lose their jobs as a result (New York Victims Service Agency, 1987; Schechter & Gray, 1988). A study of battered women seeking shelter found that their abusers destroyed an average of $10,000 in family property prior to separation, including photographs, toys, and furniture of children (Hart, 1991). Finally, domestic violence, which causes half of the homelessness of families in America (Zorza, 1991), costs the average victim who must move a minimum of $5,000 to relocate (Hart, 1991).

Because most abusers rationally decided whether they will batter, using a cost-benefit analysis (Jaffe, Wolfe, Telford, & Austin, 1986; Williams & Hawkins, 1989), restitution orders, and swift, strict sentencing can make a major difference in making abusers stop their violence.

## RELIEF THROUGH CRIMINAL ACTIONS

In every state, a domestic abuse victim can bring criminal charges against her assailant or the person who assaults her child. In the majority of states, she also can bring criminal charges against the abuser if he violates an order of protection. In some instances (e.g., if the woman was raped by her husband) it is unlikely that criminal charges would be brought against her assailant unless it is both a crime in that state and she wanted her husband charged.

Although battered women legitimately fear retaliation from their abusers if they bring criminal charges against the men, studies have found that the women are least safe when they have the charges dropped, but are by far the safest when they choose to keep pursuing the charges (Ford & Regoli, 1993).

Criminal prosecution can send a very powerful message to abusers, particularly if the system treats the crime seriously. The major drawback to criminal charges is that the crime is seen as a violation against the state, not the victim. This drawback means that the prosecutor has control over how aggressively to pursue the charges or even whether to pursue them at all. The prosecutor can negotiate directly with the assailant and/or the court to have the charges dismissed or "resolved" in a way that fails to convey the seriousness of the offense to the offender. Even when the prosecutor wishes to pursue a criminal case aggressively, the judge has the authority to acquit the defendant or, in one of many ways, determine the outcome of the case in a manner that fails to treat the case seriously. Further, even when both the prosecutor and the judge treat the case aggressively, the probation, correction, or parole officer involved make crucial decisions that determine how a sentence is to be carried out and enforced. Thus it is possible that the offender will be released quickly from jail or that no one follows up when he never goes to a court-ordered treatment for his abusive behavior and any drug or alcohol problem he may have.

**Court-Ordered Batterer Treatment**

Batterer treatment programs have had some, but only limited, success. Most success rate figures are inflated by calculating them on the basis of those who complete the training. Yet in reality those who drop out constitute the overwhelming majority of batterers. One study of batterers who were sent to an 8-month treatment program found that of 200 men who contacted the program by telephone, only 50 appeared for the intake interview, 25 participated in at least one counseling session, 12 completed 3 months, and only 2 (1% of the original callers) completed the entire 8-month program (Gondolf, 1993). Furthermore, some communities have no batterer treatment programs or have such long waiting lists for treatment that the abuser may never be sent to treatment before his probation or parole ends.

Other programs are just not effective. Some programs incorrectly assume that alcohol causes the violence and that successfully treating the abuser's drinking problem will cure him of his battering (Gondolf, 1989; Stordeur & Stille, 1989). Curing him of his substance abuse problem will not stop him from battering, but it will make it easier for him to be treated for his violence (Edleson & Tolman, 1992). Similarly, batterer treatment based primarily on anger control is unlikely to work because men batter out of a need to control women, not because they are angry and out of control (Gondolf & Russell, 1986). Likewise, couples counseling not only will be unlikely to cure his abusive behavior but actually will increase the likelihood that he will reoffend against his victim (Edleson & Tolman, 1992).

On a more encouraging front, there is a nationwide move to establish appropriate standards for batterer treatment programs, which should increase their effectiveness. Batterers should be screened before referral to the program most likely to help them. If they have substance abuse problems, those need to be treated as well.

**Other Rights of Victims**

The victim in most states now has new rights to seek compensation through the criminal justice system from state funds for many of her unreimbursed losses as a result of domestic violence if she reported the crime promptly and cooperated with the prosecution. This is true even if the offender was never convicted of any crime or cannot be located. The victim cannot be denied compensation under the Victims of Crime Act because she still is married to or living with her abuser. In most states the act allows her to seek reimbursement of her medical and treatment costs and attorney's fees that resulted from the injuries inflicted on her by her assailant. In addition, the state version of the act probably allows her to seek recovery for lost wages and most other out-of-pocket expenses such as transportation and housekeeping, although few states permit compensation for replacement of property.

If her abuser is convicted, the victim or her survivor has the right to submit a statement to the court about how the violence affected her and her family before the abuser is sentenced. These statements are known as *victim impact statements*. In some states the victim also may submit a victim impact statement to the court before the court decides whether to accept a plea bargain made by the prosecutor and the defendant, or to the parole board before the offender is to be released from prison. Some states will inform a victim before her offender is released so that she can make plans for her safety and that of her children.

Many states have enacted victim intimidation laws to protect victims and witnesses during the pendency of a criminal case from anyone, including the defendant, who attempts to interfere with their participation in the criminal matter. The court can order the defendant to stay away from or not intimidate or harass the victim and any witness. Such protections make it considerably more likely that a battered woman and her witnesses will be willing to cooperate in prosecuting the case. These protections end if the case is dropped, dismissed, or otherwise concluded. Hence the victim probably will need a civil protection order in addition to these victim intimidation protective orders.

In many states, police must inform any victim of domestic violence of his or her right to seek a civil protection order or to bring criminal charges against the assailant. In increasing numbers of states, a police officer must arrest any offender when the officer has probable cause to believe that the defendant has violated a civil order of protection or has committed any domestic violence offense, especially a felony, even when there is no civil order of protection in force.

Some states have enacted laws to consider statements made to domestic violence and/or rape counselors to be privileged so that the defendant cannot have access to them or can only have access to anything that might indicate his innocence. Such laws are usually more protective in civil cases, in which defendants have fewer constitutional rights (Rauch, 1993).

## SUING THE ABUSER

In cases in which the abuser earns a decent income, has assets worth obtaining, or carries insurance, a victim of domestic violence or the parent of an abused child may want to consider suing the abuser in civil court for tort damages for all of her and her children's expenses and sometimes for pain and suffering.

If a battered woman sues her abuser, the court probably will give him access to her doctor's and therapist's records. If she has any minor children, she will want to discuss with her attorney, before bringing the tort suit, whether any information the abuser may get could hurt her in a custody fight.

Many attorneys are willing to bring a tort case for a percentage of the damage amount the court awards to the victim. Even if the victim wins her case, however, she may not be able to collect from the abuser if he quits his job or spends or hides his assets.

## CONCLUSION

Battered women and their children need protective orders, custody orders, criminal enforcement of domestic violence laws and court orders, and monetary restitution to effectively protect them. Battered women also need the assurance that they will not be sent to inappropriate mediation or joint counseling and that their abusers will be given, at most, supervised visitation with their children. The legislatures must amend the UCCJA and PKPA to better protect battered women and their children. Similarly legislators must strengthen laws that make domestic violence a factor in custody cases and write new laws to take the violence into account when a battered custodial parent seeks to move. Likewise legislators should abolish friendly parent provisions or, at least, make them irrelevant in custody cases in which women or children are abused. In addition, legislators must determine realistic standards for batterer treatment programs and supervised visitation programs so that such programs provide meaningful, long-term protection from further abuse. These new laws plus ongoing mandatory training for judges, police, attorneys, doctors, and therapists will enable the professionals, police, and the courts finally to respond appropriately to the needs of battered women and their children.

Battered women and their children will be helped most when all communities have coordinated responses to domestic violence. All of a community's professionals must understand domestic violence, including how both parents minimize and deny it and how severely the violence affects the children. They must make a commitment to protect all of its victims, including the child witnesses. To do this, they must work together so that each part of the system engages, communicates with, and reinforces the rest. It is only when battered women and their children are free from further abuse that they can begin to heal.

## NOTES

1. In *Michael G.* the court stated, "No cases exist in which a father, custodial parent or not, was denied the right to move wherever and whenever he pleased" 1 *New York Family Law Update* 93 (1991).

2. Arizona, California, Colorado, Florida, Illinois, Kentucky, Michigan, Minnesota, Missouri, New Hampshire, New Jersey, North Dakota, Rhode Island, Washington, West Virginia, and Wyoming.

3. Everywhere except Delaware.

4. Everywhere except Arkansas and Wisconsin.

5. Only Arizona, Connecticut, Delaware, Indiana, Nebraska, Oklahoma, Virginia, and Wisconsin are silent as to custody and visitation.

6. Finn and Colson (1990, pp. 12-13) note that at least 43 states protect threats of physical abuse.

## REFERENCES

Abrams, R. I., & Greaney, J. M. (1989). *Report of the gender bias study of the Supreme Judicial Court.* Boston: Supreme Judicial Court.

Adams, D. (1989). Identifying the assaultive husband: You be the judge. *Boston Bar Journal, 33*(4), 23-25.

Bryan, P. E. (1992). Killing us softly: Divorce mediation and the politics of power. *Buffalo Law Review, 40*(2), 441-523.

Canadian Department of Justice. (1993). *Custody and access: Public discussion paper.* Ottawa: Department of Justice,Communications and Consultation.

Crean, S. (1989). *In the name of the fathers: The story behind custody.* Toronto: Amanita.

Dempsey v. Dempsey, 292 N.W.2d 549 (Mich. 1980).

D'Onofrio v. D'Onofrio, 144 N.J. Super. 200, 365 A.2d 27 (1976).

Edleson, J. L., & Tolman, R. M. (1992). *Intervention for men who batter: An ecological approach.* Newbury Park, CA: Sage.

Finn, P. (1991). Civil protection orders: A flawed opportunity for intervention. In M. Steinman (Ed.), *Woman battering: Policy responses* (pp. 155-189). Cincinnati: ACJS/Anderson.

Finn, P., & Colson, S. (1990). *Civil protection orders: Legislation, current court practice, and enforcement.* Washington, DC: National Institute of Justice.

Ford, D. A., & Regoli, M. J. (1993). The criminal prosecution of wife assaulters: Process, problems, and effects. In N. Z. Hilton (Ed.), *Legal responses to wife assault* (pp. 127-164). Newbury Park, CA: Sage.

Furstenberg, F. F., Jr., & Cherlin, A. J. (1991). *Divided families: What happens to children when parents part.* Cambridge, MA: Harvard University Press.

Garska v. McCoy, 278 S.E. 357 (W.Va. 1981).

Gondolf, E. W. (1989). *Man against women: What every woman should know about violent men.* Blue Ridge Summit, PA: TAB.

Gondolf, E. W. (1993). Treating the batterer. In M. Hansen & M. Haraway (Eds.), *Battering and family therapy* (pp. 105-118). Newbury Park, CA: Sage.

Gondolf, E. W., & Russell, D. (1986). The case against anger control treatment programs for batterers. *Response, 9,* 2-5.

Goodman, R. M. (1992). *Domestic violence: The hidden crime.* Albany, NY: Senate Committee on Investigations, Taxation, and Government Operations.

Halliday v. Halliday, 134 N.H. 388, 593 A.2d 233 (1991).

Harlow, C. W. (1991). *Female victims of violent crime.* Washington, DC: Bureau of Justice Statistics.

Hart, B. (1991). *Cost of domestic violence.* Harrisburg: Pennsylvania Coalition Against Domestic Violence.

Hart, B. J. (1992). State codes on domestic violence: Analysis, commentary, and recommendations. *Juvenile and Family Court Journal, 43*(4), 3-80.

Jaffe, P. G., Wolfe, D. A., Telford, A., & Austin, G. (1986). The impact of police changes in incidents of wife abuse. *Journal of Family Violence, 1*(1), 37-49.

Jaffe, P. G., Wolfe, D. A., & Wilson, S. K. (1990). *Children of battered women.* Newbury Park, CA: Sage.

Kirkwood, C. (1993). *Leaving abusive partners.* Newbury Park, CA: Sage.

Landau, B., & Charbonneau, P. (1993). *Report from the Toronto Forum on Woman Abuse and Mediation.* Waterloo, Ontario: Fund for Dispute Resolution.

Liss, M. B., & Stahly, G. B. (1993). Domestic violence and child custody. In M. Hansen & M. Haraway (Eds.), *Battering and family therapy: A feminist perspective* (pp. 175-187). Newbury Park, CA: Sage.

Magana, H. A., & Taylor, N. (1993). Child custody mediation and spouse abuse: A descriptive study of a protocol. *Family and Conciliation Courts Review, 13,* 50-64.

M.(B.P.) v. M.(B.L.D.E.), 42 Reports of Family Law 349 (Ontario Court of Appeal 1992).

McGraw J. M., & Smith, H. A. (1992). Child sexual abuse allegations amidst divorce and custody proceedings: Refining the validation process, *Journal of Child Sexual Abuse, 1*(1), 49-62.

National Center on Women and Family Law. (1993). *Mutual orders of protection.* New York: Author.

New York Victims Service Agency. (1987). Unpublished study. (Available from Victim Services/Travelers Aid, 2 Lafayette St., 3rd Floor, New York, NY 10007)

Pagelow, M. D. (1984). *Family violence.* New York: Praeger.

Parental Kidnapping Prevention Act, 28 U.S.C. §1738A.

Pearson v. Caudle, 593 So.2d 619 (Fla. App. 1992).

Pennington, H. J., & Woods, L. (1990). *Legal issues and legal options in civil child sexual abuse cases: Representing the protective parent.* New York: National Center on Women and Family Law.

Polikoff, N. D. (1987). Joint custody: Only by agreement of the parties. *Women's Advocate, 8*(1), 3-4.

Porter v. Porter, 274 N.W.2d 235 (N.D. 1979).

Rauch, S. H. (1993). *Protecting confidentiality: A legal manual for domestic and sexual abuse programs.* New York: National Center on Women and Family Law.

Roy, M. (1988). *Children in the cross-fire: Violence in the home—How does it affect our children?* Deerfield Beach, FL: Health Communications.

Schechter, S., & Gray, L. T. (1988). Understanding and empowering battered women. In M. B. Straus (Ed.), *Abuse and victimization across the life span* (pp. 240-263). Baltimore: Johns Hopkins University Press.

Stordeur, R. A., & Stille, R. (1989). *Ending men's violence against their partners: One road to peace.* Newbury Park, CA: Sage.

Sun, M., & Woods, L. (1989). *A mediator's guide to domestic abuse.* New York: National Center on Women and Family Law.

Treuthart, M. P., & Woods, L. (1990). *Mediation: A guide for advocates and attorneys representing battered women.* New York: National Center on Women and Family Law.

Trudeau v. Trudeau, 822 P.2d 873 (Wyo. 1991).

Williams, K. R., & Hawkins, R. (1989). The meaning of arrest for wife assault. *Criminology, 27,* 163-181.

Young v. Young, 19 Reports of Family Law 227 (Ontario Supreme Court 1989).

Zorza, J. (1993). *State custody laws with respect to domestic abuse.* New York: National Center on Women and Family Law.

Zorza, J. (1992). *Guide to interstate custody: A manual for domestic violence advocates.* New York: National Center on Women and Family Law.

Zorza, J. (1991). Woman battering: A major cause of homelessness. *Clearinghouse Review, 25*(4), 421-429.

# 10

# Child Protection Services for Children of Battered Women

*Practice and Controversy*

CAROLE ECHLIN
LARRY MARSHALL

Doctor Smith, a family physician, writes to a child protection worker. She states that Dan, age 10, has been deemed a gifted student but is failing in school. Doctor Smith is worried about Dan's emotional well-being. She links Dan's somatic complaints and suicidal ideation to living in an abusive environment.

Doctor Smith complains that Dan's stepfather, Bill, who is still mainlining heroin, is physically and emotionally abusive toward Dan's mother, Helen. In fact, she states that Dan witnessed Bill trying to strangle Helen last weekend. The doctor reminds the child protection worker that this is the third letter she has written about her concerns and notes that Helen still refuses to leave her abusive partner. The doctor demands that Dan be removed from the abusive environment.

What should the child protection worker do? What can the child protection worker do?

The response of child protection workers to the needs of child witnesses of woman abuse in Canada and the United States is as varied as the provinces and states that make up the two countries. Allegations that child witnesses of woman abuse are in need of protection often can result in inconsistent and sometimes inappropriate responses by agencies mandated to protect children. It is no surprise, then, that a great deal of controversy surrounds the issue of how child protection workers intervene in such cases.

In the situation just presented, variations in attitudes, laws, and practices could lead to a multitude of approaches about how the child protection worker would intervene. They also could result in a militating dichotomy: If the child protection worker does not remove Dan from the abusive environment, he or she may be criticized for failing to protect the child. If the worker does remove him, he or she may be accused of revictimizing the child's mother.

In this chapter we look at the difficulties that child protection workers face when trying to make a situation safe for children who witness woman abuse. Four areas are examined: (a) the role of Child Protection Services, (b) whether a child who witnesses woman abuse can be defined as a child in need of protection, (c) how Child Protection Services currently respond to woman abuse and child witnesses of woman abuse, and (d) roadblocks and barriers in responding to child witnesses of woman abuse. We conclude the chapter with recommendations for improving the response to the needs of child witnesses of woman abuse.

## INTRODUCTION TO
## CHILD PROTECTION SERVICES

Child Protection Services represent in a tangible way a community's values and norms regarding children. Child Protection Services are mandated to protect society's customs and standards concerning child-rearing practices. Child welfare policies define when and how the state should intervene in a family's life. In Canada and the United States, it is the responsibility of Child Protection Services to receive and investigate reports of suspected child abuse and neglect. Child Protection Services are supportive and directed at strengthening the family unit. Services include individual, couple, family, and group counseling. In-home support services also may be offered. If services do not exist within the Child Protection Service agency, child protection workers attempt to link clients with community resources. Clients involved with Child Protection Services have either a voluntary or involuntary relationship with the agency.

Child protection workers employed by child welfare agencies are empowered by law to act as agents for the government. They are given the authority to take whatever action is deemed necessary to protect a child living in a dangerous situation (Vayda & Satterfield, 1984). When voluntary services are ineffective at protecting children, child protection workers can use the power vested in them by the state to protect children from harm. Within the framework of *parens patriae* (the protector of subjects unable to protect themselves) and *loco parentis* (the power to stand in the place of the parents), the state has the authority to act in the best interests of and for the protection of children (Wilkerson, 1973). For example, if a child's level of care falls below the minimum community standard set out in legislation, the child protection worker can remove a child from the parent's care. In these cases it is expected that the rights of the parents should be abrogated only when there is compelling evidence that the child is at risk of harm while in the parent's care. When removal of a child is seen as the only alternative for protecting him or her from harm, child protection workers must weigh the impact of moving the child into a system that is plagued with problems against leaving the child in an abusive environment.

Protecting children from harm is complex, fast-paced, risky work. Child protection workers must be able to quickly investigate, identify, assess, and treat a problem in a systematic and creative way, often despite the resistance of the people for whom help is intended. Unlike other areas of social work in which clinical skills are the primary focus, a child protection worker must be able to investigate like a police officer, think like a lawyer, and treat like a social worker (Vogel, 1987).

## CHILD WITNESSING AND CHILD ABUSE

Are child witnesses of woman abuse abused children? *Child abuse* has been described as any form of physical harm, emotional deprivation, neglect, or sexual maltreatment that can result in injury or psychological damage to a child (Dawson, 1990).

Children who have been abused typically exhibit patterns of maladaptive behaviors. Although some of the behaviors are seen commonly in all children at one time or another, when they are pervasive and lasting, rather than isolated and temporary, they may indicate child abuse. Behaviors that describe children who have been physically, emotionally, or sexually abused fall into four broad categories. Abused children may (a) be overly compliant, (b) be extremely aggressive, (c) demonstrate overly adaptive behaviors, and (d) experience lags in their development. Other general behaviors that characterize abused children include an inability to form trusting relationships, role reversal, suicidal ideation, low self-esteem, learning problems, and oppositional or behavioral disorders such as rebellion, running away, lying, and stealing (Dawson, 1990).

Children who witness woman abuse exhibit symptoms similar to children who have been physically, sexually, or emotionally abused (Hershorn & Rosenbaum, 1985; Jaffe, Wolfe, Wilson, & Zak, 1986; Wolfe & Mosk, 1983). Studies have shown that exposure to woman abuse can result in internalizing behavior problems such as depression, low self-esteem, and withdrawal and externalizing behavior problems such as rebellion, hyperactivity, and delinquency (Jaffe, Wolfe, & Wilson, 1990; Moore, Pepler, Mae, & Kates, 1989; Pressman, 1989; Sinclair, 1985).

Jaffe et al. describe in their book *Children of Battered Women* (1990) the devastating effects that witnessing woman abuse can have on a child's cognitive, emotional, social, developmental, and physical well-being. They state that a child's response to woman abuse varies according to age, gender, stage of development, and role in the family. They identify other factors that affect the child's response to witnessing woman abuse, including the frequency of the violence, economic and social disadvantage, repeated separations and moves, and special needs that a child might have (Jaffe et al., 1990).

In addition to psychological, cognitive, and behavioral adjustment problems, researchers have found that children from violent homes are at increased risk of being injured themselves (Carlson, 1984). Layzer, Goodson, and deLange (1986) found that 70% of the children admitted to shelters were direct victims of abuse and neglect. Shelter studies also show that children exposed to woman abuse may be at risk of neglect or abuse by their mothers, who are suffering from the cumulative stress of being victimized (MacLeod, 1987).

Perpetuating violence also has been identified as possibly related to a history of witnessing woman abuse, suggesting a cause-and-effect relationship between the two (Pagelow, 1984; Rosenbaum & O'Leary, 1981). Some studies have found male children who witnessed woman abuse to be at an increased risk of becoming perpetrators, and female children who witnessed woman abuse to be at an increased risk of becoming victims (Hughes & Hampton, 1984).

So are child witnesses of woman abuse abused children? Yes. Review of the literature shows that they exhibit symptoms similar to those of other abused children, who are at risk of physical harm, and are likely to perpetuate violence. Although not necessarily the direct victims of violence, their exposure to woman abuse should define them as children in need of protection. Yet millions of children who suffer the effects of witnessing woman abuse (Carlson, 1984) are not adequately protected by Child Protection Services. Unfortunately the phrases "child abuse" and "child witnessing of woman abuse" mean different things to different people. This variability can result in a haphazard response to children exposed to woman abuse.

## CURRENT RESPONSES BY CHILD PROTECTION SERVICES

Responses of Child Protection Services to children who witness woman abuse are often dramatically different from their responses to children who have been neglected or who have been physically, sexually, or emotionally abused. Confusion around whether a child who is witnessing woman abuse is an abused child and in need of protection results in varied responses. Consider the following three cases.

Mrs. S contacts the Child Protection Service agency to report ongoing fighting between her neighbors. She has heard glass breaking, children crying, a male shouting obscenities, and a female begging not to be hit again. Mrs. S is worried about the safety of the three preschool children living in the home. The child protection worker asks Mrs. S whether she has ever seen either of the parents hitting the children or noticed whether the children had any injuries. When Mrs. S says that she has not, the child protection worker says the children are not being abused. The case is closed.

A school psychologist contacts Child Protection Services to report that Harry, age 11, is having a number of problems in school. She describes Harry as an aggressive child who is impulsive and quick tempered. She reports that Harry's severe temper tantrums have kept him from establishing positive relationships with other school children. The psychologist states that Harry has above-average ability but is failing academically. She adds that Harry recently disclosed that he saw his father trying to strangle his mother. The psychologist believes strongly that Harry is in need of protection. The child protection worker shares the psychologist's concerns, contacts the family, and offers services. But the family refuses them. Because Harry is not seen as being at risk of harm according to the law, the case is closed.

A local police officer contacts Child Protection Services while investigating a case of woman abuse. He reports that Mrs. T, mother of three children, was physically assaulted by her partner, Mr. D, the previous evening. He states that Mr. D left the home and his whereabouts are unknown. The police officer states that he plans to arrest Mr. D when he finds him and that he will obtain an order to prohibit Mr. D from accessing Mrs. T and her children. The police officer states that Mrs. T told him she and her children would be at risk of physical harm if Mr. D returned home. Mrs. T also stated that she would be unable to prevent Mr. D from entering the home if he returned. Mrs. T stated she was not prepared to call the police when Mr. D showed up.

A child protection worker investigates the report and offers to help Mrs. T relocate to a shelter for battered women. Mrs. T refuses to leave the house. The child protection worker then suggests that the children be

placed with family or friends. Mrs. T turns down the suggestion. Deciding
that the children would be at risk of physical harm if Mr. D returned to the
family home, the child protection worker removes the children from Mrs.
T's care.

These examples represent typical responses by Child Protection Services
to cases of woman abuse in both Canada and the United States. The variation
in responses illustrates how an imprecise mandate and a child protection
worker's lack of knowledge can result in some child witnesses of woman
abuse being protected and other children who were exposed to woman abuse
falling through the cracks of the system. Why is this happening?

Not much has been written about the response of Child Protection Services
to child witnesses of woman abuse or their mothers. What has been written
is very disturbing. Gordon, in her book *Heroes of Their Own Lives: The
Politics and History of Family Violence* (1988), describes the various responses of Child Protection Services to woman abuse in the Massachusetts
Society for the Protection of Children between the years 1880 and 1960.
Gordon found that some child protection workers attempted to avoid wife-
beating cases, blamed the women for the violence, and tended to use gender-
neutral euphemisms such as "marital discord" and "marital disharmony"
when describing woman abuse. Her research also showed that women in the
1940s were encouraged by child protection workers to remain in abusive
situations and were counseled to alter their behavior to alleviate the violence!
What is particularly amazing is the finding that, because of the inadequacy
of police protection, battered women continued to ask child protection
workers for help despite their outrageous responses.

Callahan (1993), in Wharf's book *Rethinking Child Welfare in Canada,*
also discusses the child welfare system's response to battered women. She
exposes the victimization that battered women experience when their children are removed by Child Protection Services because the mother has failed
or is predicted to fail to protect them from the abusive partner. She also
describes the battered women's loss of self-esteem, loss of child tax credits,
reduction of social assistance, and ineligibility for housing. Finally Callahan
criticizes the child welfare practice for ignoring the poverty and powerlessness of battered women.

Questions arise about why Child Protection Services have failed to intervene consistently and appropriately in families in which woman abuse is
occurring. One possible explanation may be related to lack of understanding
by some child protection workers of the dynamics of woman abuse. Another
major problem seems to be the lack of a workable definition of child abuse
that includes children who witness woman abuse.

For example, in the United States no federal or state laws specify that child witnesses of woman abuse are abused children (Peled, 1993). However, virtually all states include emotional abuse, mental injury, or impairment of emotional health as a reportable condition in their child abuse laws (Younes & Besharov, 1988). Unfortunately, many child witnesses of woman abuse have not been protected by this section of the statutes. Defining a child as in need of protection does not seem to be a problem if the case is clearly outrageous by any standards of acceptable parenting—for example, a child witnessing its mother being tortured, locking a child in the basement for days at a time, or tying a child to a bedpost. The difficulty seems to arise with those cases in which the abuse is not obvious, where the abuse occurs incrementally, and there is no actual or reasonably foreseeable injury to the child. Conceptualizing the meaning of *emotional abuse* seems to be a major obstacle. Although there appears to be common agreement that a child who witnesses woman abuse is being emotionally maltreated, most state legislatures have failed to develop comprehensive statutory definitions instructing when and how Child Protection Services should intervene in those cases. In the few states that have developed statutory definitions of psychologically abusive behaviors (e.g., habitual scapegoating, humiliation of the child, violent acts producing fear or guilt on the part of the child), judges seldom are presented with cases in which only psychological maltreatment is alleged (Melton & Davidson, 1987). It seems to be very difficult to state with certainty that the parent's behavior created severe emotional harm to the child.

Under these circumstances Child Protection Services in the United States are left to decide when and how they should intervene. Given the impreciseness of the definition of emotional abuse, the difficulty proving in court that the behaviors of the child are the result of psychological maltreatment, and the difficulty proving that the psychological maltreatment was the result of a parent's behavior, it is not surprising that there is little uniformity among the responses of Child Protection Services in the United States to allegations that children who are witnessing woman abuse are themselves being abused.

In Canada each province has its own child abuse legislation. Six of the 10 provinces stipulate that a child who has witnessed woman abuse can be found to be in need of protection. Legislation exists in the provinces of Saskatchewan (Family Services Act Saskatchewan, 1978), Prince Edward Island (Family and Child Services Act, 1988), Newfoundland (Child Welfare Act Newfoundland, 1990), New Brunswick (Family Services Act New Brunswick, 1980), Alberta (Child Welfare Act Alberta, 1984), and Nova Scotia (Children and Family Services Act Nova Scotia, 1990). For example, in Alberta:

a child is emotionally injured if there is reasonable and probable grounds to believe that the emotional injury is the result of . . . exposure to domestic violence or severe domestic disharmony. (Child Welfare Act Alberta, 1984, pp. 2-3)

In Nova Scotia

a child is in need of protective services where the child has suffered physical or emotional harm caused by being exposed to repeated domestic violence by or towards a parent or guardian of the child and the child's parent or guardian fails or refuses to obtain services or treatment to remedy or alleviate the violence. (Children and Family Services Act Nova Scotia, 1990, p. 10)

The Family Service Act New Brunswick (1980) states:

The security and development of the child may be in danger when the child is living in a situation where there is severe domestic violence. (p. 14)

Although these laws to protect child witnesses of woman abuse are a step in the right direction, they are also problematic. The definitions are too vague, too broad, and not inclusive enough. Some of the laws specify emotional harm to the child; others do not. Some address the developmental and physical harm of the child; others do not. The majority of the legislation uses the term "severe domestic violence" but offers no guidelines on how to define what is meant by "severe."

Another problem with all of the legislative acts is the use of the gender-neutral terms "domestic violence" and "domestic disharmony." Defining the act of violence so that the perpetrator is not identifiable disguises the fact that the victims in "domestic violence" are almost always women and children. Gender neutrality also obscures the attribution of responsibility to the battering male. Currently the laws present a distorted picture. The acts do not portray the picture of a man beating a woman and thus the children being hurt because of it. Is this accidental or deliberate?

Given the above criticism, it is not surprising that these sections of the provincial child protection legislation are rarely used. Child protection workers from the provinces that have this type of child abuse legislation suggest that (a) the difficulty proving the damage experienced by a child who has witnessed woman abuse and (b) the lack of judicial support results in these cases being ignored and other abuse cases with a clearer mandate getting priority. These workers recognize and state with frustration that unlike children who have been neglected, abandoned, or sexually or physically abused, children who witness woman abuse rarely have their right to be protected from harm exercised.

This discussion demonstrates the importance of the child protection worker's knowledge of the dynamics of woman abuse and of a precise definition of child abuse (especially as it pertains to child witnesses of woman abuse) in providing appropriate intervention to victims of woman abuse. However, the lack of a clear mandate or lack of knowledge about the dynamics of woman abuse should not excuse, but can explain, the inconsistent and inappropriate response by Child Protection Services to child witnesses of woman abuse. Whether Child Protection Services should have a mandate to intervene in cases of woman abuse, however, is very controversial. This controversy has created additional roadblocks to effective intervention with child witnesses of woman abuse.

## FURTHER ROADBLOCKS
## TO BETTER INTERVENTION

Why has there not been better child protection intervention with child witnesses of woman abuse? Researchers have identified the trauma they experience; the parallels with children who are physically, sexually, and emotionally abused have been well documented; and some child welfare legislation to protect child witnesses of woman abuse, although problematic, has been in place for more than 20 years. Three major barriers to the intervention of Child Protection Services with child witnesses of woman abuse seem to be (a) an ongoing lack of awareness of the effects of woman abuse, (b) an overwhelmed child protection system, and (c) a strong resistance by advocates for battered women to legislation and to Child Protection Services. These roadblocks, which have interfered with the development of more and better interventions for child witnesses of woman abuse, are the focus of this section.

### Lack of Public Awareness

Despite the intense efforts of many people, woman abuse and its effect on children have not been identified as a serious social problem in Canada and the United States. Although millions of dollars have been spent in both countries on massive public education programs, they have been unsuccessful in increasing public awareness. Government studies have focused on identifying the number of women and children living in abusive situations, factors that contribute to woman abuse, and possible solutions to the problem.

Recently, a Panel of Violence Against Women, appointed by the Canadian government, spent more than $10 million dollars examining the problem of woman abuse. Particularly disheartening was its finding that despite ongoing intensive efforts to educate the public, there still exists a lack of awareness regarding the staggering levels of violence against women (Canadian Panel on Violence Against Women, 1993). Without social acknowledgment of the pervasiveness and seriousness of woman abuse as a social problem, the likelihood of receiving adequate resources to meet the needs of children who witness woman abuse is very dismal (Peled, 1993).

Lack of knowledge about the dynamics of woman abuse and its impact on children is found within Child Protection Services and affects the provision of services for child witnesses of woman abuse. Training about woman abuse in general and child witnesses of woman abuse in particular is usually minimal, if at all available.

## Overwhelmed Child Protection System

Child protection systems in both the United States and Canada can be described as underfunded, overworked, and overwhelmed. Yet reports of child abuse and neglect continue to grow in alarming numbers. Overburdened by an increased demand to protect children from being hurt, many Child Protection Services and their workers are being severely tested (Zellman & Antler, 1990). In their struggle to meet their mandated roles, Child Protection Services are closing the doors on cases considered "less serious" or "voluntary" (Kamerman & Kahn, 1990). These agencies are being forced to turn away cases unless they fit a very narrow definition of what is meant by an abused child. Unfortunately, limited resources have created a cruel and vexing reality: Child abuse cases are being triaged. Priority is being given to abused and neglected children who show visible signs of neglect or abuse (Peled, 1993). Child witnesses of woman abuse do not fit this definition. Their wounds do not show. It is scandalous that Child Protection Services, through necessity, have become an empty promise for these abused children!

An overtaxed system and a lack of knowledge about woman abuse and its impact on children have hindered the development of programs for child witnesses of woman abuse. At a time when governments at all levels should be increasing funding to Child Protection Services, they are freezing or cutting back on their annual allocations. With these tough economic times, Child Protection Services have been forced to narrow their scope of services in order to meet their existing mandate, rather than expand on or develop new services (Kamerman & Kahn, 1990). With limited funds for training, resources have been directed mainly toward increasing the knowledge of child protection workers about the dynamics of physical and sexual abuse and neglect and how to respond better to these allegations.

Many Child Protection Services are reluctant to address the issue of woman abuse. To do so may open a Pandora's box. By providing training that would result in increased awareness, caseloads would swell and the cry for program development would be heard throughout both nations. This provision would likely result in draining already limited resources. Consequently Child Protection Services seemed to have developed an arms-length approach to protecting child witnesses of woman abuse issue and have abdicated their responsibility to protect them. Frequently, the policy of many Child Protection Services is to become involved in only those cases of woman abuse in which there is actual evidence that the child has been physically injured.

## Resistance by Advocates for Battered Women

Advocates for battered women have also been instrumental in thwarting Child Protection Services from involvement in the area of woman abuse. Their resistance to the development of specific legislation regarding child witnesses of women abuse is based on the following reasons.

State interventions contravenes the principles of the feminist movement (Walker, 1990). Feminists are concerned that state intervention will mirror the abused women's experience; legislators, who primarily have been male, are likely to continue developing child welfare policies and practices traditionally built on the oppression of women (Hutchinson, 1992). Battered women and their advocates are worried that such legislation will include mandatory reporting, which, in turn, may dramatically change their relationship.

Mandatory reporting may cause battered women, who already have trouble talking about the violence in their lives, to become more reluctant to disclose the violence or be more selective in what they say so as to not risk losing their children. Under a mandatory reporting law, advocates for battered women may be viewed as agents of the state, rather than allies of the battered women. Such a law could put the advocates in the unenviable position of having to report a victim of woman abuse to Child Protection Services and thus collaborate in her revictimization by a patriarchal system perceived as insensitive to the battered woman's needs.

Advocates for battered women realize that battered women and their children are not a priority for Child Protection Services. They recognize that child protection workers have limited or no training on the issue of woman abuse and realize that this has resulted in an inconsistent response to child witnesses. As mentioned above, when reports of woman abuse and possible risk to the children are received, they are met with an array of responses. In some cases women are told that woman abuse is not within the service's mandate and that they are ineligible for services. In other cases, on the opposite end of the continuum, are child protection workers who respond by blaming the woman for putting her child at risk. Battered women report that child protection workers fail to recognize the battered woman's history of victimization and minimize or ignore the responsibility of men who batter. In regions where legislation exists, advocates for battered women have been frustrated by Child Protection Services' lack of clout to protect women and children and to remove abusive men from the home.

## PROTECTING CHILDREN EXPOSED TO WOMAN ABUSE

In this chapter, we have described the role of Child Protection Services and shown that a child who witnesses woman abuse is indeed a child in need of protection. Weaknesses and roadblocks in the current system have been examined. Recognizing that child witnesses of woman abuse are abused children and should be protected by society, we offer the following recommendations.

First, the continued efforts of advocates for battered women must be acknowledged, and woman abuse must be accepted as a serious social problem. The impact it has on women and the consequences for society are devastating. Woman abuse is not likely to decrease until its existence is recognized. Everyone has a role in combating its spread.

Second, the impact of witnessing woman abuse on children must be recognized as a serious social problem. We cannot continue to consider woman abuse as a problem between two adults, but rather must acknowledge that it affects children who witness it. Ongoing research is necessary to further document the short- and long-term implications that witnessing woman abuse has on children.

Third, clear, consistent legislation in both countries needs to be enacted to ensure that the needs of children witnessing woman abuse are protected. Discrepancies in current legislation must be resolved. We recommend that legislation do the following:

- Acknowledge that woman abuse and its subsequent impact on children are social problems.
- Clearly define child witnesses of woman abuse as children in need of protection.
- Allow for funding and development of programs to prevent and treat the child victims of woman abuse.

- Allow ordering perpetrators of woman abuse out of the home until they have completed treatment successfully.
- Allow child protection workers to remove children when all of the lesser intrusive methods of supporting the family have failed.
- Mandate education and training of workers on feminism, woman abuse, and the impact that woman abuse has on children.
- Promote and fund research in this area.
- Increase public awareness and promote public education on woman abuse.

Participation of advocates for battered women in the drafting of such legislation is necessary. Their expertise will be essential in developing a clear working definition of woman abuse and guidelines to assist Child Protection Services in creating intervention strategies for women and children affected by woman abuse. Advocates for battered women can also assist in developing responses necessary to address the needs of women from high-risk groups.

Fourth, Child Protection Services in both countries have to accept woman abuse and child witnesses of woman abuse as part of their mandate. They are confronting cases of woman abuse daily, and they can no longer attempt to place the responsibility for them on the shoulders of women's advocates. Child Protection Services need to (a) develop their own protocols for the identification of cases in which woman abuse is occurring, (b) document the impact that exposure is having on the children, and (c) develop programs to service children, battered women, and men who batter.

Fifth, education and training of child protection workers on feminism, woman abuse, and the impact of that woman abuse must be mandated. Child protection workers need to be made aware of the current research on child witnesses of woman abuse and the parallels with children who have been physically, sexually, and emotionally abused. The dynamics of woman abuse and the impact of victimization on parenting need to be stressed, as well as the total responsibility for the violence and its consequences being placed on the men who batter. Further, child protection workers need to receive training on how to work cooperatively and effectively with advocates for battered women.

Sixth, prevention of woman abuse must become a universal priority. All levels of government must earmark funding for woman abuse prevention efforts. Prevention entails improving the socioeconomic conditions of children and their families. It also involves promoting the belief that violence is never acceptable. Violence awareness must be incorporated into the curricula of the school systems, and violence in the media must be eliminated.

Seventh, all communities in both countries need to develop a coordinated response to victims of woman abuse. Necessary participants include judges, law enforcement departments, crown attorneys, child protection workers, shelter workers, advocates for battered women, mental health workers, medical professionals, politicians, educators, and any other disciplines working with or involved with the victims of woman abuse. A coordinated response must ensure that all of the systems work together to protect women and children in their own homes from men who abuse them. Communities must recognize that woman abuse is a crime and identify men as being responsible for the violence. A coordinated response will allow for the development of protocols among agencies and permit better access to services to women, children, and men who batter.

## CONCLUSION

Once Child Protection Services in both countries implement the suggested recommendations, a positive response to the cases presented at the beginning of this chapter would be possible. Dr. Smith would be answered that Child Protection Services should and could become more involved with Dan. Child Protection Services could facilitate services for the child, mother, and stepfather that focus on woman abuse. Child Protection Services could also link up the stepfather with substance abuse programs. The various agencies involved with the family—family physician, school, and a children's mental health center—would meet regularly to monitor the family's progress and the risks to the child and mother. If it was thought that the situation was deteriorating and that the child was still at risk of harm, the police and child protection court could become involved in removing the stepfather from the home until he had successfully completed his treatment programs. Would this plan work?

In Duluth, Minnesota, and London, Ontario, coordinated responses that include Child Protection Services have been developed to protect child witnesses of woman abuse. Although the models are different, both involve a number of agencies in their communities constantly working together to improve the plight of battered women and their children. Representatives of these agencies meet regularly to review the delivery of services to women, child victims of woman abuse, and men who batter. Their goal is to improve the coordination of these services. They are concerned about agency accountability, advocacy, and research. Specifically, child protection workers are included in the committees in both communities, and the inclusion of these workers has

184          ENDING THE CYCLE OF VIOLENCE

resulted in the development of a planned response and services to the problem
of woman abuse.

## REFERENCES

Canadian Panel on Violence Against Women. (1993) *Changing the landscape: Ending violence—achieving equality.* Ottawa: Ministry of Supply and Services Canada.

Callahan, M. (1993). Feminist approaches: Women re-create child welfare. In B. Wharf (Ed.), *Rethinking child welfare in Canada* (pp. 172-209). Toronto: McLelland & Stewart.

Carlson, B. E. (1984). Children's observations of interparental violence. In A. R. Roberts (Ed.), *Battered women and their families* (pp. 147-167). New York: Springer.

Child Welfare Act Alberta, S.A. (1984), c. C-8.1.

Child Welfare Act Newfoundland, R.S.N. (1990), c. C-12.

Children and Family Services Act Nova Scotia, S.N.S. (1990), C.5.

Dawson, R. (1990). *Child sexual abuse: 1. Investigation and assessment.* Toronto: Institute for the Prevention of Child Abuse.

Family Services Act New Brunswick, S.N.B. (1980), c. F-22.

Family Services Act Saskatchewan, R.S.S. (1978), c. F-7.

Family and Child Services Act, R.S. P.E.I. (1988), c. F-2.

Gordon, L. (1988). *Heroes of their own lives: The politics and history of family violence.* New York: Penguin.

Hershorn, M., & Rosenbaum, A. (1985). Children of marital violence: A closer look at the unintended victims. *American Journal of Orthopsychiatry, 55,* 260-266.

Hughes, H. M., & Hampton, K. L. (1984, August). *Relationships between the affective functioning of physically abused and nonabused children and their mothers in shelters for battered women.* Paper presented at the Annual Meeting of the American Psychological Association, Toronto, Canada.

Hutchinson, E. D. (1992). Child welfare as a woman's issue. *Families in Society: The Journal of Contemporary Human Services, 73,* 67-76.

Jaffe, P., Wolfe, D. A., & Wilson, S. (1990). *Children of battered women.* Newbury Park, CA: Sage.

Jaffe, P., Wolfe, D. A., Wilson, S., & Zak, L. (1986). Promoting changes in attitudes and understanding of conflict resolution among child witnesses of family violence. *Canadian Journal of Behavioral Science, 18,* 356-365.

Kamerman, S. B., & Kahn, A. (1990). If CPS is driving child welfare, where do we go from here? *Public Welfare, 48,* 9-13.

Layzer, J. I., Goodson, B. D., & deLange, C. (1986). Children in shelters, *Response, 9*(2), 2-5.

MacLeod, L. (1987). *Battered but not beaten: Preventing wife battering in Canada.* Ottawa: Canadian Advisory Council on the Status of Women.

Melton, G., & Davidson, H. A. (1987). Child protection and society. When should the state intervene? *American Psychologist, 42,* 172-175.

Moore, T., Pepler, D., Mae, R., & Kates, M. (1989). Effects of family violence on children: New directions for research and intervention. In B. Pressman, G. Cameron, & M. Rothery (Eds.), *Intervening with assaulted women: Current theory, research, and practice* (pp. 75-91). Hillsdale, NJ: Lawrence Erlbaum.

Pagelow, M. D. (1984). *Family violence.* New York: Praeger.

Peled, E. (1993). Children who witness women battering: Concerns and dilemmas in the construction of a social problem. *Children and Youth Services Review, 15,* 43-52.

Pressman, B. (1989). Power and ideological issues in intervening with assaulted women. In B. Pressman, G. Cameron, & M. Rothery (Eds.), *Intervening with assaulted women: Current theory, research, and practice* (pp. 21-45). Hillsdale, NJ: Lawrence Erlbaum.

Rosenbaum, A., & O'Leary, K. D. (1981). Children: The unintended victims of marital violence. *American Journal of Orthopsychiatry, 51,* 692-699.

Sinclair, D. (1985). *Wife assault: A training manual for counselors and advocates.* Toronto: Ontario Government Bookstore.

Vayda E., & Satterfield, M. (1984). *Law for social workers.* Toronto: Carswell.

Vogel, R. (1987). The legal aspects of child protection. In *Child protection: Part 1. Investigation and assessment resource material.* Toronto: Institute for the Prevention of Child Abuse.

Walker, G. A. (1990). *Family violence and the women's movement.* Toronto: University of Toronto Press.

Wilkerson, A. (Ed.). (1973). *Emergent concepts in law and society: Rights of children.* Philadelphia: Temple University Press.

Wolfe, D. A., & Mosk, M. D. (1983). Behavioral comparisons of children from abusive and distressed families. *Journal of Consulting and Clinical Psychology, 51,* 702-708.

Younes, L. A., & Besharov, D. J. (1988). State child abuse and neglect laws: A comparative analysis. In D. J. Besharov (Ed.), *Protecting children from abuse and neglect: Policy and practice* (pp. 353-490). Springfield, IL: Charles C. Thomas.

Zellman, G. L., & Antler, S. (1990). Mandated reporters and CPS: A study in frustration. *Public Welfare, 48,* 30-37.

# 11

# Doing More Harm Than Good?

## *Some Cautions on Visitation Centers*

MARTHA McMAHON
ELLEN PENCE

In March 1981 Duluth, Minnesota, became the first city in the United States to put in place an integrated community response project as a way of protecting battered women from continued acts of abuse. The Domestic Abuse Intervention Project (DAIP) coordinated a set of police, court, social, and health service responses to domestic violence. The project was designed and monitored by a local victim advocacy organization. The results were immediate and visible. Arrests of batterers increased dramatically, conviction rates soared, and the number of women seeking protection orders tripled. Offenders who used violence in their relationships were court-ordered to attend group-based rehabilitation programs. Those who dropped out or reoffended were arrested and incarcerated. Every reported case of domestic abuse now could be monitored by the victim advocacy organization, from the first call to the police, through to the final outcome.

A culturally specific companion project, Mending the Sacred Hoop, was organized by activists in the Native American community. Media attention placed the tiny Minnesota city of Duluth and the Fond Du Lac Reservation in the center of the national debate on the role of the community in protecting women and children from domestic violence.

However, the success of the Duluth projects in improving community and civil and criminal court interventions in domestic assault cases has not yet been matched by a similarly coherent approach to the visitation and custody issues that usually accompany the end of a violent relationship. Children who witness violence in their homes are also its victims. When an abused woman leaves a violent partner, issues raised about children are not simply those of custody but also of responding to the totality of harm that violence has done to the children. The community, we argue, rather than individual women, has the responsibility to respond to this harm.

For women who have been battered, separation from an abuser often shifts the site of the conflict from the privatized setting of the home to the public arena of the judicial system. Custody and access workers report that abusive men are more likely than nonabusive men to fight for physical custody of their children (Taylor, 1993); evidence suggests that they are also more likely to receive favorable rulings from the courts (Saunders, 1993). As Cain and Smart (1989) emphasize, children and child custody issues are now a significant part of the politics of gender. A violent man's relationship with his children, we argue, entails a power relationship with the children's mother, played out through the issues of custody and visitation.

Not surprisingly, the time period in which child custody and visitation issues are being negotiated is also the period of greatest risk for women. Women leaving violent relationships face the greatest risk of death or serious injury in the months following separation.[1] Thus children who may once have been observers of violence in their homes become central to the conflict between separating couples (Shepard, 1992).

In this chapter we use the experience of one Minnesota community to argue that advocacy and shelter programs for battered women and their children have a central role to play in the development of visitation centers for children. We also argue that the visitation centers now being established across the United States and Canada can play an important role in protecting children from violence, distress, and harm as their primary relationships are reordered. However, we must develop a clearer understanding of the role that violence and power play in shaping the social relationships of families; otherwise these centers may become administrative and managing agencies of a legal system that makes visitation centers new sites of damage to children and their mothers.[2]

In emphasizing the visitation center's mandate as one of both protecting women and children and responding to the harm done to them by violence, we propose some guidelines for battered women's activists to consider when participating in their communities' efforts to protect the children of abused women. Violence, however, must be conceptualized in its totality. The harm done to children who witness violence cannot be separated conceptually or empirically from the harm done to their mothers who are beaten. We argue that we cannot conceptualize children or the "best interests of the child" as if children stand alone and are not integral to the power relations that are part of violence against women. In Duluth the decision by the shelter movement to insert itself into these efforts from the standpoint of victims of family violence comes from its history of grassroots activism and from the experience of organizing and coordinating Duluth's first visitation center.

## THE DULUTH VISITATION CENTER

The Duluth Visitation Center opened in December 1989, 13 years after women in that community organized a shelter for battered women and their children and 8 years after the beginning of the Intervention Project. It currently employs two coordinators and six to eight volunteers. The center is located at the YWCA building in downtown Duluth, where several family rooms, play areas, and a gym are available for its use. It is open 3 days per week, including Sundays.

Age-appropriate resources and facilities are available. Included are special places for babies and relatively accident-free, toy-laden space for toddlers, the gym to run about in, and a room for older children to read in. Colors, furniture, toys, and games were selected with children in mind, and much effort goes into making the environment pleasant and nonthreatening.

The center's work is organized around five main activities: (a) arranging families' use of the center, (b) overseeing visits and child exchanges, (c) parent groups, (d) indirect involvement in custody and visitation decisions, and (e) advocating for a coherent, just, child-centered community response to custody and visitation issues.

The center is still in its formative stage. Its mandate, activities, involvements, and day-to-day procedures are the objects of ongoing debate, reflection, and revision.

Fully 95% of the referrals to the center are made through a court order or by a county social worker.[3] An abused woman seeking a protection order, for example, may petition the civil court for mandated use of the visitation center. Criminal court judges may order the center's use as a provision of an offender's probation. Visiting or noncustodial parents have usually not freely chosen to use the center.[4] The court specifies conditions such as whether visits are to be on-site or off, their frequency, the extent to which the visits are to be monitored, the violent parent's attendance at parenting groups, and the terms and date of the case review. As a condition of using the center, parents who have battered their partners are required to attend three group parent sessions; the court may order further attendance. Classes for mothers are thus usually obligatory only if the women have harmed their children, but weekly group meetings are available to support custodial parents in helping children harmed by violence. The courts usually require both parents to contact the Visitation Center within 2 days of the hearing at which the use of the Center is mandated. Thus the Center is used most in the high-risk period immediately after a woman leaves a violent man.

Center staff draw up contracts separately with both parents prior to the first visit. These contracts detail the terms of visitation arrangements, the nature of information to be recorded for court purposes, and parent-group attendance.

What follows is a description of a "typical day" at the Duluth Center. Although expressed in the words of one staff member, it fits the other accounts gathered from those who work at the center. We include this account as a description of the center's day-to-day workings and because these day-to-day workings are the topic of our later analysis.

> We might have 15-20 families use the Center [on a Sunday]. Usually half of them stay on site and the other half just use us as an exchange place. Some visits are set up for a couple of hours and others for the whole day, so it's not like we ever have 12 families there all at once. . . .
>
> The mother will bring the kids to the Center through . . . the side door and wait with the kids in the lunchroom. We let her know when the father has arrived. Once in a while he'll have some discussion with her or her with him about the kids, so we will take the kids off and stay nearby while they talk. . . . If it needs a big conversation, we usually set up something at the office or maybe ask a social worker to facilitate a meeting if one is involved in the case.
>
> I have to say it doesn't always go smooth. We've had a few situations where we had to call the police or step in because it looked like he was going to hit her. It really makes you wonder what was happening before we started this place. What the kids were seeing and hearing and how scary the whole thing must have been for them. You know how kids can take on the blame. So their mother's upset and crying and their dad is yelling while they stand there waiting to go out for the day with their father. It's just so easy for the kids to think "all this is my fault." Just a few incidents we've had here makes me get a glimpse of what has been going on.

The center's staff discovered that they cannot assume that children will experience the visits the way adults expect:

> Once the father arrives and the mother leaves, there is this period of time in which the father and the children are somewhat negotiating the visit. Sometimes it's very easy. The kids are glad to see their fathers, and they immediately start to talk and find a space for themselves in the center. In other cases, it is very difficult. It might be that the kids don't want to see him; it might be that the

father has a very difficult time trying to figure out what to do in this environment, with us hanging around trying to look like we are not noticing. Some fathers have never spent time actually playing with their children. . . . It's not our job to organize the time for them, but sometimes we do step in and show the father and the kids some of the games. . . . The only other time we step in is if something harmful to the children is going on.

The Center's role, however, is a problematic one:

This is very difficult, deciding when to step in. We try to make it very clear before the first visit that we have to step in if the parent is talking abusively to a child or pumping a child for information or being physically intimidating or abusive. But all of these conditions for the visit are open to interpretation and somebody's judgment. As workers, we don't all agree on when to call the father or mother aside and say, "Wait, this is inappropriate." We've spent a lot of time on this in our monthly meetings and in our ongoing training sessions. We all have our points of view about these things, and it's important for us to have an understanding of parenting as something that is influenced by our class, race, and sex. I think the groups for parents has helped a lot. You can tell the difference when a guy has gone to the groups. It's a lot easier to approach him about something you're seeing that's inappropriate.

Where children have witnessed violence, can the Center have a "neutral" role that also means "being there for the children"?

There was a big discussion [about videos]. Some of us felt that we shouldn't be allowing this time to be spent watching TV. But then it became obvious to us that some of the older kids felt the safest when they could just watch TV with their fathers. For some of them, the visit was compulsory. That's where it all gets confusing; we're supposed to be there for the kids. We make this the least traumatic, most nurturing space possible, given the circumstances of their parents' relationship. But there is still this eerie silence about what has gone on: I mean the violence.

Staff are daily confronted with the realization that "being there for the children" implicates the Center's activities in legal and bureaucratic processes in ways over which they have no control and that may distort their role of responding to violence.

[After the visit] we make a note in the log if anything went on worth noting. It's that term "worth noting" that causes the problems. We've had so many discussions about what to record. These records have been subpoenaed by attorneys on both sides of really brutal custody fights. So we all feel uncomfortable about what to record.

We thought we solved the problem by agreeing to only record exactly what we saw. Still, just selecting which 2 or 3 things of the 30 things we've observed should be logged was a problem. Should we only comment on things the visiting parents do that are negative? If we put in the log "He was always on time and respectful to us and his former partner and seemed to be attentive to the children's needs and feelings," what would be the purposes and use of this comment later in a courtroom when lawyers make their cases?

## Some Unanticipated Issues

Although the Duluth Visitation Center originally was designed as a safe place through which to facilitate parental visitation, advocates for battered women gradually came to understand that its role was far more complex and problematic.

In its day-to-day practice, the Duluth Visitation Center operates as a mediator and organizer of family relationships. The Center's role is located at the margins of a complex bureaucracy. In its totality, this bureaucracy represents the state's and community's involvement in reordering family relationships after separation or divorce. This bureaucracy is not organized by a single discourse, but rather by multiple and competing discourses that direct its various practitioners. We see that conflict over children and child custody produces particular tensions when the judiciary acts as a defender of parents' rights through the legal discourse, and social work professionals act through a psychological discourse as protector of children's welfare. For example, a tension between justice and welfare norms, Cain and Smart (1989) argue, is expressed in the waning role of the judiciary in favor of the professional judgments of welfare officers in and around child custody issues.

Both discourses, however, are problematic for women. On the one hand, the discourse of rights obligates women to allow fathers access to or custody of children, with little regard for the women's own safety. On the other hand, the discourse of welfare obligates women as mothers to protect their children from harm done by the fathers' violence.

The organizers of the Duluth Visitation Center confronted the tensions of competing discourse in a very practical way, considering such questions as: What exactly was the Center to do? Was the Center to organize visitations, record information, and submit it to the courts and human service agencies? And if so, what information would be documented and about whom? To take the role of objective recorder would be to act as if such data had no social significance and as if the Center itself could act as a neutral social actor.

The past experience of advocates for Duluth's battered women had been that the assumption that the state acts as a neutral arbitrator of competing rights and interests does not hold in social contexts of systemic gender inequality.

How precisely, then, was the Center to constitute itself as a safe place for children? In what ways was it to respond to the harm that violence does to children? What services would it offer? Who would decide?

Organizers of the Duluth Visitation Center gradually came to the realization that part of the Center's role was to intervene in and influence the process of reordering family relationships from the standpoint of those who had been harmed by violence. This decision put the children's viewpoint at the center of the program's focus, but in a way that did not treat children as separable from their primary relationships.

To understand this decision and its implications for communities who wish to respond to the harm that violence does to children, we have to see how children's interest and women's issues are connected. We begin by looking at their historical connection in the origins of the Duluth Visitation Center.

## Origins of the Duluth Visitation Center

Duluth is a small, working-class city of about 90,000 people located in northeastern Minnesota. In 1975 three women who were attempting to leave abusive relationships founded a group that 1 year later opened Duluth's first shelter for battered women and 13 years later opened its first visitation center for children.

In the past 12 months, eight persons have been murdered in this small city. Six of these murders were linked directly to women leaving abusive partners.[5] Nine Duluth children have had their lives scarred by the murder of their mothers and the associated suicide or imprisonment of their fathers. One 4-year-old boy apparently witnessed his father hack his mother to death with a machete. His father subsequently committed suicide by jumping in front of a bus.

In retrospect, it is somewhat surprising that a center had not been established earlier. From the start, the shelter movement has been as much about children as it has been about their mothers. Kathy, one of the organizers of the Duluth shelter, in an interview done at the shelter's fifth anniversary, described the meetings from which battered women decided to open a shelter:

> We would show up at the meetings and immediately start talking about what it took [us] just to get there. You know, lies, coverups, excuses. Because none of us could say, "I'm going to a meeting to get a shelter going for battered women, dear. Be back at 10:30 or so."

Most of us brought our kids. When I think back on it, I realize that we were all single parents in our marriages. Half were leaving for the kids; the other half were staying for the kids. I think the whole deal about how everything was affecting our kids was a big motivation for us to get this place. But it was an exciting time. We knew we were doing something that was going to change everything for us and our kids. I think the fear was overcome by the sheer magnitude of what we were doing. (Kathy, Duluth, 1983)

Early domestic assault intervention programs did not initially appreciate all of the ways children are drawn into violent relationships. Children often are used as a strategy of control. A child witness recalls:

My father held a gun to my mom's head one night. She was begging him to stop. She kept yelling at me to get out of the house, but he said if I ran he'd shoot her. He was screaming at her about all sorts of things—how she had ruined him, how she had tried to undo everything he's working for . . . anyway, that night, he finally put the gun away and started laughing about how it wasn't loaded. He was just fooling around to see what we'd do. He was making fun of me for crying, and then he said he just wanted to see if I'd run for help if my Mom needed it. (Jason, child witness)

Although institutions dealing with domestic violence often take precautions to protect both the women they serve and the agency workers, there is almost no protection for women and children outside these institutions. Shelters usually are wired to elaborate alarm systems, and police usually operate a priority response system. Participating institutions take care not to overlap appointments with abusers and victims, and courts offer separate seating for perpetrators and victims waiting for hearings.

Yet a man who has battered his partner, and a woman who has been battered, are expected to negotiate a visitation schedule, organize intricate details of exchanging children, meet somewhere, and exchange the children without threat, conflict, or dispute. As the Duluth experience tragically shows, this discounting of the reality of violence puts women and children at risk.

## BEATEN NOT JUST AS WIVES, BUT ALSO AS MOTHERS

Duluth shelter organizers and workers realized that women are not beaten just as wives, but also as mothers. But it took some years to respond to the full implications of this reality. Women come to shelters attached to children who are implicated in the violent relationship. In a Canadian Advisory Council on the Status of Women (CACSW, 1987) national study, women who had been battered by their partners reported that their partners had abused their children physically (26%), psychologically (48%), and sexually (7%). The abuse of their children, this study noted, usually has devastating psychological effects that remain with the women even after they remove their children from the abuse. The children, too, appear to remain at increased risk for the development of adjustment problems (Jaffe, Wilson, & Wolfe, 1988; Shepard, 1992). United States research suggests an even higher correlation between woman abuse and child abuse in families. Saunders (1993) reports that abusive husbands are seven times more likely than nonabusive husbands to abuse their children. Battered women are twice as likely as nonbattered women to abuse their children, although once out of the relationship, the odds of them abusing their children are reduced (Saunders, 1993). If, as structural analyses of wife assault strongly suggest, the roots of violence against women are located in society, rather than simply in individual psychology (Adams, 1988; Walker, 1992), then the community, not simply the individual woman, should share the responsibility and provide resources to protect children.

Yet protection of children falls on individual women. And because it is seen as a "natural" part of a mother's role, a function of the "private" sphere (Lopata, 1993), women are offered little social support in caring for their children. Rather, mothers are penalized if they "fail to protect" or are unable to.

From the start, conversations with battered women in Duluth's shelter made clear the extent to which children were central to their responses to violent situations. Janice, a mother of two, explained:

> I stayed way too long with him, for my kids' sake. I can see that now. They have all sorts of problems from what they were living with. Now I feel guilt cause I think I thought I was staying for them, but it was really cause I was scared. I was scared of living alone, of what he'd do, like just up and leave me with all the troubles and the bills, and he'd be off with some other woman like he didn't even know us. That's pretty much what ended up happening, too. (Janice, mother of two, 1992)

For the children of abused women, separation does not end the violence and uncertainty with which they have lived (Shepard, 1992). Rather, the site of struggle shifts and the experience of abuse changes. In the Duluth experience, children of battered women were drawn directly into the violence and conflict with which issues of custody and visitation were negotiated.

Police records in Duluth document, and individual women testify to, the ways abusers, excluded from their homes by protection orders or probation agreements, use their visitation with children as an opportunity to harass or physically assault their estranged partners. In 1988, almost one third of the violations of civil court protection orders or domestic assault probation agreements in Duluth occurred while parents were picking up, visiting, or dropping off the children.[6]

One of the unforeseen consequences of the "profathering" movement in the United States, according to Ehrensaft (1990), has been the ways many fathers have disempowered mothers in brutal custody battles. Support for shared parenting or involved fathers is laudable in principle. In practice, however, such support often is based on the mistaken premise that both parents have been involved in caring for the children prior to separation and will be equally responsible afterward (Pollock & Sutton, 1985). Ehrensaft (1990) notes that in approximately two thirds of contested custody cases before judges in the United States, fathers will win even if mothers have been the primary caregivers prior to divorce and independent of whether or not the father pays child support after separation.

Although some men indeed are motivated by the child's best interests, many also are concerned to maintain control of "their" families: their children and former wives (Arendell, 1992; Ehrensaft, 1990; Pollock & Sutton, 1985). Being in control, as a CACSW (1991) report points out, is a characteristic highly valued by men who abuse their wives.

## THE BEST INTERESTS
## OF FAMILIES AND CHILDREN

Children turn a couple into a family. Behind the unifying image of family, however, lies a "his" and "hers" experience of marriage (Bernard, 1974) and parenthood (Cowan et al., 1985). After the couple relationship breaks up, parental and family relationships do not necessarily end. As in the case of divorce (Arendell, 1992), after an abused woman leaves a violent partner, a whole array of taken-for-granted relationships and practices are pulled into question. These include the often hidden practices of such extrafamilial institutions as the judicial and economic systems in regulating family life, but also the familiar character of family life itself—parenting and domestic arrangements (Arendell, 1992). Most critically put into question are gender identities and the implicit meanings of family relationships (Arendell, 1992).

Men who were court-ordered into batterers' groups in Duluth spoke freely of their frustrations and anger around problems associated with access to their children and of their difficulty establishing positive relationships with the children after separation. Women's continued responsibility for the

day-to-day care of children in two-parent homes means that fathers' relationships with children, even in nonviolent families, are mediated in a variety of
ways by their partners' domestic, emotional, and caring work (Daly, 1991;
Hochschild, 1989). Fathers' communication with children may be indirect or
implicit. Indeed, fathers may be socially constructed as the disciplinarian by
both parents, making their taking of a broader or nurturant parent role after
separation difficult for all involved. Similarly mothers often both interpret
children for their fathers (LaRossa & LaRossa, 1981) and, in turn, interpret
fathers for their children, often in a sympathetic way. Women leaving a violent
relationship, however, may be disinclined to continue this facilitating role.

Thus many men experience the rupture in the relationship with their
children that comes with separation from the mother as a violation of their
rights, as something the woman "took" from them (Arendell, 1992). Family, in
the masculinist discourse of divorce, Arendell continues, becomes "a broken
family" made up of two parts—the male self and the wife-and-children—and
referred to as "me" and "them": It is experienced as a loss of power and authority.
Men often angrily blame women, the courts, and the human services agencies.
An assumption of control is so embedded in such men's construction of self
as husband and father, Arendell (1992) notes, that the complexity of family
relationships can be collapsed into a discussion of rights.

> I am a strong advocate for father's rights, for men's rights. I had to fight for
> my rights as a father; and it cost me over twenty thousand dollars to win the
> custody fight. But I had to show my ex that I was still in control here, and that
> she couldn't deny me my basic rights just because she got the divorce she
> wanted. By winning the custody battle, I showed her that I was still in charge.
> But I knew all along that I would let my son go back to live with his mother
> once this was over. (divorced father in Arendell, 1992, p. 166)

Divorced men, as Arendell shows, tend to construct fatherhood in terms
of "rights" to children, rather than as responsibility for children. Motherhood, in contrast, is cast culturally as a relationship of responsibility, rather
than of rights (Rothman, 1989). Social workers, for example, may conceptualize women primarily in terms of their family responsibilities, rather than
as individuals. In contrast, Arendell (1992) argues, a rhetoric of individual
rights is basic to divorced men's understanding of family and men's place in
it and their postdivorce actions, perspectives, and relationships with their
children and former partners. This rhetoric of rights, she continues, is
appropriated from political and legal theory and practice and is widely
available in the culture at large. The rhetoric of rights, we suggest, does not
address men's responsibility for the harm done by their acts of violence.

These constructions of fatherhood and motherhood, we argue, also are embedded in many of the intervention practices surrounding custody and visitation arrangements. However, they have damaging consequences for children in that they falsely locate children within a set of competing rights and interests and discount the significance of violence. These constructions tend to reflect the standpoint of state or social welfare agencies, rather than children's experience.

In contrast, we suggest that children need to be understood as living within an ensemble of social relationships within which the damage of violence happens. The literature on visitation and custody often makes primary the "best interests of the child" as if children somehow stand alone. Taking the standpoint of the child, however, means that we need to think about the day-to-day meaning of family, rather than abstract notions of parenthood. Perhaps we need to rethink notions of parents' rights and children's interests, seeing children instead as being located within a set of kinlike relationships in which they cannot conceptually separate themselves from the harm done to mothers, brothers, and sisters with whom they feel connected.

Similarly, in taking the standpoint of the child, perhaps we need to rethink parenthood for both men and women, to understand it as a culturally shaped relationship that implies a social commitment to nurture, protect, foster growth, and adequately prepare a child for life in his or her society (Ruddick, 1990). Violence in the web of children's primary relationships violates the commitment and responsibility that constitutes parenting, even if the violence is directed at a child's mother, rather than at him- or herself. Taking the standpoint of children, therefore, means attempting to undo the harm of violence within the broad web of children's significant relationships. But this is not what typically happens.

## SHIFTING THE SITE OF STRUGGLE

Children are central to the ways the judicial system intervenes to respond to family violence. Ironically, in turning to the police and judiciary for protection, battered women in Duluth found their struggle had not ended but merely had moved to another arena in which they were "judged" not simply as abused wives but also as mothers of children.

I lived with him through 12 years of torture. I still can't believe that I got out alive, and I still can't believe that I didn't get out years earlier. But it's like the Kurdish women you see on TV who finally escaped the war and near extermination to end up on a refugee camp where they were raped. My ex-husband is

still in my life every day, threatening to take away my children, to leave me
penniless, to do whatever he can think of. He used to beat me in the bedroom;
always in the bedroom, now it's in the courtroom. (Lillian, mother of 2, 1992)

How is it that abusive men receive favorable court rulings in their fights
for custody of their children? It would be far too simplistic to say that such
puzzling rulings are a reflection of sexist attitudes of court practitioners.
They are more likely the result of institutionalized ways of thinking about
and acting on conceptions of family, parenting, violence, and children's
interests. To the women involved, however, these practices can feel like
abuse (CACSW, 1991). Jane put it like this:

We were surprised at how similar our problems were. It was almost like our
partners had gone to some kind of school on how to batter. We could literally
finish each other's stories. But we were shocked at how many of us were facing
the same problems with the police, the courts, or the welfare department. It
seems like they went to the same school as our husbands. (Jane, battered
women's organizer)

Women come to believe they can trust neither the courts nor social service
agencies. These agencies have, like the men who abused them, the power to
separate them from their children, characterize them as unfit mothers, and
interpret the meaning of their experience and behavior. And, as in the abusive
marriage, women's experience of violence may be discounted or ignored in
constructing notions of the best interests of the child and appropriate parenthood. Thus the site of conflict shifts, as do the ways in which children are
involved.

## DISCOUNTING VIOLENCE IN
## CONSTRUCTING A CHILD'S BEST INTERESTS

Through a wide variety of practices, human services and courts discount
the reality of violence in conceptualizations of parenthood and children's
welfare and interests. These practices, we argue, fail to see the harm that
violence does to both battered women and their children and thus threaten
the welfare of both. Such practices, for example, include psychological
assessments, data gathering, report writing, and the training of agency and
court staff.

It is not unusual in many United States courtrooms that when a woman
has left a man who has sexually, emotionally, and physically assaulted her,
the man claims that she is an unfit mother and asks the court for custody of

the children. In such and other cases, the court usually will order psychological evaluation of both parties. The interpretations of these psychological assessments typically become central to lawyers' arguments and judges' deliberations on issues of custody, visitation, and children's interests.

Not infrequently, battered women's psychological assessments will suggest significant dysfunctions, and a battered woman will be constructed as a less than fit parent, as someone who could put her children at risk, perhaps. Indeed, a battered woman's relationship with a violent man itself may be constructed as a "failure" to protect her children. Thus the victim, rather than the perpetrator of violence, is perceived to have exposed the children to harm. Psychological assessment, as Broverman, Broverman, Clarkson, Rosencrantz, and Vogel (1970) show, frequently carries serious gender bias. Yet assessment methods themselves seldom become an issue of court or human services consideration.

Similarly, in assessing an abused woman as a mother, courts and intervention agencies may take little or no account of the fact that she, at the time of intervention, is recovering from years of brutalizing violence. Victims of abuse suffer psychological damage, low self-esteem, and guilt (CACSW, 1991), which no doubt affect the results of psychological assessments and home visits by case workers. An equitable community response to the totality of harm done by violence attempts to undo the harm, rather than to punish its victims for its consequences.

Perhaps more important, however, are the ways violence and its consequences for men, women, and children are conceptualized. A man's violence toward his partner may be considered of little relevance in discussions of his claims as a father. Sletner's (1992) study of battered women going through divorce proceedings, for example, found that in the preparation of court reports, 64% of respondents were not asked by the guardian ad litem whether they had been abused by their partners, and 75% were not asked about the impact the abuse had on the children. Even when a child protection worker was involved with the family, 47% of abused women were not asked by the worker whether they had been abused, and 60% were not asked what impact the abuse had on the children (Sletner, 1992).

How is fatherhood conceptualized such that a man's violence to the child's mother is viewed as of little relevance to his relationship with the child? How is it that a violent man's parenthood is conceptualized in terms of rights to the child, rather than as responsibility to heal the harm done by violence? What do children implicitly learn when the violence they have witnessed is not addressed? Some learn, no doubt, that violence is effective and legitimate: 73% of the men who had been through the Duluth court system for battering, for example, were either physically abused as children or witnessed their mothers being abused (Domestic Abuse Intervention Project, 1987).

Programs for battered women and their children often operate within and reflect the framework of unequal social relationships that underlie violence (CACSW, 1991). Court or social service practioners, no matter how well intentioned, present a new set of risks to women who have experienced violence (especially women outside dominant culture groups), and to their children.

> I grew up on welfare, and my mother always said, "when they come, you hush up. Let me do the talking, cause one wrong word and we're in the streets." I still get that feeling today. I guess my case worker is nice enough. In fact, she's given me some good tips. She's seen what a bastard Carl can be. He's not pulling the wool over her eyes like he's done others. But I still get this feeling of one wrong word and my kids are gone. It's not just her, it's a whole bunch of people I don't even know involved in this thing. (Sarah, mother of 2, 1993)

## ADDRESSING VIOLENCE
## DIRECTLY IN COMMUNITY RESPONSES

For quite some time, advocates for battered women in Duluth thought that personnel in the court and human service system engaged in much victim blaming. Yet as the experience of the Duluth Visitation Center was to make clear to them, these personnel were often both personally and professionally committed to the welfare of the families with whom they worked.

The difficulty of responding adequately to the needs of children who had witnessed family violence and their parents arose not out of the indifference of practitioners, but out of how the practices of police, human services, and court personnel had been bureaucratized and conceptualized in ways that masked the power dynamics in violent families.

Long-standing "ways of doing things" and the discourse of the law and human service professionals were imbued with ideological practices that frequently reinforced a violent man's position of dominance over his wife and children. Consider the problem posed by a Minnesota custody evaluator at a recent state conference:

> I needed to decide custody in a family where the man has repeatedly assaulted his wife. Because of the abuse, she isn't in good shape. She is chemically dependent and is not being a very good parent. He has a job, he's sober, and he's stable. I know that it's the violence that has done this to her. But given where she's at, compared to him, how can I not give him custody? Even

though I know it's not fair to her, isn't it fair to the children? (custody evaluator, 1993)

This custody evaluator ties the child's best interest to the man's economic security, sobriety, and apparent stability. Because the evaluator's work is not structured in ways to allow him to address the totality of harm done by violence, he cannot conceptualize what children themselves need in order for the harm to be undone. Neither can he ask what the significance a father's repeated violence to the children's mother has for his ties of "kinship" and parenting with those children. Nor can he offer a father assistance in undoing the harm done by his violence.

From the standpoint of the child, the social messages around custody issues are ambivalent, contradictory, and no doubt deeply troubling. How are children to understand the ways violence apparently renders one parent "unfit" to care for them, and a violent parent apparently "fit"? Does not such a construction of their mothers constitute children themselves as psychologically, as well as physically, vulnerable to violence? What are the implications for their understandings of family and kin relationships? Whatever their sympathies, on some level children are faced with accepting the dominant negative definitions of the battered parent (as "crazy" or "unfit") or of living in fear of the power of their father. Unless violence is directly addressed, children may, self-protectively, emotionally, and psychologically distance themselves from the "weaker" parent, thus undermining her very capacity to parent. However, home visitors merely will report that the children "act up" with the mother. At the same time, validating the parental claims of an abusive man, without addressing the issue of his violence, we suggest, encourages children in a conflicted identification with the more powerful parent.

The evaluator (above) is constrained by the way his or her job is conceptually and technically organized. The evaluator is required to report to the court on specific items that the law says are relevant to the "best interest of the child." This reporting involves, for example, asking whether either parent is drinking or depressed; who can offer the child an emotionally and economically stable environment; whether the father has a new partner who will provide child-rearing labor; what are the natures of child-parent relationships and interaction; and so on.

On the surface this kind of concern with children's welfare is both reasonable and justified. However, domestic violence is itself responsible for many of the conditions and phenomena that then are used as independent grounds for assessing what represents children's welfare. In this sense, not only is violence not addressed, but its workings also are deeply and invisibly embedded in how we resolve questions of children's interests.

## THE CENTER AS AN AGENT OF CHANGE

Concerns around issues of visitation and custody led to the opening of the Duluth Visitation Center in 1987. The Center did not resolve these issues, however, but rather made them more visible and urgent. More than ever, children and their welfare were seen as being central to the community response to domestic assault. How to respond?

Two years after the Duluth Visitation Center opened, the group coordinating the interagency Duluth community response to domestic violence hired an organizer to work as part of the Center and to set up and facilitate a visitation and custody interagency committee. This committee subsequently organized a series of workshops, open meetings, and a statewide conference with the purpose of engaging a wide variety of interested parties in dialogue on issues associated with child custody and visitation. These discussions were deeply divided between those who thought the legal and court systems, child welfare agencies, and helping professions could act as neutral mediators or assessors of children's interests, and those who thought such claims to be "value free" were ungrounded or ideological. In claiming neutrality, this latter group charged, court and other professional practitioners were blind to how race, class, and gender structure the experiences and reality of those about whom they made custody and visitation decisions. Thus, rather than acting neutrally, such practitioners act, albeit unintentionally, either from the standpoint of privilege or to reproduce privilege.

Although these divisions within the committee have strained relationships, the Center and interagency committee have actively encouraged all involved with child custody and visitation issues to be self-reflective about their assumptions and practices. In particular, the committee challenges practitioners to question (a) what are the implicit conceptualizations of battered women's children with whom they work, (b) how do different interventions function to reorder such children's primary relationships, and (c) whose interests are central in practice. To this end, the Center and interagency committee have undertaken a series of community and educational projects, described below.

## ABANDONING CLAIMS TO NEUTRALITY: INTERVENING ON THE CHILDREN'S SIDE

The custody and visitation committee provides an ongoing series of lectures that the chief judge of the district encourages all those involved in custody and visitation issues to attend. These lectures examine the historical roots, and cultural, theoretical, and ideological frameworks surrounding custody and visitation issues. They also expose practitioners to research and accounts rooted in children's experience of violence, separation of parents, and visitation and living arrangements. This series is intended to assist practitioners to examine the hidden (nonneutral) codes, practices, and assumptions embedded in their own work and agency and court practices. The lecture series looks at violence and custody issues from the standpoint of children.

The committee also facilitates a multidisciplinary monthly round table discussion for practitioners working in any aspect of court assessment and for advocates of battered women. These discussions make open to debate and inspection the practices of observation, data gathering, record keeping, and assessment in the custody and visitation decision-making process. They also raise for critical discussion the ways in which notions such as family, fatherhood, motherhood, parenthood, and children's best interests and welfare are conceptualized and the ways in which family relationships do not simply refer to private, interpersonal, affectional, or biological relationships, but rather are shaped by state and community practices, often made visible only on separation or divorce. These ongoing discussions allow case workers to discuss difficult problems with a multidisciplinary team. They provide the advocates for battered women and the visitation center workers with a forum in which to attempt to make women's and children's lived experience of violence accounted for, rather than discounted, in the many practices surrounding custody and visitation.

The interagency committee is working to make the practices surrounding custody and visitation more child focused and more aware of the nature and consequences of violence. To this end, practitioners are urged to be reflective on every aspect of their prescribed practices, whether psychological assessment tools, guidelines for home visits, or the curriculum for parent groups at the Center. As we know, agency workers usually are guided by established sets of practices and procedures. These may ensure consistency between different workers and offices; however, they also profoundly shape what practitioners see, record, report, and do in their work. Agency personnel are encouraged to participate in the replacement of inadequate procedures. For example, the committee recently helped develop a new standardized assessment tool for use by custody and visitation evaluators in cases that have a history of battering (Regan et al., 1994). Built into this new assessment method is the attempt to be more child focused, to account for the role violence played in producing the conditions being reported to the courts, and to reduce the expectation that the mother be individually responsible for undoing the harm that violence has done to her children.

Finally the custody and visitation committee is exploring a model of advocacy for battered women and their children known as the *Massachusetts model*. This model provides women with resources and support as they attempt to undo the harm that violence has done to their children. The outcome is the shifting of responsibility for undoing the harm and protecting children of battered women from individual women to a partnership between them and the community, thereby acknowledging that the needs of women and children who have experienced violence are linked but not identical.

## CONCLUSION

The Duluth Visitation Center, like its counterparts in other North American cities, is struggling with the tensions created when women turn to the state for protection of themselves and their children. Such protection has historically come at a high price. As children are drawn into the politics of gender, their lives are diminished, their connections to kin altered, and their sense of security and well-being threatened. Visitation centers can be sites in which gender inequality and its destructive consequences for children are reproduced. Alternatively, they can become opportunities for a broader response to violence that resists reproducing social relations of domination and violence. Understanding the harm done by violence from the standpoint of children is central to this resistance. Advocates for battered women and their children, we argue, should be included in the design and operations of these centers as a way of making our community responses truly adequate to the reality of violence.

## NOTES

1. A battered woman's chance of being killed by her partner rises more than 30-fold after she leaves him (Barnard, Vera, Vera, & Newman, 1982). Battered women seek medical attention for injuries sustained as a consequence of domestic violence significantly more often after separation than during cohabitation. As many as 75% of the visits to emergency rooms by battered women occur after separation (Stark & Flitcraft, 1988). One investigation demonstrated that about 75% of the calls to law enforcement for intervention and assistance in domestic violence occur after separation from batterers (Langen & Innes, 1986).

2. We use the term *mother,* rather than the gender-neutral term *parent,* because the majority of those who batter are male.

3. Typical situations in which the court mandates use of the visitation center include the following:

The history of violence is such that any contact between the parents creates a danger of further violence.

The child is at risk of physical or sexual abuse by the visiting parent.

The parents have had a history of hostile or even violent arguments during the pickup and return of children.

The visiting parent has a substance abuse problem that gives the custodial parent concern for the child's welfare.

The visiting parent's living situation is unsuitable for meeting his or her children, and the parent cannot afford or does not wish to visit in commercial settings.

The visiting parent has had a difficult time getting the custodial parent to cooperate with visitation arrangements.

The courts suspect that the visiting parent may leave the state with the children.

The children are in foster care, and the parent would rather visit them at the center than in the home.

4. We use the term *noncustodial parent* loosely to imply a parent with whom the child does not usually reside.

5. Data are from the Minnesota Coalition for Battered Women in Regan et al. (1994).

6. See Regan et al. (1994) and Shepard (1992) for the ways wife abuse is continued through child visiting.

# REFERENCES

Adams, D. (1988). Treatment models of men who batter: A profeminist analysis. In K. Yllö & M. Bograd (Eds.), *Feminist perspectives on wife abuse* (pp. 176-199). Newbury Park, CA: Sage

Arendell, T. (1992). The social self as gendered: A masculinist discourse of divorce. *Symbolic Interaction, 15*(2), 151-181.

Barnard, W. W., Vera, H., Vera, M. I., & Newman, G. (1982). Till death do us part: A study of spouse murder. *Bulletin of the American Academy of Psychiatry and the Law, 10,* 271-280.

Bernard, J. (1974). *The future of marriage.* New York: World.

Broverman, I., Broverman, D., Clarkson, S., Rosencrantz, P., & Vogel, S. (1970). Sex-role stereotypes and clinical judgments of mental health. *Journal of Consulting and Clinical Psychology, 34*(1), 1-7.

Cain, M., & Smart, C. (1989). Series editor preface. In C. Smart & S. Sevenhuijsen (Eds.), *Child custody and the politics of gender* (pp. xi-xiii). New York: Routledge.

Canadian Advisory Council on the Status of Women (CACSW). (1987). *Battered but not beaten: Preventing wife battering in Canada.* Ottawa: Author.

Canadian Advisory Council on the Status of Women (CACSW). (1991). *Male violence against women: The brutal face of inequality.* Ottawa: Author.

Cowan, C., Cowan, P., Heming, G., Garrett, E., Coysl, W., Curtis-Boles, H., & Boles, A. III. (1985). Transitions to parenthood: His, hers, and theirs. *Journal of Marriage and the Family, 6*(4), 451-481.

Daly, K. (1991, May). *The social construction of fatherhood.* Paper presented to the Qualitative Analysis Conference, Carlton University, Ontario, Canada.

Domestic Abuse Intervention Project. (1987). *Year end report to Department of Corrections, 1987.* Duluth, MN: Author. (DAIP, 206 W. Fourth St., Duluth, MN 55806)

Ehrensaft, D. (1990). Feminists fight (for) fathers. *Socialist Review, 20*(4), 57-80.

Hochschild, A. (1989). *The second shift: Working parents and the revolution at home.* Berkeley: University of California Press.

Jaffe, P., Wilson, S., & Wolfe, D. (1988). Promoting changes in attitudes and understanding of conflict resolution among child witnesses of family violence. *Canadian Journal of Behavioral Science, 18,* 356-366.

Langen, P. A., & Innes, C. A. (1986). *Preventing domestic violence against women* (Bureau of Justice statistics special report). Washington, DC: U.S. Department of Justice.

LaRossa, R., & LaRossa, M. (1981). *Transitions to parenthood: How infants change families.* Beverly Hills, CA: Sage.

Lopata, H. (1993). The interweave of public and private: Women's challenge to American society. *Journal of Marriage and the Family, 55*(1), 176-190.

Pollock, S., & Sutton, J. (1985). Fathers' rights, women's losses. *Women's Studies International Forum, 8*(6), 593-599.

Regan, K. et al. (1994). *The Duluth Custody and Visitation Project.* Unpublished manuscript. (Available from Minnesota Program Development Inc., 206 W. 4th St., Duluth, MN 55806)

Rothman, B. K. (1989). *Recreating motherhood: Ideology and technology in a patriarchal society.* New York: Norton.

Ruddick, S. (1990). Thinking about fathers. In M. Hirsch & E. Fox Keller (Eds.), *Conflicts in feminism* (pp. 222-233). New York: Routledge.

Saunders, D. (1993). Custody decisions in families experiencing woman abuse. *Social Work, 39,* 51-59.

Shepard, M. (1992). Child-visiting and domestic abuse. *Child Welfare, 71*(4), 357-365.

Sletner, J. (1992). *Battered women's perspective on custody and visitation determinations.* Unpublished master's thesis, University of Minnesota, Department of Social Work, Duluth.

Stark, E., & Flitcraft, A. (1988). Women and children at risk: A feminist perspective on child abuse. *International Journal of Health Services, 18*(1), 97-118.

Taylor, G. (1993). Child custody and access. *Vis à Vis: National Newsletter on Family Violence, 10,* 3. Canadian Council on Social Development.

Walker, G. (1992). The conceptual politics of struggle: Wife battering, the women's movement, and the state. In P. Connelly & P. Armstrong (Eds.), *Feminism in action: Studies in political economy* (pp. 317-342). Toronto: Canadian Scholars Press.

# PART FOUR

# Prevention and Education in Schools and Communities

# 12

# Teach Your Children Well

## *Elementary Schools and Violence Prevention*

SARAH SNAPP

Since the mid-1980s, increasing concerns have been expressed about the effects that abuse and witnessing violence have on children. Fueled by escalating violence in our society and frustration with traditional law enforcement and mental health solutions, an array of violence prevention efforts were reported in the late 1980s. The more recent designation of violence as a public health issue has brought new people, new expertise, and new dollars to the table. In the 1990s, attention is focused on preventing violence in our communities, as well as in our families.

Prevention strategies employed with children attempt to identify the ways violent behavior may be reinforced through victimization and witnessing violence during a child's development and to counter this social learning before negative patterns of behavior are established. Interest and activity in this area have virtually exploded in the last few years. A variety of prevention strategies and programs designed for use in elementary schools have been instituted in school districts from rural communities to urban centers.

AUTHORS' NOTE: The worksheets in this chapter appear in *My Family and Me: Violence Free,* published by the Minnesota Coalition for Battered Women, 1987, and are reprinted by permission. For further information about this publication and other elementary school curriculum materials, contact the Coalition at 1619 Dayton Ave., St. Paul, MN 55104, or call (612) 646-6177.

Before exploring some of the strategies employed in elementary schools today, it is important to reiterate a point made by Prothrow-Stith and Weissman (1991) in their book *Deadly Consequences.* They state that not only will violence prevention efforts enable students to learn, but also that learning itself is violence prevention. Academic excellence for all students must be at the core of all violence prevention efforts. The critical thinking skills that come from school success are essential elements of the ability to stop, think of alternatives, analyze them, and select the best course of action. Also, school success is the pathway to better jobs, a better standard of living, and a generally brighter future. For children to think that they should make certain choices, they must believe that they have choices.

In this chapter we describe several strategies for violence prevention in elementary schools and provide examples of each approach. These strategies include peacemakers, affective education, skills education, values education, family life education, and specific education on violence itself. Following the description of these programs, an in-depth discussion of one prevention project illustrates the process of curriculum development and the challenges encountered in implementing a program in elementary schools. In the conclusion we describe an overall relationship-building and climate strategy that must be the underpinning of prevention efforts and provide examples of a new wave of projects in elementary schools.

## VIOLENCE PREVENTION STRATEGIES

### Peacemakers

Teaching children to be "peacemakers" is a widely used strategy. This approach takes a global perspective and highlights well-known peacemakers such as Dr. Martin Luther King, Jr., Mohandas Gandhi, and Mother Teresa as role models. Children are encouraged to have compassion for and feel a sense of responsibility for people all over the world. This strategy frequently is linked with environmental concerns. While providing hope and inspiration, this approach does not address underlying issues and skill deficits among the students. It is an excellent complement to a more comprehensive strategy but has limited effectiveness when it stands alone.

### Affective Education

Affective education is widely used. These types of programs do not always view themselves as exclusively or even primarily violence prevention. Many arose from the chemical health discipline and have adapted themselves to fit issues of violence. These programs strive to enhance self-esteem and to teach children to recognize and label feelings, to distinguish between feelings and behavior, and to empathize with the feelings of others (a skill perpetrators frequently lack). In elementary schools this approach typically takes the form of feelings and self-esteem groups run by the school social worker.

One limitation of this approach is that perpetrators of violence do not necessarily suffer from poor self-esteem. In fact, bullies generally score average or above average on standard measures of self-esteem (Olweus, 1991). Their violence frequently stems from a sense of entitlement and opportunity. The other core goals of this strategy, however, do address violence prevention.

## Skills Education

The next strategy is skills education. Among the skills taught are assertiveness, self-control, problem solving, and conflict resolution. When teaching assertiveness to bolster the strength of victims, it is essential that the victims not be blamed if their efforts to be assertive are ineffective or if they (wisely in some cases) choose not to be assertive with an aggressor. Similar to affective education, this approach can take the form of social skills or friendship groups run by the school social worker or psychologist.

Another way to use this approach is through a curriculum offered to all students. One widely used curriculum is *Second Step: Skill Training Curriculum to Prevent Youth Violence,* which was developed and produced by the Committee for Children (Beland, 1987) in Seattle, Washington. The curriculum, which has units for preschool through eighth grade, teaches skills of empathy, impulse control, problem solving, and anger management. Lesson plans, plots, discussions, videos, puppets, and role plays teach the identified skills. The program is designed to allow for flexible scheduling. Lessons may be taught daily or weekly.

Conflict mediator programs are particularly popular in the skills education category. In these programs, children are taught to mediate problems among their peers. The Community Board Program (Sadalla, Homberg, & Halligan, 1990) of San Francisco has an excellent curriculum to guide schools in establishing such a program. Students receive training and then are assigned times and places in which to identify and mediate problems among their peers. One of the strengths of this approach is in developing leadership skills of students who are identified by peers as being well-respected. The program empowers these student leaders by providing them with a structure and the skills needed to understand and resolve conflicts among peers. Conflict is presented as inevitable and, when managed properly, as a positive force for individual and community growth.

These programs teach skills and empower youth to work together to solve their own problems. However, two core assumptions implicit in these programs are not always true. First, they assume that violence stems from conflict. In some cases violence may be caused by roughhousing that gets out of hand for children with undeveloped internal controls. Violence may be caused also by confusing violence with entertainment (Miedzian, 1991). Some violence is caused by a person's sense of entitlement to have what he or she wants or the opportunity to attain it (Olweus, 1991). Second, conflict resolution programs assume a level playing field for all participants. Proper supervision must occur to ensure that bullies are not inadvertently given a captive audience to victimize or control. Very few schools use the conflict resolution model to settle conflicts between students and adults. One must question what message children receive when adults are not willing to use the process they are teaching.

## Values Education

During the 1990s a renewed interest in teaching values and character building has gained popularity. Programs in this category strive to remedy a perceived "moral illiteracy" in our culture. Kilpatrick (1993) calls for character education that teaches children to practice habits of courage, justice, and self-control (p. 11a). The best programs using this strategy stress that, if we are going to live together peacefully, we must find ways to celebrate and honor diversity and also identify what unites us as a community. These programs go further than the values clarification exercises of 20 years ago; they articulate and promote values they believe are universal.

One example at the secondary level of this approach is the *Community of Caring,* developed by the Joseph P. Kennedy Foundation (1988). The program endorses and promotes the universal values of caring, trust, respect, responsibility, and family. Its explicit goals are to help students avoid destructive behaviors such as early sexual involvement, teen pregnancy, drugs, alcohol, excessive school absenteeism, and dropping out of school. Although violence is not specifically included, it certainly fits into the framework of destructive behaviors. The curriculum is integrated into existing course work and connects the core values to daily life and decision-making skills.

At the elementary level, values efforts are simplified. Some schools teach values such as the "Three B's: Be Safe, Be Respectful, and Be a Learner." They teach children to examine behavior and decisions through the lens of these core values. Discipline procedures are tied to these values as well.

Support for this approach has come from the National Education Association, which has endorsed the necessity of including values education as part of school violence prevention efforts.

## Family Life Education

Other schools are teaching family life education and child development classes beginning as early as kindergarten. This approach is based on the premise that effective preparation for parenthood will prevent incidents of family violence. One such program is Educating for Parenting, described by Miedzian (1991) in her book *Boys Will Be Boys*. These programs strive to teach children about child development, set realistic expectations for the burdens of parenting (and thus decrease adolescent pregnancy), and promote the parenting skills and empathy of boys as well as girls. These programs use experiential learning by providing supervised opportunities for children to observe and interact with babies, toddlers, and preschool children.

## Violence Education

Another approach is to teach about violence itself. Typically these programs include the following core messages:

- Violence is a learned behavior and can be unlearned.
- There are alternatives to violence.
- Violence rarely solves problems and usually creates new ones.
- Violence hurts and is not entertaining, fun, or glamorous.

These programs attempt to counteract the psychic numbing that comes from overexposure to violence by helping children see the violence all around them: in the movies, on TV, in their video games, and on the playground. An example is CLIMB Theater's (1987) plays *OUCH* and *OWIE!* with accompanying curriculum for grades 3-6 and K-2, respectively. Repetitive, raplike songs are used to help children see the consequences of violence and learn self-control. The program strives to help children see violence and learn that they do have alternatives.

## MCBW SCHOOL CURRICULUM PROJECT

One of the most ambitious violence prevention efforts was launched in the late 1980s by the Minnesota Coalition for Battered Women (MCBW). The project targeted both secondary and elementary schools throughout the state and involved the development of an original curriculum for elementary students. The educational materials combined strategies from affective education, skills building, and violence education. The project provides a good case study of the challenges that practitioners are likely to encounter in organizing large-scale prevention projects, regardless of the approach or strategy adopted.

MCBW was formed by the state's battered women's shelters and programs to coordinate their collaborative efforts to address domestic violence, such as the development of new legislation and model projects with a statewide impact. In 1985, MCBW initiated the School Curriculum Project, designed as a school-based primary prevention effort. The project was funded through grants from private foundations. An educational approach was chosen because observations and research suggested that domestic violence was rooted in social learning that developed and maintained behaviors and attitudes supportive of using violence against women (Dobash & Dobash, 1979). Researchers and counselors working with batterers generally agreed that social learning played a significant role in reinforcing violence behavior against intimate partners (see Edleson & Tolman, 1992). Activists believed that prevention programs could make a substantial contribution to ending violence against women by challenging these cultural norms and teaching alternative attitudes and behaviors (Pence & Shepard, 1988).

The MCBW project was staffed by a full-time coordinator (Denise Gamache) with a background in both domestic violence programming and secondary education. Her first task was to develop plans to introduce prevention curricula into all secondary schools in Minnesota. A number of shelters had conducted educational campaigns in their local high schools and uncovered incidents of violence in teenage dating relationships. These observations were supported by several research studies published at that time (Henton, Cate, Koval, Lloyd, & Christopher, 1983; Roscoe & Callahan, 1985). Therefore the goal of the secondary school project was to prevent abuse from occurring both in adolescent dating relationships and in future adult relationships.

Because all students are at risk of being abusive or abused in a relationship, the coalition was committed to reaching all students. It was understood, however, that the prevention project would also provide opportunities for intervention if adolescents experiencing violence in their relationships or witnessing it in their homes were prompted to seek assistance as a result of exposure to the curriculum. To prepare for this possibility, the project stressed the importance of increased ties between the school districts and programs for battered women in a local area. Funds supporting the curriculum project were partially distributed to local programs for battered women to cover staff time spent on teacher recruitment and training. A program's participation also included a commitment to assist the school in responding to teens or families experiencing violence. Although ties between some programs and their local schools were already strong, project support provided the first opportunity for outreach to schools in some areas of the state.

An existing secondary curriculum *Skills for Violence-Free Relationships* (Levy, 1984) was chosen as the basic text, and the staff added specific information about dating violence and local community services. A 1-day training session included background information about violence in dating and family relationships, an overview of the curriculum materials, and information about local community resources. During the next 3 years, staff disseminated educational materials and provided free training to more than 400 teachers and support personnel from 210 junior and senior high schools. A follow-up survey of teachers found that the curriculum was being taught to more than 20,000 Minnesota students annually. Schools in 146 of the 430 public school districts were participating in the project.

The project was evaluated by comparing pre- and posttests of students exposed to the curriculum with a matched control group. Findings indicated that knowledge about dating and family violence increased. Measures of attitude change were not significant, though this result may have been due to the attitude measure used in the research (Jones, 1991).

## Development of
## MCBWs Elementary Curriculum

The secondary school project directed attention to the need for a similar effort at the elementary level. Children's advocates and teachers believed that attitudes promoting the use of violence needed to be countered before students reached junior high school. Advocates stressed that a school-based program would provide another opportunity for intervention and that early identification of children living in violent homes would improve the community's ability to provide supportive services that might end the abuse or, at minimum, would mitigate the effects of witnessing violence.

Project staff believed that an elementary curriculum would be accepted by elementary administrators and teachers. Around the state, other related prevention materials were being incorporated into elementary schools. Some of the most popular were programs aimed at physical and sexual abuse prevention (*Touch; Red Flag, Green Flag People*) and chemical dependency prevention (*Project Charlie*). None of these materials incorporated domestic abuse information, and project staff believed that teachers could be persuaded to view domestic abuse prevention as a natural complement to their current prevention programming. In addition, contacts with school district personnel during the secondary curriculum project indicated that schools would cooperate in a similar elementary project.

Several features of the secondary project that had been particularly successful were incorporated into the new initiative. The elementary project, too, would focus on training teachers to implement prevention materials in regular classrooms. This was seen as the most efficient means of reaching a large number of students. Collaborative arrangements for staff support from local programs for battered women were again negotiated. It was especially important to assure elementary teachers that assistance would be available for children who might disclose incidents of violence. As in the secondary project, the classroom teacher's role was educational, the role for which they were trained. They were not expected to assume counseling duties, but to refer cases to support personnel according to guidelines developed in each school. The additional support from programs for battered women was particularly helpful for small rural schools that lack on-site support staff. In some regions, four or five school districts share one elementary school social worker.

These collaborations also had proven valuable in the recruitment of teachers and in negotiations with local school districts. The local program for battered women was often aware of sympathetic personnel in the area schools. In secondary schools a wide variety of initial contact people had proven effective in obtaining a commitment to participate in the project. A unique approach had to be tailored to each of the 430 districts in the state. The project coordinator produced descriptive brochures for use in recruitment and completed several mailings to all schools. In many cases individual teachers were able to commit on their own authority; in fact, classroom teachers can exercise great latitude in their choice of educational materials. In some school districts, principals or school board members pushed to establish policies that directed or encouraged teacher involvement in the project. In some schools, support staff such as school nurses, counselors, or social workers were instrumental in urging educators to participate.

It again was expected that teachers would be most receptive to instructional materials that were flexible and provided a variety of student activities they could adapt to their particular needs. Mindful of the cost and time necessary to develop a curriculum, the staff searched for suitable elementary materials. Unfortunately the few resources located were unsatisfactory, primarily because staff believed they failed to clearly identify or define domestic violence. A typical focus was violent behavior in general, an approach that lacked instruction to specifically counter the social learning that promotes violence against women. An antiviolence message would be ultimately unsuccessful unless delivered in a context that challenged the cultural beliefs promoting violence against women. If students were not taught that the cultural targeting of certain classes of people as "appropriate victims" of domination and violence was wrong, they would be unlikely to apply their new skills toward people in these groups.

As a result of the dissatisfaction with existing materials, a decision was made to produce a new curriculum. A consultant with experience in both elementary education and prevention programming was brought to the project. A school social worker who previously had developed sexual abuse prevention curriculum was contracted to collaborate on the development and authorship of the curriculum and to assist in training teachers in its use.

## Empirical Basis of the Curriculum

The staff began the process of curriculum development by reviewing the research on children who witness violence, on children who experience other psychological traumas, and on the strategies of successful intervention efforts with these populations. The following relevant themes were identified:

*Boys and girls who witness family violence exhibit emotional and behavioral problems.* Studies of male children (Hershorn & Rosenbaum, 1985; Jaffe, Wolfe, & Wilson, 1990) found that marital violence was significantly related to behavioral and emotional problems in the witnessing boys and that this impact was similar to the adjustment problems of abused boys. In another study (Wolfe, Jaffe, Wilson, & Zak, 1985), battered women rated their children significantly higher in behavior problems and lower in social competence than a comparison group of mothers. This study also found that the impact on the child may be partially a function of maternal stress. In other research using maternal ratings by battered women and a comparison group (Jaffe et al., 1990), girls from violent families exhibited more internalizing behavior problems and lowered social competence, while boys demonstrated both internalizing and externalizing behavior problems, in addition to a lower level of social competence.

*Children are taught messages about violence when they witness assaults in their homes.* Authors of a particularly useful article (Jaffe, Wilson, & Wolfe, 1986) reviewed current research findings and summarized the lessons that children were likely to learn from violent parents: (a) Violence is an appropriate form of conflict resolution or stress management; (b) violence has a place within family interactions; (c) if violence is reported to others, such as police officers or counselors, there are few, if any, consequences; (d) sexism, demonstrated by an inequality of power, decision making, and roles within a family, is acceptable, and (e) victims must tolerate this behavior or examine their responsibility for causing the violence. These observations

raised similar questions about the impact and lessons learned from witnessing violence in the community or in the media.

*Children's recovery from difficult life experiences is enhanced by building*
*their problem-solving abilities and increasing the social supports available*
*to them.* Research on children undergoing stressful life experiences such as
divorce, medical problems, and family crises (Rutter, 1983) indicated that
children's competencies and resources were central in determining their
emotional recovery from these events. A study (Wolfe, Zak, Wilson, & Jaffe,
1986) comparing current and former shelter residents and their children to a
nonviolent community sample suggested that children from violent families
could recover from the impact of parental conflict and separation, provided
the violence is eliminated and proper supports and opportunities for recovery
were provided. The former shelter residents and their children showed no
more behavioral or emotional symptoms than the comparison community
sample. Jaffe, Wilson, and Wolfe (1986) recommended that such efforts be
extended to schools because shelters see only a fraction of the children
experiencing family violence.

These research findings provided the basic framework for the curriculum.
The teaching techniques and student activities were designed to challenge
the social messages that promote domestic violence and to build children's
problem-solving skills. These skills not only would assist children currently
involved in abusive situations but also would be of value to all children. The
project would attempt also to improve the school's ability to provide social
support by training teachers to recognize the behavioral cues likely to be
exhibited by affected students and by developing an effective school and
community response to children who disclose information about violence in
their families.

## Curriculum Development Process

A group of six consultants, including children's advocates, classroom
teachers, and multicultural education experts, were brought together for 2
days to assist the staff in the development of appropriate learning goals, to
brainstorm possible classroom activities, and to share their knowledge of
available resources. These ideas provided the initial outline used by the
project coordinator and primary consultant to begin writing the curriculum.
In addition, invaluable assistance was contributed by the proprietor of a local
children's bookstore specializing in nonviolent, nonsexist, multicultural
books, games, and educational materials. She assisted in identifying materials to match our learning goals and developed the comprehensive bibliog-
raphy of related books and resources included in the curriculum.

The curriculum was organized into separate units for primary and intermediate elementary grade levels. The project stressed that schools should begin presenting this material to students in the primary grades and follow up to reinforce these messages in a more sophisticated way at the intermediate level. On the basis of the experience with secondary schools, it was expected that individual school districts would determine the particular grade levels in which the units would be incorporated. The units were designed to complement other violence prevention curricula that might be in use.

It was important that the materials reflect the multicultural diversity of the state's population. Any written materials also needed to be visually attractive to children. An artist was chosen who could produce drawings in a cartoon, coloring book style and who previously had illustrated multicultural materials. A nice feature of this format was that teachers could have younger students color the drawings.

## Structure and Content

The curriculum was entitled *My Family and Me: Violence-Free* (Stavrou-Petersen & Gamache, 1988), with units for grades K-3 and 4-6. Both units presented six learning goals through different age-appropriate readings and activities. Each session was designed to last approximately 50 minutes, or a typical class period. To provide continuity, it was recommended that two sessions be presented each week, although teachers could adapt the unit to a different schedule as needed. A basic routine was designed for the sessions:

*Relaxation/Visualization.* Each session opened with quiet music and a brief guided imagery related to the theme for the day. The purpose was to establish a sense of a special opening that differentiated the unit from other classroom activities.

*Reading/Lecture.* Books, videos, or short lectures, delivered by the teacher directly or through the use of puppets, were used to introduce the basic concepts of the unit.

*Creative Project.* A variety of art projects, role playing, and written exercises reinforced the information presented and allowed the students to react to the material. Teachers were presented with several options from which to choose.

*Closure.* Sessions closed with a brief activity that affirmed each student's participation in the unit and reinforced the theme stressed in the session.

## Learning Goals

The six learning goals follow, with descriptions of the student activities incorporated into each unit.

1. *To raise awareness of their concept of family and the effects that problems have on all family members.* A book on different kinds of families introduced students to different family configurations. Art projects such as the creation of "family mobiles" illustrated the connections between family members and how one person can affect the rest of the family.

2. *To label and define the different forms of violence in families and to understand the effects on family members.* Teachers could choose from videos or books that illustrated incidents of physical and emotional abuse. Teacher-led discussions helped students to define emotional and physical abuse and to differentiate abuse from discipline. In the second session, sexual abuse specifically was discussed with the aid of videos or books from sexual abuse prevention programs that were already available to the teachers through the school or library system.

3. *To develop a personal safety plan to use in abusive, emergency situations.* Worksheets were provided to help teachers guide students in developing an individual plan that helps them identify whom they can go to for help in emergencies (see Figures 12.1 and 12.2). Friendly animals decorated the K-3 version. Teachers also helped students differentiate between emergency and nonemergency situations. Puppets were used to lead this discussion with younger students.

4. *To express their feelings, opinions, and behaviors based on the values of equality, respect, and sharing of power.* In the K-3 unit, several readings launched discussion about these values. Songs and games addressed sex role stereotyping. Books on identifying and expressing feelings helped children label their feelings. Worksheets (see Figures 12.3 and 12.4) or games such as Feelings Charades reinforced these ideas. Children were also taught to separate their feelings from their behavior. In particular, children learned that they can choose to express anger, frustration, or other difficult emotions without violence. A game was invented to help younger students identify healthful ways to express feelings. Older students outlined and discussed "What happened? How did I feel? What did I do?" (See Figure 12.4.)

5. *To learn and practice assertiveness skills that can solve problems nonviolently.* A monster and a mouse were used to represent aggressiveness and passivity. In class discussion and role playing, students identified assertive alternatives. The K-3 unit included a series of books that help children generate alternative, nonviolent solutions to problem situations. The 4-6 unit provided several worksheets (see Figure 12.5) and used role playing of problem situations.

6. *To gain a sense of their own uniqueness and worth, regardless of the problems that may be occurring in their families, and an understanding that*

**Figure 12.1.** Worksheet on Developing a Personal Safety Plan

*they can make different choices for themselves in the future.* Teachers led a discussion on self-esteem, how events in our families or at school can affect

**Figure 12.2.** Worksheet on Developing a Personal Safety Plan

our feelings, and how we affect others. Students brainstormed ways they can
get emotional support when they need it. Students identified their special and

**Figure 12.3.** Worksheet for Self-Expression

unique qualities (see Figure 12.6) on art projects such as magazine covers, paper bag T-shirts, and a collective collage of Polaroid pictures.

**Figure 12.4.** Worksheet for Self-Expression

### Testing and Evaluation

After preliminary drafts were developed, the staff trained 40 elementary teachers and social workers in a 2-day session. Participants represented a diverse group of schools from around the state. In addition, several out-of-state groups that had heard of the project asked to attend, expanding the test sites to small communities in Wisconsin and Ohio and to inner-city schools in Boston. The materials and training were provided free, and in return each teacher agreed to present the unit during the year, administer the pre- and posttests, and complete an evaluation of the unit.

The pre- and post-tests attempted to measure positive changes in knowledge and attitudes among students. Twenty-two teachers administered the tests in their classes (grades K-3, $N = 238$; grades 4-6, $N = 176$). Overall, students at both elementary levels showed an increase in knowledge. Measures of changes in attitude, though in a positive direction, were not statistically significant. However, it was not expected that exposure to one unit for a relatively short time period would show dramatic attitude change (Jones, 1988).

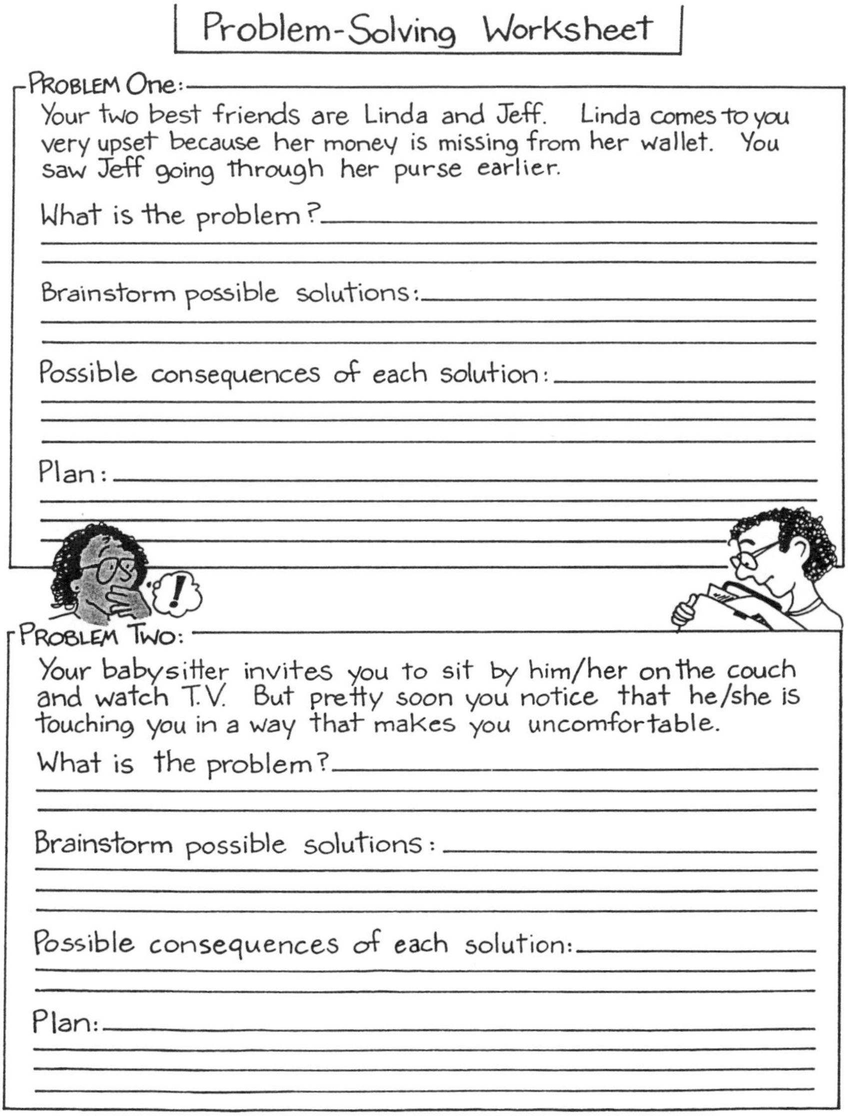

## Problem-Solving Worksheet

**PROBLEM One:**

Your two best friends are Linda and Jeff. Linda comes to you very upset because her money is missing from her wallet. You saw Jeff going through her purse earlier.

What is the problem?_____

_____

Brainstorm possible solutions:_____

_____

Possible consequences of each solution:_____

_____

_____

Plan:_____

_____

**PROBLEM Two:**

Your babysitter invites you to sit by him/her on the couch and watch T.V. But pretty soon you notice that he/she is touching you in a way that makes you uncomfortable.

What is the problem?_____

_____

Brainstorm possible solutions:_____

_____

_____

Possible consequences of each solution:_____

_____

Plan:_____

_____

**Figure 12.5.** Worksheet on Assertiveness Skills

The teachers' evaluations of the curriculum were quite positive. Teachers noted that the concepts presented in the curriculum were integrated by the

**I AM ME AND I AM GLAD**

1) I am proud of_____
2) One thing I am very good at is_____
3) My best friend is_____
4) Someone who likes me a lot is_____
5) A good thing I did once was_____
6) I like myself best when_____
7) I look best when_____
8) People like to be around me when_____
9) The best thing about me is_____
10) I am happy when_____

**Figure 12.6.** Worksheet on Developing Self-Worth

children and that some behavior change was observed as a result. The learning goals and the basic structure were well received. This held true in different types of schools. The Boston group had taught the curriculum in several sites, one of which was an elementary school serving a largely inner-city, Puerto Rican population. They translated the materials into Spanish and reported that the curriculum had worked well in these classes.

The teachers had several suggestions for improvements to the units that were incorporated into the final version. A few of the sessions had not included a range of learning activities. Teachers commented that several approaches should be available for each learning goal so that they could choose the activity appropriate for their students or in their community. This point was underscored by the one negative experience that occurred. Some parents in a small rural community objected to the film that was used in the session dealing with physical abuse in the family. The film had been developed by coalitions for battered women and had been used extensively with children in shelters. The parents thought the film was too graphic and would needlessly upset children who were not living in violent homes. The school administration decided not to proceed with the unit, particularly because the materials were still in development. Ironically another participating elementary school in town had fully completed the unit a few weeks before this teacher began her presentations. The revised units included a range of choices for the books, videos, and student activities in each session.

The curriculum had been designed for use by teachers in typical classroom settings. Many of the test sites, however, had used a team approach, most often the teacher and a social worker or an advocate from the local program for battered women. Their evaluations recommended this approach because of the nature of the information. It had been helpful to have another adult available to respond to individual children when needed. Although the staff recognized that this approach may be impossible in some schools, the recommendation of using a team was incorporated into the curriculum.

The process of curriculum development and evaluation required almost 2 years. After the final revision, *My Family and Me: Violence Free* (Stavrou-Petersen & Gamache, 1988) was produced and is marketed by the Minnesota Coalition for Battered Women. The elementary school project continued to recruit and train teachers around the state. The curriculum materials have since been incorporated into a variety of prevention programs in the United States and Canada.

## TOWARD A NONVIOLENT CLIMATE IN SCHOOLS

Particularly at the elementary level, good prevention programs in the areas of violence, chemical health, or adolescent pregnancy cover much the same ground. It is probably obvious that just as prevention disciplines overlap, strategies within a discipline overlap. Affective education includes some life skills. All violence prevention programs have some inherent values education: at minimum, the value that less violence is better than more. Evidence is growing that one additional strategy or set of strategies must serve as a foundation for any effort. This strategy can be labeled the *relationship building* and *climate approach.*

James Garbarino and his colleagues at the Erickson Institute in Chicago have studied the impact of violence on children. They have compared children living in inner-city America and children growing up in the war-torn countries of Northern Ireland, Israel, Palestine, Cambodia, and Mozambique. Garbarino has drawn on his own research, as well as the literature on resiliency, to design childcare and school programs for inner-city children. He stresses that relationship is the curriculum. Garbarino asserts, "All children, especially children at risk, learn and are able to control their behavior in the context of constructive relationships with emotionally significant adults in a school setting that is educationally enriching and developmentally appropriate" (Garbarino, Drew, Kostelny, & Pardo, 1992, p. 152).

In a similar vein, Olweus (1993), a Scandinavian researcher on the bully-victim problem, asserts that it is a fundamental democratic principle that everyone has a right to be spared humiliation, oppression, and intentional injury at school, as well as in the society at large. Olweus goes on to argue that adults must be in charge of setting the school community standard of behavior. He has established the following fundamental principles for school violence prevention:

Warm, caring relationships with adults
Firm, clear, consistent limits to unacceptable behavior
Nonhostile, nonphysical sanctions
Adults acting as authorities
Active monitoring and supervision

An underlying premise of Garbarino's and Olweus's work is that parents play a profound role and should be engaged at every opportunity. They also believe that schools can and should draw a magic circle around themselves within which they state: "In here it is different." In effect, schools can serve as the primary nurturing and limit-setting caretakers for some children.

The premise of climate approaches is that the climate, especially as expressed in the quality of adult-student relationships, provides the foundation on which to build additional programs that use the approaches discussed in this chapter. Several model programs are pursuing this approach in elementary schools.

Cool 2B Safe: A School Violence Reduction Project is being piloted by Sarah Snapp and the Wilder Foundation in St. Paul and uses Olweus's fundamental principles and Garbarino's work to build violence-free schools. It also incorporates some features of a successful school reform project organized by Dr. James Comer (1980) in inner-city New Haven (since replicated in Maryland). A core principle of his work was an interdisciplinary team that drew from the best of what educators, mental health practitioners, and parents had to offer. By providing training and ongoing consultation to the school staff, as well as engaging students, Cool 2B Safe is enriching the quality of the relationships within the school community and enhancing the staff's ability to respond to problems as they arise.

The prevention program designed by Mid-Minnesota Women's Shelter and Harrison Elementary School in Brainerd is built around such a team approach involving students, school staff, and parents. Basic methods of teaching nonviolent conflict resolution include (a) "conferences" for resolving interpersonal problems, (b) group gatherings to address major and minor issues that affect the group as a whole, and (c) modeling of appropriate problem-solving behavior by school staff. *Conferences* are guided conversations led by either the people in disagreement or an outside facilitator and occur when requested by students or staff. Students are encouraged to ask for conferences in order to prevent their conflicts from escalating or remaining unresolved. In addition, teachers incorporate a variety of violence prevention curricula into their classes that address emotional, physical, and sexual abuse, abduction, and racial or cultural harassment. Staff members meet weekly in teams to discuss how conflicts have been handled and how to improve. A project evaluation will compare several measures of behavior change at Harrison with a control school. The staff is enthusiastic about initial results, and the principal has reported that in-school suspensions, given for violations of a strict and specific behavior code, have decreased by half.

A similar program, the Violence-Free School Project, is being implemented in Duluth, Minnesota. The project, a collaboration of several domestic violence programs and the school district, aims to develop a violence-free environment at school. Beginning with one elementary school, the staff used a listening survey of students, teachers, parents, and support staff to identify the problems in the school environment. Project staff then organized the information into a diagram describing the types of abuse noted: physical abuse, emotional abuse, isolation, threats and fears, disrespect, racism, ableism, sexism, and classism. A conflict resolution curriculum is being used to teach these skills to students, school staff, and parents within a context of moving toward a set of values and behaviors that will replace the abuses. These include peaceful conflict resolution and appreciation for differences, affirmation and support, inclusiveness and community, safety, respect, multiculturalism, understanding differently abled people, gender fairness, and respect for each person's reality. The project will expand to other elementary schools in its second year, and an evaluation is planned to measure changes in incidents of violence and the response to violence, satisfaction with the project, and improvement in overall academic performance.

Similar programs have been implemented in elementary schools in Chicago, New York City, and Seattle ("Schools Try," 1993). Each involves students, teachers, and parents in changing the climate in which children learn to handle conflicts and grievances, so that peaceful interactions are valued and violence is prevented. Preliminary evaluations have demonstrated decreases in the number of fights and verbal put-downs and an increase in caring among the students.

Pete Seeger said, "Children know better than adults that what we do is more important than what we say." Any school curriculum that teaches values, attitudes, and skills must be practiced by the adults in the school community. If we want children to learn to be respectful, we must be respectful to them. If we want them to learn to resolve conflicts, we must attend to how we resolve conflicts with each other and with them. In addition, people, including children, can only learn new skills in settings where it is safe to practice them. How we develop and maintain relationships in our schools may be our most important resource for violence prevention.

## REFERENCES

Beland, K. (1987). *Second step: Skill training curriculum to prevent youth violence.* Seattle, WA: Committee for Children.

CLIMB Theater. (1987). *OUCH/OWIE!* St. Paul, MN: Author.

Comer, J. P. (1980). *School power: Implications of an intervention project.* New York: Free Press.

Dobash, R. E., & Dobash, R. P. (1979). *Violence against wives: A case against patriarchy.* New York: Free Press.

Edleson, J. L., & Tolman, R. M. (1992). *Intervention for men who batter.* Newbury Park, CA: Sage.

Garbarino, J., Drew, N., Kostelny, K., & Pardo, C. (1992). *Children in danger.* San Francisco: Jossey-Bass.

Henton, J. M., Cate, R. M., Koval, J., Lloyd, S., & Christopher, F. S. (1983). Romance and violence in dating relationships. *Journal of Family Issues, 4,* 467-482.

Hershorn, M., & Rosenbaum, A. (1985). Children of marital violence: A closer look at the unintended victims. *American Journal of Orthopsychiatry, 55,* 260-266.

Jaffe, P. G., Wilson, S. K., & Wolfe, D. A. (1986). Promoting changes in attitudes and understanding of conflict resolution among child witnesses of family violence. *Canadian Journal of Behavioral Science, 18,* 356-366.

Jaffe, P. G., Wolfe, D. A., & Wilson, S. K. (1990). *Children of battered women.* Newbury Park, CA: Sage.

Jones, L. (1988). *Report on the evaluation of the elementary school curriculum.* Unpublished report, Minnesota Coalition for Battered Women, St. Paul.

Jones, L. (1991). The Minnesota School Curriculum Project: A statewide domestic violence prevention project in secondary schools. In B. Levy (Ed.), *Dating violence: Young women in danger* (pp. 258-266). Seattle, WA: Seal Press.

Joseph P. Kennedy Foundation. (1988). *Communities of caring.* Washington, DC: Kennedy Foundation.

Kilpatrick, W. (1993, July 23). Schools must return to teaching what's right and wrong. *St. Paul Pioneer Press,* p. 11a.

Levy, B. (1984). *Skills for violence-free relationships.* Santa Monica: Southern California Coalition on Battered Women.

Miedzian, M. (1991). *Boys will be boys: Breaking the link between masculinity and violence.* Garden City, NY: Doubleday.

Olweus, D. (1991). Bully/victim problems among school children: Basic facts and effects of a school based intervention program. In D. Pepler & K. H. Rubin (Eds.), *The development and treatment of childhood aggression* (pp. 411-448). Hillsdale, NJ: Lawrence Erlbaum.

Olweus, D. (1993). *Bullying at school: What we know and what we can do.* Cambridge, MA: Blackwell.

Pence, E., & Shepard, M. (1988). Integrating feminist theory and practice: The challenge of the battered women's movement. In K.Yllö & M. Bograd (Eds.), *Feminist perspectives on wife abuse* (pp. 282-298). Newbury Park, CA: Sage.

Prothrow-Stith, D., & Weissman, M. (1991). *Deadly consequences.* New York: HarperCollins.

Roscoe, B., & Callahan, J. E. (1985). Adolescents' self-report of violence in families and dating relations. *Adolescence, 20,* 546-553.

Rutter, M. (1983). Stress, coping, and development: Some issues and some questions. In N. Garmezy & M. Rutter (Eds.), *Stress, coping, and development in children* (pp. 1-41). New York: McGraw-Hill.

Sadalla, G., Homberg, M., & Halligan, J. (1990). *Conflict resolution: An elementary school curriculum.* San Francisco: Community Board Program.

Schools try to tame violent pupils, one punch and one taunt at a time. (1993, August 19). *The New York Times,* p. A12.

Stavrou-Petersen, K., & Gamache, D. (1988). *My family and me: Violence free.* St. Paul: Minnesota Coalition for Battered Women.

Wolfe, D., Jaffe, P., Wilson, S., & Zak, L. (1985). Children of battered women: The relation of child behavior to family violence and maternal stress. *Journal of Consulting and Clinical Psychology, 53,* 657-665.

Wolfe, D., Zak, L., Wilson, S., & Jaffe, P. (1986). Child witnesses to violence between parents: Critical issues in behavioral and social adjustment. *Journal of Abnormal Child Psychology, 14,* 95-104.

# 13

# Violence Prevention Programs in Secondary (High) Schools

MARLIES SUDERMANN
PETER G. JAFFE
ELAINE HASTINGS

The problem of violence in intimate relationships concerns a majority of high school students. Sexual and physical violence in high school dating relationships has been documented to be a widespread problem (Mercer, 1987; Sudermann & Jaffe, 1993). Because at least 1 in 10 women are physically abused by their partners each year (MacLeod, 1987; Straus & Gelles, 1986), one can estimate that between 3 and 5 students in the average high school classroom have witnessed their mothers being assaulted at home. Recently the silence about this problem is ending on a societal level, and the process of naming the violence and coming to grips with its scope and depth has begun. The need for primary prevention of violence in intimate relationships is very pressing, and prevention with high school students possibly represents one of the most effective actions a community can take to reduce the incidence of violence and to ameliorate its effects. High school students represent a very broad cross section of a community's youth. Not only will many students be personally assisted by learning about violence and its consequences, but students also represent the future community health care workers, police officers, judges, neighbors, and friends of those who will be affected by violence in intimate relationships. Thus, in raising awareness and empowering adolescents to respond to violence in the community and in their own lives, the probability of effecting a fundamental decrease in violence is high.

The London Family Court Clinic is a children's mental health center that specializes in assisting children and families before the courts and that engages in research and public policy development. For more than 6 years, the London Family Court Clinic has been involved in developing and implementing school-based violence prevention programs in partnership with boards of education and other community agencies. Combining our knowledge of violence against women and skills in research with educators' expertise in implementing programs with young people has resulted in creative and effective prevention programs. We write this chapter from the point of view of an outside agency collaborating with the school system. Other community agencies such as women's shelters, sexual assault crisis centers, and children's mental health centers can use a similar approach to violence prevention for adolescents. Educators can take the lead, drawing on community agencies as needed. We have found that a joint planning committee including board of education staff and community agency representatives facilitates violence prevention efforts.

In this chapter we describe some aspects of violence in relationships and its effects on students and on the larger community. We also describe successful high school based prevention programs that have begun to make a difference. The emphasis in the programs is on partnerships—between schools and communities and between students, teachers, and administrators—and on action planning in an evolving area. The chapter includes six sections. The first section covers the scope of the problem in society, students' views of the problem, and the demands on all institutions to work together for prevention. The second section describes the groups that need to become involved in order to make violence prevention a reality in a school system and community, and the third section presents some ideas on getting started. The fourth section suggests ideas for teacher professional development. Student programs, including special awareness events and curriculum integration, are covered in the fifth section; this section also includes advice on handling disclosures of violence, locating resources, and on systemwide planning for violence prevention. The final section suggests how to evaluate and obtain feedback when implementing a high school based violence prevention program and presents evaluation results from our programs.

## WHY HIGH SCHOOLS
## NEED TO BECOME INVOLVED

We live in a very violent society in which many children learn that aggression against vulnerable individuals or groups is an accepted way to solve problems or advance one's own interests. This learning is described in other chapters of this volume, but some illustrative statistics and examples are offered here.

The feminist analysis of the underpinnings of violence in relationships has emphasized that individuals in our society learn that women and other disempowered groups are appropriate and acceptable targets of violence. Some community members or educators may believe that violence against girls and women is not a problem in their particular community or school. A closer look, however, usually will reveal significant problems. For example, wife assault is the cause of more injuries to women than are car accidents, muggings, and rapes combined (Toufexis, 1987). The commonly cited statistic of 1 in 10 women who suffer from wife assault each year is considered too low an estimate by many workers in the field. This statement is supported by a carefully conducted survey in Toronto, Ontario (Smith, 1987), that found *1 in 3* women had experienced some form of physical abuse over the course of their adult years, and 14.4% had experienced abuse in the immediately preceding year.

Children who witness violence in their homes are greatly at risk for both suffering emotional problems and getting involved in future violent relationships. A study of children exposed to wife assault has shown that the levels of emotional and behavioral problems displayed by them are comparable to those of children who are themselves physically abused (Jaffe, Wolfe, Wilson, & Slusczarzck, 1985). Children who witness violence at home display emotional and behavioral disturbances as diverse as withdrawal, low self-esteem, nightmares, and self-blame, and aggression against peers, family members, and property. For males, growing up in a violent home is the strongest predictor of becoming a batterer in teen and adult years (Dutton, 1988). Males who grow up in a violent home have 10 times the rate of wife beating, compared with males from nonviolent homes (Straus, Gelles, & Steinmetz, 1980). (It is important to note that the majority of boys who witness violence will *not* become abusers as adults.) For females, the relationship between growing up in a violent environment and having a violent partner in adulthood is less straightforward. It appears that girls who grow up witnessing wife assault are not more likely to choose a violent mate but that once they are in a violent relationship they are less likely to leave (Jaffe, Wolfe, & Wilson, 1990).

Children growing up in violent homes may also absorb many negative and dysfunctional messages about the acceptability of violence as a problem-solving strategy, about the worth of women relative to men, and about responsibilities in relationships. These are known as the *subtle symptoms* of living in a violent home as a child (Jaffe et al., 1990). These beliefs and attitudes may become evident in the school environment in the form of negative attitudes toward female teachers and in a propensity to solve peer disagreements with violence.

A major contributing cause of woman abuse and violence in relationships is lack of equality of women and girls in society in terms of empowerment and resources. Devaluation of women and girls is the underlying substrate that allows violence against women to be tolerated and to flourish. Power inequality for females in high schools often is reflected in sexual harassment. Staton and Larkin (1993) have documented the frequency and impact of sexual harassment of girls at school.

Dating violence is another key area to address with high school students. Recent studies show that rates of sexual abuse in dating relationships are very high. For example, Head (1988) found that 25% of female students in her high school sample had been victims of forced intercourse. Koss and her colleagues found that 1 in 4 women in a national U.S. college sample had been victims of rape or attempted rape (Koss, Gidycz, & Wisniewski, 1987). In our own study of students in two high schools, over 21% of female students who were dating reported physical abuse, and 23% reported sexual abuse (Sudermann & Jaffe, 1993).

High schools are, in part, a reflection of a larger society that still condones and promotes violence as an acceptable solution to problems and as legitimate entertainment. Gender inequality in high schools also reflects the gender inequality in society. Prime examples of the prevalence of violence are the media and sports. Videos, movies, music lyrics, television shows, magazines, advertising, and video games are all rife with violent images, and in particular, violence against women.

High school students are well aware of the problems of violence in society and in their own lives. In our discussions with students, we have found that many are concerned about potential violence in dating relationships, peer violence at school, and violence in society in general. A recent large-scale survey of Ontario high school students showed that 82% of students agreed or strongly agreed that schools should have a role in violence prevention (Jaffe, Sudermann, Reitzel, & Killip, 1992).

Given the salience of the problem of violence in intimate relationships and the importance of solving this problem, increasing demands are being made on all institutions and groups to address the issue. Many people are asking how the damage can be avoided before it begins. High schools are uniquely positioned to become involved to change the basic attitudes, values, skills, and learned behavior patterns that underlie and potentiate acts of violence against women and other vulnerable individuals and groups. Schools transmit the knowledge and values of our culture, have access to a large proportion of the young people in our society, and are staffed with professionals whose skills include the ability to influence young persons. High school age youth are in a crucial stage of their development in which they are defining their individual identity and values, as well as forming intimate relationships. Therefore, high schools, in partnership with other community groups, are uniquely positioned to prevent violence.

## SCHOOL-COMMUNITY PARTNERSHIPS: WHO NEEDS TO BECOME INVOLVED?

Successful high school based prevention programs for violence in intimate relationships involve key groups both within the school system and in the community, including students, teachers, parents, school administrators and trustees, survivors of violence, and community agencies that deal with abuse victims and perpetrators.

### Students

Students are key players in any prevention effort and, in our experience, can contribute a great deal in terms of suggesting directions, planning interventions, and presenting interventions to other students. Peer counseling and obtaining student feedback are other ways students can participate. Students respond best to interventions presented, at least in part, by fellow students and also turn to peers for advice and support in far greater numbers than they approach adult counselors. For these reasons, involving students is an invaluable component of planning a prevention program.

### Teachers

Teachers also have a key role in school-based prevention programs. Committed staff can inspire and reinforce students' efforts; conversely, resistant teaching staff members can create confusion for students and severely hamper programs. Professional development, therefore, is of prime importance in creating an atmosphere in which prevention efforts have maximum impact.

### Support Staff

School support staff, including counselors, social workers, and psychologists, are another obvious group to involve. Although many in this group will be aware of the relevance of the topic of violence in relationships, professional development presentations are often necessary to fully inform and involve them. This is because professional education, until very recently, often did not include sufficient preparation in the area of violence in intimate relationships. Secretaries and custodians frequently have one-to-one contact with students and other staff, which makes them important to include in any school professional development activities on the topic of violence in relationships, including how to respond to disclosures of abuse.

## Parents

Parents, when appropriately informed about school-based prevention efforts, are very supportive of prevention efforts for violence in relationships. Presentations at home and school association (or parent-teacher association) meetings and newsletters to parents are two ways to involve and inform parents and prepare them for what their children are about to learn. Parents can participate in planning programs and can serve as resource persons.

## Administrators and Board Members

Support of school administrators and school board members is necessary in developing a sustained and comprehensive violence prevention program. As with teachers, awareness presentations are very important in developing support of these groups. School board meetings may offer an opportunity for a presentation by concerned groups of parents, community members, and administrators. One effective type of presentation is the description of a successful local program. Fear of parents' negative reactions may be a problem that keeps administrators from developing programs, but in our experience, parents are generally a very supportive group.

## Survivors

Survivors of abuse are an important community group to involve in school-based prevention programs. Survivors who have overcome their situations as victims of abuse can make some of the most effective speakers in prevention efforts. Often a survivor who is also a member of the target audience, such as a teacher or administrator, is the most effective choice. Clearly the person involved must feel comfortable in speaking out in this very public manner and should not be pushed into this role under any circumstances.

Within any school system are many unidentified survivors and victims of abuse, and sensitivity to the needs of these persons is important in planning interventions. Sensitivity can be shown through personal support, by making available referrals to counseling as well as excused absences.

**Community Agencies**

Community agencies and groups with expertise in intervention in violence are important groups to involve and are an excellent resource. Local women's shelters, children's aid societies, counseling agencies, and police services are groups to consider. Some communities have coordinating committees of community service agencies that deal with responses to violence against women or children, and these are excellent resources. Community agencies can provide assistance with information, speakers, classroom discussion leaders and can participate in planning and evaluating an intervention.

## GETTING STARTED

Violence prevention can be started in a number of ways. To achieve a large-scale, effective, integrated program, changes must occur at both the classroom and administrative levels, so the best approach may include both top-down *and* bottom-up strategies. Getting started is best done by a person or community agency knowledgeable about violence issues, in partnership with interested persons in the educational system. *Raising awareness* of the issue of violence in relationships with teachers, administrators, or the board of trustees is an excellent starting point. Presentations at regular meetings of these groups can be planned. Helpful components of such a presentation include facts about violence in relationships, the extent of the problem, and the effects on students who witness or are victims of violence. Video resources can be effective in introducing the topic and in showing the educational relevance. For example, the video *The Crown Prince* (MacDonald, Yetman, & Johnston, 1988) is a powerful choice. Beyond the presentation of facts, it is important to make connections between students witnessing violence at home and their behavior and ability to learn at school, between issues of gender inequality and violence against girls and women, and between witnessing violence as a child or teen and becoming an abuser or accepting violence as normal in relationships.

Another good strategy for working with teachers, administrators, and trustees is to have teachers or administrators who already have implemented a violence prevention activity speak about their activity, why they initiated it, what they did, and what student and parent responses were.

Starting with a small-scale program for students in one school or class-room is another good starting point. A community speaker can be invited. One of a number of violence-prevention curricular resources can be used. A review of such materials and ordering information is found in *A.S.A.P.: A School-Based Anti-Violence Program,* a manual for school-based violence prevention (Sudermann, Jaffe, & Hastings, 1993).

Forming a school-based committee to assess a school's needs in violence prevention and to plan a special project in violence prevention can be another excellent starting point. Such a committee serves to raise awareness, provide peer support, and adapt the program to the school. Successful formats for student special events for violence prevention are described in the next section.

## SUCCESSFUL PROGRAMS:
## WHAT WORKS?

Successful programs for preventing wife assault, dating violence, and other forms of violence in relationships are multifaceted and address the root causes of violence, including gender inequality, sex role stereotyping, and acceptance of violence in our culture. In our experience the most successful school-based programs raise awareness and gain support from the broadest spectrum of participants in the school system and the community and are continuing rather than one-time efforts. Important components include teacher and staff professional development, special awareness events for students, integration into the curriculum, and policies and support for handling disclosures of violence by students and teachers.

### Teacher, Staff, and
### Administration Professional Development

Professional development for teachers, staff, and administrators is an essential component for a primary prevention program. Although in most schools some individuals will be knowledgeable and supportive of violence prevention, a larger group will be uninformed, while another group typically will be resistant to the topic at first. Teacher professional development may be viewed as a process in which basic awareness is the starting point, knowledge and skill development come next, and the end goals are attitude change and empowerment for leadership.

Successful basic awareness programs for teachers do the following:

Break the silence around violence in relationships

Give permission to address the issue of violence in school

Present relevant information

Explain how violence fits into existing curriculum

Motivate teachers to become involved at the school level

Connect to existing teacher values and skills (e.g., the concept of teaching the
    whole child, emotional and cognitive development)

Handle resistance in a positive manner

Identify a network of staff committed to this issue

A sample agenda for a large-group basic awareness session for teachers
and administrators is provided in Figure 13.1. Although specific activities
can be adapted to the needs and resources of a particular school or board of
education, several key elements are illustrated in this model. Presentation of
information about wife assault and dating violence, connection of the issue
of violence in relationships to the educational context and the needs of
students, opportunity for small group discussion to process the information
and reactions of the participants, and the use of action planning to involve
the participants in implementing student-oriented activities are all useful
components of such professional development events. At the close of the
event, recruitment of a committee to plan interventions for students can be
undertaken.

**Advanced Teacher Professional Development**

Teachers, like other groups, frequently need several exposures to professional development about violence prevention to move beyond awareness to
attitude change, skill development, and action on behalf of students. Additional topics that can be addressed include handling student disclosures of
violence; dating violence; dealing with violence within the school and
classroom and at extracurricular activities; media literacy and media violence; developing prosocial behaviors and skills with students; and particularly, curriculum resources for violence prevention.

**Resources for Teacher Professional Development**

Resources available to assist in teacher professional development include
videos; fact sheets on wife assault, dating violence, and effects on children
of witnessing wife assault; sample school codes of conduct that address
violence and sexual harassment at school and at school events; sample school

---

**BASIC AWARENESS**
Sample Agenda
Large Group Session for Teachers: 1/2 day to full day

| | |
|---|---|
| INTRODUCTION: | "Why violence prevention is an educational issue" (by school board administrator) |
| PRESENTATION: | Myths and facts about violence in intimate relationships (by community expert or knowledgeable staff member) |
| VIDEO: | *The Crown Prince* <br> Topics include students who witness abuse at home, dating violence, disclosure at school, school and community response. |
| SMALL GROUP DISCUSSION: | Topics from "Discussion Questions" for use with *The Crown Prince* |
| REPORT BACK TO MAIN GROUP: | By small group recorders |
| ACTION PLANNING: | What can we do toward violence prevention at our school? (Give list of ideas) (In small groups) |

**GOALS:**

1. To inform teachers about the prevalence and dynamics of wife assault and dating violence.
2. To illustrate how children and teenagers who witness violence at home are affected in their emotions and school adjustment.
3. To make connections between school and community responses.
4. To stimulate discussion and action planning for school violence prevention programs.
5. To prepare teachers to consider school-based protocols for handling disclosures of violence.

---

**Figure 13.1.** Sample Agenda for Large-Group Basic Awareness Session.

disclosure policies and protocols; sample school brochures listing community resources; and reviews of violence prevention curricula that can be integrated in a wide variety of school subjects at the high school level. These materials and/or source addresses are available in the manual *A.S.A.P.* (Sudermann et al., 1993). Examples are *65 Friendly Lessons on Violence Prevention* (Board of Education for the City of London, 1993), brochures for educators (Victoria County Board of Education, 1989), and the video *The Power to Choose* (National Council of Jewish Women of Greater Minneapolis, 1988).

## Handling Disclosures of Violence

Teachers and administrators need to learn how to handle disclosure of violence from students who are witnessing violence in their homes or who are victims of violence in dating situations. Although many school boards now have protocols for the reporting of child abuse disclosures, disclosures of the above types are often not addressed in school policy. Once basic awareness professional development has been achieved, many teachers will recognize the signs of children who may be witnessing violence; and once student awareness sessions are held, disclosures inevitably happen. Teachers may feel inadequate to handle such disclosures and may fear doing the wrong thing in response. School protocols and information brochures have been developed by a number of boards, and these usually suggest that teachers should:

Listen calmly to the student

Take the information seriously

Reassure the student that he or she is not to blame and that he or she is not alone in having this problem

Be supportive of the student

Never promise confidentiality or "quick fixes" or make other promises that cannot be kept

Avoid displaying strong emotional reaction of shock, disgust, and so forth

Involve appropriate school or system staff (while respecting student's privacy as much as possible)

Consult with local agencies serving victims of violence

Take appropriate action as needed

Seek support for themselves in handling this situation

Action to be taken after disclosures vary according to the situation, the individuals involved, and the resources available. An interview with the student's mother may be indicated; referrals for assistance may also be necessary. To best serve these students, school staff need to discuss the issues and options and then develop a protocol that meets the needs of students and that is complemented by local resources. Staff of women's shelters may be helpful in developing a local protocol. A more complete discussion of this issue can be found in the *A.S.A.P.* document (Sudermann et al., 1993).

**Employee Assistance Programs**

Teachers and staff, too, are victims, survivors, and perpetrators of violence in their intimate relationships. School administrators should take steps to ensure that existing employee assistance programs become attuned to issues of violence in relationships and can offer appropriate counseling and referral to specialized programs. Both administrators and the employee assistance counselors need to be aware of community resources such as women's shelters, legal advice services sensitive to battered women's issues, and programs for batterers. Many administrators and teachers initially are not aware that professionals such as teachers and administrators could be in need of such services, but the need is there. Often a school awareness program will give staff members the impetus to address their own issues in a new way.

## STUDENT PROGRAMS

Two main approaches to student programs are special awareness events and curriculum-based approaches. Both approaches are needed in order to have maximum impact. Special, large-scale awareness events involving the whole school are most effective in breaking the silence around violence in relationships and can provide basic information and start attitude change. More in-depth work can be accomplished by integrating violence prevention issues into different subject areas, including health, English or literature, history, physical education, family studies, studies of law and sociology, personal life management, and others.

**Student Violence Awareness Events**

Large-scale awareness events for high school students are one of the most exciting aspects of violence prevention work. Students usually find the topic of high relevance, and their support and responses tend to be enthusiastic. Students know and will acknowledge that the issue of violence in relationships is a familiar and important issue for them. An illustrative exercise for doubtful teaching staff is to have them ask students in their high school classes how many of them know of violence in dating relationships in their peer group.

Although the grade and age levels included in high school vary across different areas, we have found that the concepts discussed here work well for grade 7 through the most senior grades of high school. Modifications sometimes are needed for grades 7 and 8 or for students in special classes, depending on the social maturity of the group.

The basic format we have employed is a half-day event covering basic awareness around the issues of wife assault, dating violence, and other violence in relationships and including a large group (auditorium) presentation followed by classroom discussion with specially trained facilitators. The large group presentation can consist of a video or a film, or a combination of speakers and video presentations, or a dramatic production by a professional or student drama group. After the auditorium presentation, students return to their classrooms, discuss the issues raised by the presentation, and engage in action planning to address the issue. Facilitators for the discussions may be teachers or school support staff who have received training in this area or community volunteers from agencies that work with issues of violence in relationships and who have also received a training session.

## School Planning Committees

To organize a special event for violence awareness, the formation of a school planning committee is recommended. The committee can begin several months in advance with setting goals for the event, reviewing and booking presentation resources, contacting presenters and community facilitators, and putting other necessary planning in place. This committee can be the same committee that organizes teacher professional development, plans training sessions for the facilitators, and puts together handouts for students and teachers. Representatives of the administration, student counseling services, and students should be included in a planning committee if possible, and consultation with community agencies with expertise in dealing with violence in relationships is recommended. Consideration should be given to informing parents of the special event and to providing such information in an existing newsletter to parents or home and school association meeting. A final meeting of the committee after the event is recommended in order to evaluate the event and the reaction of students and staff.

## Content of Large-Group Violence Awareness Events

We highly recommend having a student introduce the topic in the large group assembly, along with an administrator or a teacher. Introductory remarks are best kept brief. It is usually best if a person who is very knowledgeable about the issues assists the student(s) to prepare the remarks. Dramatic presentations or videos addressing the issues of the impact on children and teens of witnessing wife assault, dating violence, date rape, sexual harassment, and violence and sex role stereotyping in the media are most useful. In our experience, videos or plays that address mainly wife assault issues are not perceived as very relevant by teens. We also have tried speakers from agencies that deal with violence in relationships, such as shelter workers or leaders of treatment groups for batterers. We have found that these talks work better in small group sessions as follow-up to the large-scale awareness sessions. Dramatic presentations by student groups or professional theater groups readily capture student interest. If an original script is developed for the purpose, an advisor who is knowledgeable about issues of violence in relationships can be very helpful. Videos are excellent, both in capturing student attention and in getting considerable information across in a relatively brief time period.

We have found the best student response with a play entitled *Whenever I Feel Afraid* performed by the Toronto theater group Company of Sirens (Grant & Seagrove, 1990). This play deals with events in the lives of two adolescent students, a sister and brother, whose father was abusive to their mother. Issues addressed are wife abuse and its emotional and behavioral impact on adolescents, date rape, sexual harassment in high school, sex role stereotyping, violence in the media, and peer support. Excellent student feedback and attitude change has resulted also with the use of videos such as *Crown Prince* (MacDonald et al., 1988) and *Right From the Start* (Victoria Women's Transition House, 1992). Other videos useful in this context are *Break the Cycle* (Cartmer, 1987) and *Heart on a Chain* (Advanced American Communications, 1991). A review of these videos, together with source addresses and ordering information, is provided in the manual *A.S.A.P.* (Sudermann et al., 1993).

An alternative for the large group presentation is to have an adult survivor of an abusive relationship speak about her or his experiences. High school students have responded well to this voice of experience. Good speakers will feel comfortable sharing their experiences with a large group, have good speaking skills, and be able to talk about their experiences in the dating phase of the relationship and how they gradually became isolated and trapped in the abusive relationship.

## Small Group Discussions

Discussions with students in the classroom setting after the auditorium presentation is a vital component of the prevention program. Students need to process the information and impressions they have received, share views, clarify concepts, and discuss the implications of what they have learned. Information about school and community resources that offer help to victims and perpetrators of violence is also best provided in a small group setting. Handing out a brochure with names and telephone numbers of helping agencies to each student is an excellent step and allows students to share information with family members.

Many students feel pessimistic about solving the problems of violence in relationships unless they have the opportunity to share ideas about action that students and schools can take to address the issue. Therefore, it is helpful to end the small group discussion session with the brainstorming and sharing of ideas on what students can do to end violence in relationships. For example, actions that students have taken include having school poster contests on a theme of ending violence in relationships; producing a play to inform other students and parents about issues of violence in relationships; engaging in fund-raising—car washes, sponsored runs—for a women's shelter; and involving peer counseling programs at school in becoming more attuned to issues of dating violence.

Facilitators of discussions should be knowledgeable about issues of violence in relationships, have good skills for stimulating student discussions, and be sensitive to students who may be having difficulty handling the topic for various reasons. We have had good results by pairing community agency personnel (volunteers) or school support staff with the classroom teacher. Students from school peer support groups also have been employed with success.

Classroom teachers who volunteer to be trained as facilitators for the program have been used successfully. However, it is important not to compel all teachers to take the lead in the small group discussion. Some teachers will not wish to do this because they have personal issues with the topic; others simply may feel unqualified. It is helpful to provide classroom facilitators with a training session covering information that students are likely to ask about and techniques in facilitating discussions. The type and scope of training needed depends on the background of the facilitators. Handouts for facilitators, including background information, suggested discussion questions and techniques, and forms for recording student action planning suggestions, can be distributed at the training session. Evaluation forms for students and/or facilitators and teachers to fill out after the intervention can be included in the handout package.

## Curriculum Integration

The inclusion of violence prevention in regular classroom courses and activities allows for an ongoing, in-depth approach to violence prevention. As mentioned previously, the subject areas in which violence in relationships and related topics can be included are as diverse as health, English literature, family studies, sociology, and history. In addition to imparting basic information about the prevalence and dynamics of violence in relationships, students need to learn the definitions of physical, emotional, and sexual abuse. Dating situations, avoiding being a perpetrator or a victim of date rape, and development of healthy communication in dating relationships will capture students' interest.

An important component to include is the connection between women's lack of personal and economic power and rights throughout history and society's acceptance of violence against women. The impact of changes in the legal and political systems on women's rights and equality can be studied. Topics such as assertiveness, conflict resolution, and other social skills can be taught. Sex role stereotypes and acceptance of violence in media and literature can be taught at appropriate points in the curriculum.

A number of curricula and curricular resources are available to assist the teacher and school that wish to integrate violence prevention in the curriculum. These can be free materials authored by school boards, departments of education, and teachers' federations, or purchased materials. A review of available materials, together with ordering information, appears in *A.S.A.P.* (Sudermann et al., 1993).

## ROADBLOCKS AND HOW TO OVERCOME THEM

Resistance is to be expected when the issue of preventing violence in relationships first is raised in a school or in a school board. It is important to remember that resistance accompanies most major changes in a school system. Handling resistance in a positive and assertive manner is important. A few common issues and possible responses are listed in the following subsections.

### Male Defensiveness

Some teachers, both men and women, will feel that addressing the issue of violence in relationships is "male-bashing" or picking on men. It is important to deal with this perception. Responses include the following:

- Emphasize the role that nonviolent men can play in finding solutions to the problem.
- State that most men do not batter their spouses.

- Focus on responsibility, not blame.
- Suggest that men will benefit from a less violent school and society.

## Insufficient Resources

Some teachers initially will say, "The curriculum is too crowded already; why do we have to address this issue?" They will point out that they do not think they have the expertise to address violence prevention. A response may include the following points:

- Violence prevention is a fundamental need for the functioning of both schools and of teachers, students, and society. Without a safe environment, learning cannot take place.
- Violence prevention can be incorporated into current subject matter in almost all areas.
- Resources are available both within the educational materials and within the community to address issues of violence.
- This is an issue too important to leave to "experts"!

## Relevance

Teachers may believe that violence prevention is not an educational issue. An effective response is to remind teachers of the following:

- Students who are not in a safe home, peer, and school environment may be severely impaired in their ability to learn.
- The child who comes to class after being bullied in the hallway, or after witnessing wife assault at home, or after being abused by a date will not learn effectively, if at all.

Teachers often will be able to identify issues of violence that affect their students once they reflect and discuss the topic. Examples in addition to the personal violence issues raised above include verbal abuse, media violence, and violence in sports. When teachers ask their *students* about the relevance of these issues, the response often convinces the teachers.

## EVALUATION

Evaluation of newly implemented violence prevention programs serves a number of important functions. Evaluation can facilitate the collection and incorporation of feedback from students, teachers, parents, facilitators, and others in the development and refinement of programs. Evaluation of students' and teachers' learning and attitude change also facilitates planning for improvements and allows demonstration of positive results. Other uses of evaluation of our violence prevention programs have been to ascertain the experiences of students and teachers with violence in their own lives, to demonstrate the relevance of the issue for students, to detect areas of backlash and resistance, and to adapt programs to the needs of special groups.

In evaluating school-based violence prevention programs, it is important to distinguish between *process* and *outcome*. Both should be evaluated if possible. *Process evaluation* might seek the opinions of participants about various components of the intervention; *outcome evaluation* might evaluate changes in knowledge, attitudes, and behavioral intentions from before to after the intervention and at a delayed follow-up. With limited resources and without skilled evaluation consultation, it is often best to keep evaluation simple.

One simple but effective strategy we have used is to ask students to write their comments in response to the following question: What feedback and suggestions do you have for the organizing committee of the Violence Prevention Event? This query allows the committee to obtain a wide variety of opinions on both the process and outcomes of the event, which can be used to improve further events. Instruments designed to collect feedback and measure knowledge and attitude changes after prevention programs are contained in the manual *A.S.A.P.* (Sudermann et al., 1993).

## Evaluation Results of Existing Programs

Prevention programs for violence in relationships are so new that only a few evaluations have been done. One program that has been evaluated is of the Coalition for Battered Women School Curriculum Project (Jones, 1987). This program consisted of 5 or 6 days of intervention for students in grades 7 to 12, during which both attitudes and knowledge about wife assault and dating violence were targeted. Results showed positive changes in knowledge, but no attitude changes. This result may reflect on the relatively brief, five-item assessment measure that was employed.

Two large-scale evaluations of programs conducted in the London, Ontario, schools have shown very encouraging results. The first study (Jaffe et al., 1992) evaluated a primary prevention program for wife assault and dating violence undertaken jointly by the Board of Education for the City of London, the London Family Court Clinic, and numerous community agency volunteers. The intervention involved professional development of teachers and administrators, as well as special violence prevention awareness events for all high school students in the system. The evaluation focused on the violence prevention program for students. The intervention involved a large-group auditorium presentation, followed by classroom discussions facilitated jointly by knowledgeable community professionals and teachers. Two schools employed a full-day intervention, and two schools employed a half-day intervention. The auditorium presentations varied somewhat from one school to another, depending on the input of school-based planning committees. Speakers from community agencies, videos on wife assault and the effects on teens who witness wife assault, plays by professional and student theater groups, and talks by a survivor of abuse were employed.

A random sample of subjects for the study were selected from four high schools. A total of 737 students completed the evaluation surveys. A 48-item questionnaire—the London Family Court Clinic Questionnaire on Violence in Intimate Relationships—was employed. This questionnaire was designed to tap knowledge about wife assault, beliefs and attitudes about violence in marital and dating relationships, and behavioral intentions to intervene in dating violence situations. Questionnaires were administered 1 week prior to intervention, about 1 week after intervention, and, at two schools, also at 6 weeks after intervention.

Results indicated significant changes in the desired direction for female students on 11 of the 48 items and no changes in the undesired direction, with stability of these positive changes at follow-up. Knowledge, attitudes, and behavioral intentions all showed areas of positive change for females. For males, 8 of 48 items showed significant change in the positive direction, including changes in knowledge, attitudes, and behavioral intentions. However, seven attitude items and one behavioral intention item showed change in the undesired direction for males, with the majority of these negative changes relating to attitudes about dating violence.

Significant and consistent differences were found in students' attitudes about violence in intimate relationships, with females having more positive attitudes than males both at pre- and postintervention. Also more females than males were aware of violence in their own or a peer's dating relationships (60.5% of females vs. 47.5% of males). These findings indicated that females may be more sensitive to issues of violence in relationships and more supportive of women's equality in intimate relationships. The results also indicated that females benefited more than males from the intervention, and that, in particular, females showed more positive attitude change after the intervention. This study, together with reports of classroom facilitators, suggested that future directions for intervention might include adaptations to reduce male defensiveness and backlash. The study also showed that both student knowledge and attitudes can be positively affected by a relatively brief intervention.

A second evaluation of an intervention program for violence in intimate relationships was completed in two high schools from two Ontario school boards (Sudermann & Jaffe, 1993). These two schools—one from the public board of education and one from the Roman Catholic separate school board in London, Ontario—joined together in planning a half-day program on prevention of dating violence. The program had a high level of student input in planning and organizing the events. Peer support groups from each school, together with school administrators, presented separate programs for the junior grades (9 and 10) and senior grades (11 to OAC [grade 13]). The junior group viewed a video on dating violence prevention (*Right From the Start*) and saw a play (*I Love You, But . . .*) by an amateur drama group. Classroom discussion followed. Senior students attended their choice of two workshops from offerings by 22 community presenters on topics related to prevention of violence in relationships.

All students at each school completed a revised 32-item version of the London Family Court Clinic Questionnaire on Violence in Intimate Relationships both before and after the intervention. Students also wrote comments and suggestions about the program at posttest. The total sample was 1,547 students: 672 in grades 9 and 10, and 875 in grades 11 to 13. Of these, 1,112 were present at the pretest, intervention, and posttest occasions, and this smaller sample was retained for analysis, yielding 488 in grades 9 and 10 and 624 in grades 11 to 13.

For grades 9 and 10, significant positive changes in knowledge, attitude, and behavioral intentions occurred for both females and males. Female results showed positive changes on 8 of 29 items; male results showed positive changes on 7 of 29 items. For males, only one item showed significant change in the undesired direction ("Poverty causes family violence"). This question was not a specific target of the particular intervention, which was focused on dating violence, rather than on family violence.

For grades 11 to 13, positive changes occurred on 7 of 29 items for females, and for 2 of 29 items for males. Changes in the undesired direction occurred on one attitude item for males and a different one for females in grades 11 to 13. These were again family violence items, which were not emphasized in the dating violence intervention. For both junior and senior students, marked sex differences in attitudes were found, with females having more positive attitudes pre- and post-intervention.

Also of considerable interest were the results of three questions addressing experience of violence in dating relationships. Females reported experiencing considerable verbal, physical, and sexual abuse in dating relationships. Of 44.3% females who indicated they were currently dating, 57.3% reported experiencing verbal abuse in a dating relationship; 23.3%, sexual abuse; and 21.4%, physical abuse. The comparable percentages for boys were 32.6%, verbal abuse; 3.3%, sexual abuse; and 7.2%, physical abuse. Student comments about the intervention were overwhelmingly positive and supported the relevance of the topic for adolescents. A few extremely hostile comments were also noted. A few comments indicated indifference.

Taken together, the results from this study show positive results for the intervention for the male and female junior students and positive results for the female senior students. Senior male students did not respond as positively. This may be because some older male students are already entrenched in violent dating patterns, and so the program causes them to feel defensive and resistant. Another explanation may be that the video/play format was more effective for males than the elective workshop format employed with the older students.

Future directions suggested by this study are that the confounding of age and type of intervention need to be disentangled in future research designs. It also seems well worth studying the benefit of intervention with younger, predating males, possibly in grades 7 and 8.


## CONCLUSION

Preventing violence in relationships is an important issue for high schools to address. Preventing violence is an issue that the vast majority of students identify as an important topic to learn about in school. High school students are in a crucial stage of their lives, in which they are experimenting with relationships and forming their beliefs and values. High schools are uniquely positioned to reach a large proportion of our communities' youth, to challenge and shape their attitudes, and to teach them skills for nonviolent relationships. Effective programs exist that have proven their value in addressing the issue of violence in relationships. Although questions still remain to be addressed regarding the long-term effects of such programs and the need for secondary prevention for students who already are deeply entrenched in violent relationship patterns, the potential of primary prevention in high schools is clearly great. As with the issue of drinking and driving, large-scale attitude changes can be achieved regarding violence in relationships. Adolescents can play a critical role in shaping a nonviolent society and in offering assistance to peers trapped in violent relationships.

# REFERENCES

Advanced American Communications (Producer). (1991). *Heart on a chain: The truth about date violence* [Videotape No. 5735]. Oakville, Ontario: Magic Lantern Communications Ltd. (Tel. No. 416-827-1155)

Board of Education for the City of London. (1993). *65 friendly lessons on violence prevention.* London, Ontario: Author.

Cartmer, D. (Producer). (1987). *Break the cycle* [Videotape]. St. Catherines, Ontario: Esprit Films. (Tel. No. 905-685-8336)

Dutton, D. G. (1988). *The domestic assault of women: Psychological and criminal justice perspectives.* Boston: Allyn & Bacon.

Grant, C., & Seagrove, S. (Writers). (1990). *Whenever I feel afraid* [Play]. Toronto: Company of Sirens, Theater Action in Education. (Tel. No. 416-975-9642)

Head, S. (1988). *A study of attitudes and behaviour in dating relationships with special reference to the use of force.* Scarborough: Board of Education for the City of Scarborough.

Jaffe, P. G., Sudermann, M., Reitzel, D., & Killip, S. M. (1992). An evaluation of a secondary school primary prevention program on violence in relationships. *Violence and Victims, 7,* 129-146.

Jaffe, P. G., Wolfe, D. A., & Wilson, S. K. (1990). *Children of battered women.* Newbury Park, CA: Sage.

Jaffe, P. G., Wolfe, D. A., Wilson, S. K., & Slusczarzck, M. (1985). Similarities in behavior and social maladjustment among child victims and witnesses to family violence. *American Journal of Orthopsychiatry, 56,* 142-146.

Jones, L. E. (1987). *Dating violence among Minnesota teenagers: A summary of survey results.* St. Paul: Minnesota Coalition for Battered Women.

Koss, M. P., Gidycz, C. A., & Wisniewski, N. (1987). The scope of rape: Incidence and prevalence of sexual aggression and victimization in a national sample of higher education students. *Journal of Consulting and Clinical Psychology, 55,* 162-170.

MacDonald, J., & Yetman, C. (Producers), & Johnston, A. K. (Director). (1988). *The crown prince* [Videotape No. 113C 0188037]. Ottawa: National Film Board of Canada.

MacLeod, L. (1987). *Battered but not beaten: Preventing wife beating in Canada.* Ottawa: Canadian Advisory Council on the Status of Women.

Mercer, S. L. (1987). *Not a pretty picture: An exploratory study of violence against women in high school dating relationships.* Toronto: Education Wife Assault.

National Council of Jewish Women of Greater Minneapolis (Producer). (1988). *The power to choose* [Videotape]. Toronto: Kinetic. (Tel. No. 416-963-5979)

Smith, M. D. (1987). The incidence and prevalence of wife abuse in Toronto. *Violence and Victims, 2,* 173-187.

Staton, P., & Larkin, J. (1993). *Sexual harassment: The intimidation factor.* Toronto: Green Dragon.

Straus, M. A., Gelles, R. J. (1986). Societal change and change in family violence rates from 1975 to 1985 as revealed by two national surveys. *Journal of Marriage and the Family, 48,* 465-479.

Straus, M. A., Gelles, R. J., & Steinmetz, S. (1980). *Behind closed doors.* Garden City, NY: Doubleday.

Sudermann, M., & Jaffe, P. G. (1993, August). *Violence in teen dating relationships: Evaluation of a large-scale primary prevention program.* Paper presented at the Annual Meeting of the American Psychological Association, Toronto.

Sudermann, M., Jaffe, P. G., & Hastings, E. (1993). *A.S.A.P.: A school-based anti-violence program.* (Available from London Family Court Clinic, 254 Pall Mall St., Suite 200, London, Ontario CANADA N6A 5P6) (ISBN 1-895953-01-04)

Toufexis, A. (1987, December 21). Home is where the hurt is: Wife beating among the well-to-do is no longer a secret. *Time, 138*(25), 68.

Victoria County Board of Education. (1989). *Wife assault: Family violence, an educational issue* [Brochure]. (Available from Victoria County Board of Education, P.O. Box 420, Lindsay, Ontario, CANADA K9V 4S3; Tel. No. 705-324-6776)

Victoria Women's Transition House (Producer). (1992). *Right from the start* [Videotape]. Toronto: Kinetic. (Tel. No. 416-963-5979)

# 14

# Strategies to Address Violence in the Lives of High-Risk Youth

DAVID A. WOLFE
CHRISTINE WEKERLE
DEBORAH REITZEL
ROBERT GOUGH

The need to develop effective prevention strategies to reduce violence toward women and children is critical. Research surveys indicate that approximately 3 to 4 million American households (National Center on Child Abuse and Neglect, 1988; Straus & Gelles, 1990) and 500,000 Canadian households (MacLeod, 1987) experience a significant degree of violence directed at women and/or children every year. Adolescents, both male and female, represent a major high-risk group for sexual abuse and sexual assault victimization and offenses. The victimization rate for women, for example, peaks in the 16- to 19-year-old age group (Koss, Gidycz, & Wisniewski, 1987). A recent Canadian study revealed that 42% of 202 college-age men had engaged in some form of courtship violence (Barnes, Greenwood, & Sommer, 1991), which concurs with the majority of U.S. studies indicating that between 15% and 25% of male college students (Malamuth, Sockloskie, Koss, & Tanaka, 1991) and between 9% and 39% of high school students (Girshick, 1993) engage in some level of sexual or physical aggression toward women. Moreover, male adolescents account for about one quarter of sexual abuse offenders (Rogers, 1990).

Recently our understanding of the causes and the developmental course of violence against women and children has grown significantly, allowing prevention efforts to be generated from a reasonable knowledge base (Health and Welfare Canada, 1989). For example, a consistent finding is that children with a history of family disruption and violence are at an elevated risk of becoming victims or perpetrators of violence toward others, especially during mid to late adolescence (Dutton, 1988; Widom, 1989). Abuse experiences in one's family of origin create a vulnerability for further victimization by others (especially among young women), as well as a propensity to use power and control as a means of resolving conflict (especially among young men). In addition to prior abuse experiences, the risk of becoming a victim or perpetrator of violence increases as a result of negative influences from peers (condoning violence), the absence of compensatory factors (e.g., success at school; a healthy relationship with siblings and friends), and the relative lack of alternative sources of information, all of which serve to counteract existing biases, attitudes, and beliefs (Jessor, 1993).

Processes associated with adolescent development and dating experiences suggest that this period of development may be crucial to the formation of healthy, nonviolent relationships later in life. Adolescence is a period of development in which many of the risk factors relating to interpersonal violence become more pronounced. Today's youth grow up in a world of mixed messages, in which popular television shows and musical groups glamorize violence and present it as a commonplace and acceptable means of dealing with problems. As well, youth are beginning to form intimate and dating relationships, and they inform us that they would be unlikely to disclose victimization experiences to an adult, mostly because they are poorly informed of what is normative dating behavior and what resources and actions are available for victims and offenders (Reitzel & Wolfe, 1993). Such relationships, however, often put pressure on the teen to conform to gender-specific roles (Windle, 1992). Typically boys are socialized to be strong, uncommunicative, competitive, and in control, and girls to be submissive, responsible for the well-being of relationship/family, other-oriented, and to not express anger (Serbin, Powlishta, & Gulko, 1993). These stereotypical roles, in turn, become salient during adolescence and serve to reinforce negative attitudes and power imbalances in male/female relationships (Dobash & Dobash, 1979). Yet adolescence also represents important learning opportunities. The transitional nature and normal disequilibrium that accompany adolescent development may represent an especially sensitive and hence opportune time for early intervention and enhancement experiences (Kazdin, 1993).

For these reasons, dating violence may represent a bridge between experiences of maltreatment and witnessing wife assault in childhood and the occurrence of similar personal violence or victimization in adulthood, and consequently offers a prime opportunity to educate around issues concerning relationships. For example, studies reveal that abuse among teen dating partners is almost as widespread and frequent as in adult relationships (Girshick, 1993) and resembles adult patterns as well: a building of tension, an explosion of anger, and a honeymoon period of making up (Walker, 1989). Such behavior most often appears around 15 or 16 years of age (Bethke & DeJoy, 1993) and includes a broad spectrum of physically and sexually violent acts ranging from slapping and pushing to beating or threatening the other partner with severe violence. Sudermann and Jaffe (1993), for example, recently reported that in a sample of 1,547 high school students in Canada, more than 50% of the girls and 30% of the boys reported some form of verbal and emotional abuse by dating partners. Among the 9th and 10th graders, 40% of females reported having experienced emotional or verbal abuse from boys they were dating casually, while 59% reported having experienced physical abuse and 28% having experienced sexual abuse in a steady dating relationship.

The degree of acceptance of violence among teens is reflected in Sudermann and Jaffe's findings that about 20% of *male* students said that forced intercourse was all right "if he spends money on her," "he is stoned or drunk," or "if they had been dating for a long time." Roscoe's (1985) survey of 126 *female* college students found a similarly high level of acceptance: 70% of the sample listed at least one form of violence as acceptable in a dating relationship, and 80% mentioned situations in which physical force was tolerable. Although slapping was cited as acceptable most often (49%), punching was seen as acceptable by a full 21%! In explaining their choices, these young women thought violence was acceptable in self-defense, to get a partner's attention, and when acting out of jealousy. It is also noteworthy that 18% of these women thought violence was acceptable if the couple was "playing," and 17% thought violence was acceptable if the partner was "out of control." These findings help us understand that the relatively "low level" acts of violence that are commonplace among teen relationships may be a reasonable point of entry in educating young men and women about the significance and risk of coercion and abuse of power and control during the formative stages of dating.

What indications do we get from interviews and surveys of the causes or risk factors associated with such violence? In a review of survey data, Girshick (1993) reports that jealousy and alcohol consumption are the most common proximal reasons for violence in relationships proffered by the teens themselves (other reasons included other drugs, anger, sexual rejection, pushing for sexual favors, friends, and family). Researchers, on the other hand, emphasize the fact that teens live in a society where violence is relatively commonplace and often is considered a normal and acceptable means to an end. Moreover, violence is expressed in our culture through racism, sexism, and classism that justifies group superiority and reinforces the myth that victims are to blame for their own abuse (Levy, 1991).

In light of these concerns, the scope of this chapter involves a delineation of social/developmental risk factors derived from feminist and social learning theories regarding violence against women and children. We underscore that no single cause or etiologically common pathway will suffice in conceptualizing such behavior, and thus it is essential to combine and integrate different, yet compatible, perspectives on the problem into a multilevel conceptual framework. Our approach to the prevention of gender-based violence presented herein combines psychological literature with feminist theory. The psychological literature identifies those factors that increase the risk of youth violence, while feminist theory identifies the abuse as gender-specific (male to female). Following discussion of these prominent risk factors, we present a prevention focus specific to violence in relationships among youth, along with pilot findings of our early intervention program.


## RISK AND PROTECTIVE FACTORS
## IN ADOLESCENT RELATIONSHIPS

Causes and correlates of violence in adolescent dating and peer relationships have been likened to the same processes associated with violence against adult women (Makepeace, 1981; Walker, 1989), such as the abuse of power and control over one's partner and an inability or reluctance to leave the abusive partner. Disturbingly, teen victims of violence often behave in a manner not unlike that of battered women; that is, they have particular difficulty recognizing their own abuse and leaving abusive relationships (Girshick, 1993). This behavior may be due to processes of socialization of girls, such that they are more likely to believe that they—not males—are responsible for maintaining relationships. Thus some teens are adjusting to violence as a normal course of intimate relationships, which serves as a beginning to an unhealthy pattern of intimate interaction that extends into adulthood.

The beginning stages of the abuse of power and control, coercive or violent behaviors in relationships, and similar exploitative or power assertive behaviors, define what we mean by "risk" of becoming involved in a violent relationship during adolescence. Several of the more critical risk and protective factors associated with an adolescent's social environment, family and peer environment, personality formation, and behavioral adjustment are discussed below in an effort to develop a prevention focus specific to violence in relationships among youth.

## Social Environment

Prevention initiatives directed at ending violence in relationships must attempt to incorporate an analysis of the social environment where the violent behaviors are learned and reinforced. The existing literature points to the acceptance of male violence, gender inequality, and patriarchal social institutions as major social factors that can be linked to adolescent and adult violence against women and children (see Dobash & Dobash, 1979; Health and Welfare Canada, 1989). In particular, prevention and educational efforts should include a discussion of those areas where some groups in our society hold disproportionate power to corresponding groups and where this power is abused. The connections should be made clear between sexism that underlies violence against women and other forms of oppression and intolerance of differences among people (e.g., adultism, ageism, heterosexism, ableism, classism, racism; Creighton, 1990).

Access to community resources, public education and awareness about violence, antiviolence education in schools, social action promoting antiviolence messages, and values of cooperation and mutual support have been suggested as positive ways to combat the influence of existing and pervasive negative socialization agents. For example, evidence suggests that, to counter values of individualism and competitiveness with values of cooperation and mutual support, youth can be empowered to oppose the various forms of violence and oppression that surround them. The active agent in empowerment is participation, and a cooperative peer model encourages youth to support one another while providing a venue to model positive attitudes and values. The essential qualities of healthy relationships are developed where youth have the opportunity to work together toward common goals in a respectful, supportive group setting.

A growing, yet still minority, perspective on youth places less emphasis on their wrongdoings and takes more interest in how youth serve as resources to their families, schools, and communities. In this regard, youth must be supported with the information and skills needed to be actively involved in working toward prosocial change in the youth subculture and in their broader environment. Recent evaluations of cooperative learning programs and those programs that place peers in teaching positions indicate increases in social interaction, peer acceptance, and greater acceptance of peers with physical and/or mental disabilities after such learning opportunities (e.g., Johnson &

Johnson, 1986; Maheady, 1988; Mesch, 1986; Strain, 1985) and between white and nonwhite peers (Rooney-Rebeck & Jason, 1986; Slavin & Oickle, 1981).

## Family and Peer Environment

The pathways through which caregivers and peers may influence an individual's expression of aggression and violence in relationships are complex. Although no clear evidence points to which factors are necessary and sufficient and how they may exert their influence over time, several important risk factors connected with this domain merit consideration. Dix (1991), for example, notes the similarities in parenting styles among abusive, depressed, and distressed parents. Increased negative affect and the use of arbitrary, restrictive, and punitive strategies are common, with a concomitant decrease in positive affect or positive control strategies. Such a child-rearing environment fails to promote cooperative or healthy relationships or to foster empathic or altruistic responses to others and is strongly linked to child antisocial behavior (Greenberg, Speltz, & DeKlyen, 1993; Vuchinich, Bank, & Patterson, 1992; Wahler & Dumas, 1986).

The backgrounds and peer relationships of violent adolescents are similar to those above, marked by high rates of abuse, neglect, and parental deviance, as well as low rates of positive communication and emotional expression (Loeber, Weissman, & Reid, 1983). Lower levels of family adaptability and cohesion among families with an adolescent assaultive offender also have been found, suggesting rigid family structures in which members are emotionally disengaged (Blaske, Borduin, Henggeler, & Mann, 1989). Such negative family experiences and low emotional investment, in turn, prompt the youth to become attached more closely to his or her peer group, which, unfortunately, has an increased likelihood of social deviance and aggressivity (Elliot, Huizinga, & Ageton, 1985). It is our contention that a similar process may explain the formation of perpetrator behaviors or victimization that emerges in the course of dating relationships (see also Burke, Stets, & Pirog-Goode, 1989).

## Personality and Behavior

Another domain of risk and protective factors associated with violence against women concerns various personality characteristics and disorders. The personality features of violent *adult males* that have received some empirical support relate to dimensions concerning *the need for power and control, hostility toward women, poor emotional control and excessive jealousy, and traditional sex role attitudes* (Reitzel & Wolfe, 1993). Although clinically reported, empirical evidence for the significance of self-esteem, impulsivity, intolerance of others, and low empathy is limited at present (Holzworth-Munroe, 1992). Moreover, despite tentative links between several identified personality dimensions and wife assault, no causal mechanisms or explanations can be readily drawn from these findings at present (Dutton, 1988; Walker, 1989).

Power issues frequently are described by male batterers attending treatment programs. Batterers interpret female independence as a loss of their control, leading the men to persuade or coerce their spouses into adopting the batterers' definition of relationship structure and function (Dutton & Browning, 1988). For example, domestically violent couples engage in interactions in which the husband makes increased demands for power or authority in the context of spousal withdrawal more often than do nonviolent distressed or control couples (Babcock, Waltz, Jacobson, & Gottman, 1993). In addition to a need for power and control, violent men also show a significant lack of assertiveness skills. Such lack of skill in expressing emotion, it is reasoned, results in chronic feelings of frustration and increased likelihood of violent means to attain greater control in the relationship (Dutton & Strachan, 1987; Holtzworth-Munroe, 1992).

Researchers and clinicians (e.g., Dutton, 1988; Gondolf, 1985) have theorized also that violent men have difficulty acknowledging and expressing feelings other than anger and that men in general are more likely to label any form of arousal as anger. This view is congruent with the descriptions provided by battered women of their partners, in which anger and jealousy frequently are mentioned as instigating factors. Jealousy produces a range of behavioral responses, such as aggression and increased vigilance, as well as affective reactions, such as rage and depression (Dutton, 1988). Moreover, sexual jealousy (a form of expressing power and control) is one of the most commonly reported features of the battering relationship (Walker, 1989).

The manner in which some men are invested in stereotyped, traditional gender roles has been studied in relation to trait characteristics of male batterers. Despite the appeal (and perhaps validity) of a sex role socialization explanation for woman abuse, however, in a recent review of this literature Reitzel and Wolfe (1993) concluded that as many studies substantiate this theory as do not find such a relationship. This ambiguity was clarified partially by a recent study in which a path analytic procedure was used to predict severe marital violence. Stith and Farley (1993) demonstrated that *sex role egalitarianism* and approval of marital violence both had direct effects on violent behavior; moreover, sex role egalitarianism and the observation of marital violence as a child had indirect effects on violence by

several pathways as well. These findings, coupled with the emergent literature on early childhood experiences and dating and peer behavior, reveal the
importance of socialization influences on the formation of stable beliefs and
behavior patterns that condone violence in relationships.

## AN EARLY INTERVENTION
## PROGRAM FOR YOUTH

The scope of violence in adolescent and adult relationships and the ensuing
mental health problems, coupled with the magnitude of effort required once
the problems have crystallized, make prevention a critical priority. Prevention and early intervention efforts aimed at related problems among youth
(e.g., alcohol and drug programs, delinquency, smoking) have convinced us,
however, that although information and educational efforts are extremely
important, such efforts may be insufficient by themselves in bringing about
future changes in behavior (Dryfoos, 1990). The most promising strategy in
this regard appears to be directed at youth at a point in time prior to the onset
of the problem behavior, in an attempt to educate and inoculate persons with
information and skills that counter sociocultural influences. Effective programs follow from an understanding of likely causes and risk factors, draw
on theories and models of human behavior that direct the focus of intervention, use intervention techniques that are known to change behavior, and
monitor implementation rigorously (Kazdin, 1993).

From the general framework of risk and protective factors described above,
we developed an early intervention strategy to prevent violence in relationships
among at-risk youth. Ours is a proactive, competency-enhancement approach, rather than a "treatment" per se, which was designed to build strengths,
resilience, and coping skills as a way of enhancing functioning. Every aspect
of the program, from the material presented to the relationships between
facilitators and participants, was designed to model appropriate use of power
and to support youth empowerment.

### Facilitators

Group facilitators possess varying degrees of power and privilege (e.g.,
white, male, adult, group facilitator), and it is essential that they have a clear
understanding of their use of this power. We inform them that we have videos,
information, and skills to give them so that they can let us know what is most
helpful. We also provide them with the skills and information they need to
help themselves and other teens who are at risk of experiencing or perpetrating

abuse. After all, empowerment is about sharing information and resources to enable one to help oneself. This strategy stands in sharp contrast to many existing programs whose goal is to "change" or "fix" youth and that may, in fact, model precisely the violence or power struggles they are hoping to end. When we invite youth involvement, therefore, it is important to be honest about our desire to learn from them about how to stop violence in relationships.

Establishing a "teen-centered" environment is also essential to the success of a group program on violence prevention. More important than the content of information and skills is the integrity of the facilitators in their honesty and their modeling of noncontrolling communication. Program staff should outline clearly the purpose of the group and present the information they will cover during their time together. They should frame a group agreement around what the *youth* want in order to create a safe environment and to discuss sensitive and sometimes personal information. Thus, at the outset of the group, the facilitators must acknowledge directly the power and privilege they hold; although facilitators present information and help guide discussions, the group belongs to the youth. The facilitators will not punish or try to control, but will support what the group chooses to do in response to disruptive behavior or problems that arise during the group.

## Group Structure and Procedures

The program described is operated as a 16-week group format that meets 1 day per week for 2 hours. Typically 8 to 12 male and female participants are in each group, selected on the basis of teacher nomination or referral, self-referral, or random selection from the open caseloads of child protective services (see Wolfe & Wekerle, 1993, for research design details). The program format is organized around three main goals: (a) to *raise awareness* of cognitive foundations of proaggressive attitudes and beliefs toward women and self-awareness of the same, (b) to support *skill and behavior development* regarding noncontrolling, nonviolent communication skills, and (c) to consolidate learning of new attitudes and skills and to increase competency through *community involvement and social action*. An overview of these goals, the background literature supporting them, and the specific objectives and intervention plan corresponding to each weekly session is included in Table 14.1.

*Understanding and Awareness of Violence.* The first section of the program is aimed at establishing an understanding of gender stereotypes, negative attitudes toward women, and a reduction in tolerance (or acceptance) of men's violence in intimate relationships. People often do not define violence

**Table 14.1**   Promoting Healthy, Nonviolent Relationships

---

Overview of Project
**SECTION I**

GOAL:   TO RAISE AWARENESS OF COGNITIVE FOUNDATIONS OF
PROAGGRESSIVE ATTITUDES AND BELIEFS TOWARD
WOMEN, AND SELF-AWARENESS OF SAME

Background:   Recent literature has shown that violence against women (e.g., wife
assault, date rape) is defined as the use of power of men over
women to control or dominate them. Myths (e.g., it is a private
family matter; women enjoy the abuse or would leave; alcohol
causes the abuse) about violence against women serve to minimize
and perpetuate the problem. Negative images about women are
promoted in advertising and the media and are modeled in our
culture. Boys are socialized to be strong, uncommunicative,
competitive, and in control. Girls are socialized to be submissive,
responsible for the well-being of relationship/family,
other-oriented, and not to express anger. It is clear that these
stereotypical roles reinforce negative attitudes and power
imbalances in male/female relationships.

Education and raised awareness concerning the facts about myths
and stereotypes are seen as key intervention strategies to counter
negative attitudes and beliefs toward women and male/female
relationships.

Constructs:   Power and Control

Myths About Abuse

Stereotypical Roles

Attitudes Toward Marriage

| Objectives | Intervention Plan |
|---|---|
| Define wife assault, clarify myths, and counter "just deserts" belief | Raise awareness and counteract myths (re: wife assault, date rape) |
| Examine social acceptance of violence | Define violence as control/abuse of power |
| | Inoculation: show how negative attitudes are disguised as acceptance through media, comedy, music |
| Review, assimilate, and strengthen learning gained to date | Rehearsal and repetition of prosocial responses through activities designed by youth (video debate, "Degrassi talks," talk show format) |
| Awareness of how we choose partners | Explore how we choose partners (Same as friendships? If not, why? How are expectations and roles different?) |
| Examine gender and family role rigidity | Discuss how sexist stereotypes are linked to men's violence in relationships |

**Table 14.1** *Continued*

## SECTION II

GOAL: TO EXAMINE AND MODIFY BEHAVIORAL AND AFFECTIVE APPROACHES TO CONFLICT AND TO THE USE OF CONTROLLING METHODS OF MALE/FEMALE COMMUNICATION AND SEXUAL BEHAVIOR

Background: Behavior and communication must be consistent with attitude changes and the balance of power in equal male/female relationships. To counter stereotypical roles, boys must learn to identify and express feelings assertively, recognize and respect the personal rights of female partners and own responsibility for their behavior. Girls must be supported in their personal rights, learn to take care of their own safety, and to express themselves assertively. Modeling and rehearsal of negotiation skills, effective communication skills, healthy egalitarian relationships and responding to negative attitudes is essential to counter controlling behaviors in abusive relationships and to reinforce positive attitudes.

Constructs: Responsibility

Safety

Effective, noncontrolling communication

Inoculation re: negative attitudes and beliefs

Constructive communication

Noncoercive sexual behavior

| Objectives | Intervention Plan |
|---|---|
| Develop skills to counter sexist attitudes and stereotypes, as well as to inoculate against negative peer pressure | Role-play alternative responses to "locker scene" |
| | Explore appropriate and inappropriate expression of anger (anger is a healthy feeling and does not cause the abuse) |
| | Personal inventories (self-awareness) of how individuals respond to anger and other feelings |
| | Learning to identify and express feelings |
| Define, discuss, and practice: a. being clear (personal safety) | Examine costs of abusive behavior: toward commitment against violence |
| | Inoculation: skills practiced to counter negative attitudes and pressure from peers |
| b. noncontrolling communication skills | Teach and role-play noncontrolling communication skills (esp. for boys) and personal safety (esp. for girls), e.g., assertiveness skills, "saying what you mean," negotiating skills |

**Table 14.1**   *Continued*

| Objectives | Intervention Plan |
|---|---|
| Increase social competence | Rehearsal and repetition of prosocial responses: |
| | a. Role-plays in dating situations to practice saying or accepting "no" to sexual advances, define consent |
| | b. Inoculation: skills practiced to counter negative attitudes/pressure from peers |
| | Peer modeling of prosocial attitudes through involvement of past group members |
| Explore "self-emphasis" belief (getting own needs met with no regard for others) | Define date rape, male responsibility for consent, hearing "no" messages |
| | Examine limitations and alternatives to sexist stereotypes |

in the same way. In particular, high-risk youth who may have witnessed or experienced violence at home may define only the more extreme forms of physical abuse as "violence." Furthermore, myths about violence against women (e.g., It is a private family matter; women enjoy the abuse or they would leave; when women say no, they really mean yes) serve to minimize and perpetuate the problem, and negative images about women are promoted in advertising and the media and are modeled in our culture. It is therefore important to begin at this stage to have a consistent working definition of abuse for the purposes of the group. A commonly accepted definition of violence is any act or behavior that is an attempt to control or dominate another person, a definition we augment by defining the various forms of abuse used to control others. The "Power and Control Wheel" developed by the Domestic Abuse Intervention Project in Duluth, Minnesota (Pence & Paymar, 1993), is an excellent illustration of the various forms of abuse used as tactics of control by men in abusive relationships.

   The definition of abuse must be placed in the broader social context by defining power and nonpower groups that exist in our culture as a result of power imbalances and labels placed on individuals. A helpful visual presentation

**Table 14.1** *Continued*

---

### SECTION III

GOAL: TO CONSOLIDATE LEARNING OF NEW ATTITUDES
AND SKILLS AND TO INCREASE COMPETENCY
THROUGH COMMUNITY INVOLVEMENT AND SOCIAL
ACTION

Background: To increase social competency, teens need to be empowered to
create change in their own lives and to have a positive impact in
their community. Research into meaningful work and community
service with adolescents has shown that "such opportunities help
young people to feel connected and needed, and to demonstrate
their competence" (Pransky, 1991).

When young people are seen as meaningful and contributing
members of the community, there follows an improvement in
self-respect and in the perception of the young by the community.
Through exposure to community services available to abused
women and their families, the ability of young people to access
these services for themselves or their friends is increased. Being
involved in a meaningful community activity is a source of pride
for young people and builds on their investment to end violence
against women.

Involvement in social action and promoting a "cause" they
believe in motivates attitude change and the incorporation
of noncontrolling behaviors learned in the program.

Follow-up support for individual needs and group activities for
young people toward ending violence in their lives and in the
community further reinforces and integrates commitment to
long-term change.

Constructs: Social competence

Social action

| Objectives | Intervention Plan |
|---|---|
| Identify and rehearse accessing community resources | Introduction to and practice in accessing community resources to resolve given scenarios |
| | Share experiences of agency visits and group discussion of action plans of each scenario |
| Discuss and act on what we as individuals and as a group can do to end violence against women in our community | Community involvement to reinforce nonviolence (fund-raiser for local women's shelter) |

of this concept was developed by Creighton (1990); the following is an adaptation of this table:

| Power Groups | Nonpower Groups |
| --- | --- |
| white | people of color |
| men | women |
| adult | youth |
| adult | elderly |
| rich | poor |
| heterosexual | gay/lesbian/bisexual |

It is important to acknowledge the different power and privilege ascribed to some groups because the abuse experience for some individuals may be more systemic and complex than others. For example, a disabled native woman would face far more barriers than a white adult man. In one instance, a teenage girl in the group denied that the white male facilitator held any more power. It was important for her and other participants to hear that if we fit into one of these nonpower groups, this does not mean that each of us does not have personal power—we do! It is helpful for us to see how our culture labels and places someone in a down position. We talk about the different forms of violence experienced by the nonpower groups, usually at the hands of the corresponding power group, and we identify this as oppression. Also worth noting is that each of us, at some point in our lives, has been in a nonpower group. Finally facilitators point out that the power relationship between men and women will be the focus of this group.

Defensiveness begins to surface early in the group as boys and girls attempt to generalize the power imbalance at the root of men's violence against women (e.g., "What about women who abuse men?" "Girls pick fights at school, too"). It is important to acknowledge that this does occur and that when it does, it is a crime no matter who perpetrates violence. Because of the cultural power imbalance between men and women, however, we are talking about a major social problem in which men's violence against women far exceeds the reverse. Statistics follow that clearly show that violence is not gender neutral but largely perpetrated by men. Several exercises are used to show how we come to learn these gender roles even if we do not like the effects. These exercises also highlight how we are forced, through coercion and abuse, to conform to these stereotypes. Some additional methods of diffusing this defensiveness include predicting it before it happens or as it starts; talking about why this happens and why this is difficult to talk about; and a male facilitator discussing his own process of raised awareness and feelings of defensiveness. A formerly abused woman is invited to tell her story to the group. This visit provides an important opportunity to dispel myths about "why women stay" and is an effective way for youth to empathize with the position of an abused woman. Date rape and wife assault videos are also helpful to further increase understanding of the effects of violence on the victims. Because the precursor to violence is objectification, a closer look at the impact of abuse on survivors helps counter the desensitization that occurs in a sexist culture.

A key area of socialization influence on young people is the media. Through discussions of how women and men are portrayed in rock videos, television, and advertising, teens understand further where these stereotypes are reinforced. The group members learn to deconstruct these images and decode the messages. They are tied to the same system of images and beliefs that objectify women and promote violence against women. The teens then discuss the specific effects of these images in real life. These skills, together with skills to counter sexism in the community, are rehearsed to provide an inoculation to attitudes that promote woman abuse and violence in relationships.

*Skill Development.* In the light of the complexity of the societal creation of attitudes and beliefs that promote the acceptance of violence in relationships, change is required at the personal, institutional, and cultural levels. During the skill development section of the program, we address change at the individual level—that is, the personal relationships (present and potential) between boys and girls in this group and their girlfriends/boyfriends. It is essential, given the patterns of relating based on gender stereotypes that affect us throughout our lives, that boys learn noncontrolling communication skills and that girls learn personal safety skills.

The motivation to develop effective communication skills begins with an awareness of the many choices one may make in response to a given situation and the recognition that an individual is responsible for the choice he or she makes. It follows, then, that it is not true to say it was "an automatic response" or "I lost control." In fact, the choice to use violence is a deliberate choice to gain control of a situation. If assault or coercion were not a part of our belief system and repertoire of behaviors, it would not represent the *pattern* of responses we choose. If the violence were not a choice and we were not responsible for our actions, it would not be expected that a person could change this behavior.

It is also important to recognize the "personal rights" of all individuals to encourage youth to act assertively on their own behalf. Rights such as the right to say no, the right to change one's mind, and the right to make mistakes, which often are disallowed by ourselves and others, are discussed. We can see the empowerment behind these rights, particularly if we consider a young woman in a date rape situation who is often blamed by others and herself for being in that position. Assertiveness training follows. A definition of assertiveness is best understood in comparison with the more familiar and often used passive and aggressive behaviors. Concrete skills provide tools for the rehearsal of assertive, clear interactions and responses to unclear situations. Also discussed are the respective responsibilities of males and females around the issue of sex in dating situations. A male must be clear that there is consent on the part of his date and must seek clarity if there is any confusion or ambiguity. A female should be aware of her safety in potentially dangerous situations and should seek to be clear in her intentions. It is important to note that in a rape situation the man is wholly responsible for his behavior. To facilitate the development of many of these interactive skills, we have two pairs of teens serve as nonparticipatory observers of the group for about half an hour each week. During this time they learn to be more objective in listening to their peers and, more importantly, then are asked to provide feedback to others in the group in a constructive and assertive manner about their observations. This procedure not only teaches members to be better communicators but also teaches other group members how to listen more effectively and respond to comments and feedback without aggression or withdrawal.

Finally, skills are taught and rehearsed to assist in responding to sexist remarks in the community. This rehearsal allows for inoculation against negative peer pressure and further reinforces personal change. At the same time, preparation for developing teens as agents of change within the teen culture and the community is beginning. The risks involved in "speaking up" and deciding when it is worth it are important areas of discussion to support youth in this endeavor.

*Social Action.* Several exercises are designed to develop social competence among participants in responding to violence in relationships and in challenging the acceptance of violence in their community. For example, the group discusses how to help a friend who is being abused find safety and how to help an abusive male friend stop the violence. Participants learn that if everyone reaches out to help, the abuser will not continue to think it is his right, and an attitude of intolerance for the violence will grow. Members learn that police, shelters, and other resources are available to intervene to stop the violence if necessary.

To conduct these exercises, teens are paired and provided with a problem relationship scenario (e.g., pregnant teen being abused by partner). They must begin with the telephone book and their own knowledge to find the resources they need. Brochures and community service directories are added, and teens develop a plan of action. The next step is to rehearse telephone contact with the "key" agency required and to call to arrange a visit (local agencies have been contacted in advance and have agreed to participate in this regard). The teens prepare questions and visit the agency to interview a staff person. Their action plans are revised when needed, and the pairs present their plans to the full group. This exercise prepares youth to help themselves or friends if they should be in an abusive relationship in future. It builds on their success, pride, and confidence and reinforces their learning to date.

The group next begins to talk about what we as individuals and as a group can do to end violence against women. After discussing how we can influence those in our personal lives, the group turns its attention to planning a "social action" or fund-raiser in the community. A past group chose to set up a display in a local shopping mall as a fund-raiser for the Sexual Assault Centre of London. They rehearsed and staged short skits to counter myths and provide accurate information about abuse. They sold buttons and T-shirts and provided face painting for children. They felt a tremendous sense of accomplishment to have raised funds and presented them to the Centre. Time is taken within the group for planning, making posters, and sharing tasks. Other options are "social actions" that can be done within their schools or in the community (e.g., develop and display antiviolence posters, distribute literature, organize assemblies).

## CONCLUSION

We have been exploring the benefits of the above prevention-focused strategy in a series of several pilot studies involving at-risk youth beginning in 1990. On the basis of a pretest sample of 19 girls and 16 boys (Wolfe, Wekerle, Gough, Reitzel, 1993), we determined that the needs of adolescent girls differed substantially from those of boys; that is, girls in our pilot sample were demonstrating elevated adjustment problems, compared with the normal population (which is not surprising, given that they were chosen from a protective service population), and they reported significantly more sexual victimization in comparison with the amount of sexual coercion reported by the boys.

On the basis of an initial controlled pilot study ($N = 10$ treatment; $N = 9$ controls) in which teens were assigned randomly to these conditions, we found important trends supporting the value of psychoeducationally based intervention. In terms of conflict resolution, teens who received the 16-week program reported significantly less use of blame tactics (although other forms of conflict resolution were not significant in this small sample). Importantly, girls in the treatment condition reported less sexual victimization experiences over the previous 6 months, relative to the control sample. Changes in attitudes and beliefs about violence against women also were found, primarily in terms of the treatment group endorsing fewer myths about violence in the family, and not endorsing the belief that violence is a private, family matter. Moreover, this pilot sample evidenced significant change in terms of social action. Youth commitment to end violence was evidenced by their changes in attitude, their challenging of one another on sexist language, and their ability to communicate their concerns to a role-play partner in a nonblaming, nonthreatening fashion.

In sum, violence prevention must incorporate an understanding of power imbalances in individual relationships, and this understanding must be placed in the broader social context if we are to have an impact in promoting healthy, nonviolent teen relationships. Prevention must include discussions of power relationships and must promote empowerment consistently in every aspect of program content. Furthermore, every interaction that program staff have with youth—from the invitation to become involved through to the social action work of the youth—must model appropriate use of power and support empowerment. We believe that such efforts on the part of communities, schools, mental health providers, and others will make a significant impact on the lives of both young adults and their future children.

## REFERENCES

Babcock, J. C., Waltz, J., Jacobson, N. S., & Gottman, J. M. (1993). Power and violence: The relation between communication patterns, power discrepancies, and domestic violence. *Journal of Consulting and Clinical Psychology, 61,* 40-50.

Barnes, G. E., Greenwood, L., & Sommer, R. (1991). Courtship violence in a Canadian sample of male college students. *Family Relations, 40,* 37-44.

Bethke, T. M., & DeJoy, D. M. (1993). An experimental study of factors influencing the acceptability of dating violence. *Journal of Interpersonal Violence, 8,* 36-51.

Blaske, D. M., Borduin, M., Henggeler, S. W., & Mann, B. J. (1989). Individual, family, and peer characteristics of adolescent sex offenders. *Developmental Psychology, 5,* 846-855.

Burke, P. J., Stets, J. E., & Pirog-Goode, M. A. (1989). Gender identity, self-esteem, and physical and sexual abuse in dating relationships. In M. A. Pirog-Goode & J. E. Stets (Eds.), *Violence in dating relationships: Emerging social issues* (pp. 72-93). New York: Praeger.

Creighton, A. (1990). *Teens need teens: A manual for adults helping teens stop violence.* New York: Hunter House.

Dix, T. (1991). The affective organization of parenting: Adaptive and maladaptive processes. *Psychological Bulletin, 110,* 3-25.

Dobash, R. E., & Dobash, R. P. (1979). *Violence against wives: A case against the patriarchy.* New York: Free Press.

Dryfoos, J. G. (1990). *Adolescents at risk: Current prevalence and intervention.* New York: Oxford University Press.

Dutton, D. G. (1988). *The domestic assault of women: Psychological and criminal justice perspectives.* Boston: Allyn & Bacon.

Dutton, D. G., & Browning, J. J. (1988). Power struggles and intimacy anxieties as causative factors of wife assault. In G. W. Russell (Ed.), *Violence in intimate relationships* (pp. 163-175). New York: PMA.

Dutton, D. G., & Strachan, C. E. (1987). Motivational needs for power and spouse-specific assertiveness in assaultive and non-assaultive men. *Violence and Victims, 2,* 145-156.

Elliot, D. S., Huizinga, D., & Ageton, S. S. (1985). *Explaining delinquency and drug use.* Beverly Hills, CA: Sage.

Girshick, L. B. (1993). Teen dating violence. *Violence UpDate, 3,* 1-2, 4, 6.

Gondolf, E. W. (1985). *Men who batter: An integrated approach to stopping wife abuse.* Holmes Beach, FL: Learning Publications.

Greenberg, M. T., Speltz, M. L., & DeKlyen, M. (1993). The role of attachment in the early development of disruptive behavior problems. *Development and Psychopathology, 5,* 191-213.

Health and Welfare Canada. (1989). *Family violence: A review of theoretical and clinical literature* (Cat. No. H21-103/1989E). Ottawa: Minister of Support Services Canada.

Holtzworth-Munroe, A. (1992). Social skill deficits in maritally violent men: Interpreting the data using a social information processing model. *Clinical Psychology Review, 12,* 605-617.

Jessor, R. (1993). Successful adolescent development among youth in high-risk settings. *American Psychologist, 48,* 117-126.

Johnson, D., & Johnson, R. (1986). Mainstreaming and cooperative learning strategies. *Exceptional Children, 52,* 553-561.

Kazdin, A. E. (1993). Adolescent mental health: Prevention and treatment programs. *American Psychologist, 48,* 127-141.

Koss, M. P., Gidycz, C. A., & Wisniewski, N. R. (1987). The scope of rape: Incidence and prevalence of sexual aggression and victimization in a national sample of students in higher education. *Journal of Consulting and Clinical Psychology, 55,* 162-170.

Levy, B. (Ed.). (1991). *Dating violence: Young women in danger.* Seattle: Seal Press.

Loeber, R., Weissman, W., & Reid, J. B. (1983). Family interactions of assaultive adolescents, stealers, and nondelinquents. *Journal of Abnormal Child Psychology, 11,* 1-14.

MacLeod, L. (1987). *Battered but not beaten . . . Preventing wife battering in Canada.* Ottawa: Canadian Advisory Council on the Status of Women.

Maheady, L. (1988). A classwide peer tutoring system in a secondary resource room program for the mildly handicapped. *Journal of Research and Development in Education, 21,* 76-82.

Makepeace, J. M. (1981). Courtship violence among college students. *Family Relations, 30,* 97-102.

Malamuth, N. M., Sockloskie, R. J., Koss, M. P., & Tanaka, J. S. (1991). Characteristics of aggressors against women: Testing a model using a national sample of college students. *Journal of Consulting and Clinical Psychology, 59,* 670-681.

Mesch, D. (1986). Isolated teenagers, cooperative learning, and the training of social skills. *Journal of Psychology, 120,* 323-324.

National Center on Child Abuse and Neglect. (1988). *Study findings: Study of the national incidence of and prevalence of child abuse and neglect.* Washington, DC: DHHS (OHDS).

Pence, E., & Paymar, M. (1993). *Education groups for men who batter: The Duluth model.* New York: Springer.

Pransky, J. (1991). *Prevention: The critical need.* Springfield, MO: Burrell.

Reitzel, D., & Wolfe, D. A. (1993). *Attitudes and beliefs of high school students concerning dating violence and wife assault.* Unpublished manuscript.

Rogers, R. (1990). *Reaching for solutions* (Summary report of the Special Advisor to the Minister of National Health and Welfare on Child Sexual Abuse in Canada). Ottawa: Ministry of Supply and Services.

Rooney-Rebeck, P., & Jason, L. (1986). Prevention of prejudice in elementary school students. *Journal of Primary Prevention, 7,* 63-73.

Roscoe, B. (1985). Courtship violence: Acceptable forms and situations. *College Student Journal, 19,* 389-393.

Serbin, L. A., Powlishta, K. K., & Gulko, J. (1993). The development of sex typing in middle childhood. *Monographs of the Society for Research in Child Development, 58,* Serial No. 232.

Slavin, R., & Oickle, E. (1981). Effects of cooperative learning teams on student achievement and race relations: Treatment by race interactions. *Sociology of Education, 54,* 174-180.

Stith, S. M., & Farley, S. C. (1993). A predictive model of male spousal violence. *Journal of Family Violence, 8,* 183-201.

Strain, P. (1985). Programmatic research on peers as intervention agents for socially isolated classmates. *The Pointer, 29,* 22-29.

Straus, M. A., & Gelles, R. (1990). *Physical violence in American families: Risk factors and adaptations to violence in 8,145 families.* New Brunswick, NJ: Transaction Books.

Sudermann, M., & Jaffe, P. (1993, August). *Dating violence among a sample of 1,567 high school students.* Paper presented in a symposium titled Violence in Adolescent Relationships: Identifying Risk Factors and Prevention Methods (D. Wolfe, Chair), at the Annual Convention of the American Psychological Association, Toronto.

Vuchinich, S., Bank, L., & Patterson, G. R. (1992). Parenting, peers, and the stability of antisocial behavior in preadolescent boys. *Developmental Psychology, 28,* 510-521.

Wahler, R. G., & Dumas, J. E. (1986). Maintenance factors in coercive mother-child interactions: The compliance and predictability hypotheses. *Journal of Applied Behavior Analysis, 19,* 13-22.

Walker, L.E.A. (1989). Psychology and violence against women. *American Psychologist, 44,* 695-702.

Widom, C. S. (1989). Does violence beget violence? A critical examination of the literature. *Psychological Bulletin, 106,* 3-28.

Windle, M. (1992). A longitudinal study of stress buffering for adolescent problem behaviors. *Developmental Psychology, 28,* 522-530.

Wolfe, D. A., & Wekerle, C. (1993). *Promoting healthy, nonviolent relationships: A prevention program for youth.* Grant application submitted to the National Health Research and Development Program, Health and Welfare Canada. (Available from the authors at the Department of Psychology, University of Western Ontario, London, Ontario, Canada N6A 5C2)

Wolfe, D. A., Wekerle, C., Gough, R., & Reitzel, D. (1993, August). *Promoting healthy, nonviolent relationships: A prevention program for youth.* Paper presented in a symposium titled Violence in Adolescent Relationships: Identifying Risk Factors and Prevention Methods (D. Wolfe, Chair), at the Annual Convention of the American Psychological Association, Toronto.

# 15

## Aboriginal Canadian Children Who Witness and Live With Violence

### CLAUDETTE DUMONT-SMITH

Aboriginal peoples face many obstacles in achieving a lifestyle comparable to the rest of the Canadian population. They are beset by myriad problems for which there are no rapid and easy solutions. Five hundred years of living under the rule of a foreign and dominant society has taken its toll on aboriginal peoples who once were proud, healthy, self-governing, and self-sufficient.

Parents, children, grandparents, aunts, uncles, and cousins made up the aboriginal family. It was the role and duty of all adults of the family to look after the well-being of the child. Children were regarded as gifts from the Creator and had a very "special" place in aboriginal culture. In present-day society, aboriginal children live in poverty and frequently are depressed and live in violent surroundings. Aboriginal children are in need of care and healing. This chapter is focused on the benefits of traditional healing for aboriginal children who are witnessing violence or living in a violent environment.

## SOCIOHISTORICAL CONTEXT

The Constitution Act of 1982 referred to Indians, Inuit, and Metis collectively as the "aboriginal peoples of Canada" (Woodward, 1989, p. 3). Aboriginal peoples representing all three groups make up 3.7% of the total Canadian population, with 625,710 lawfully registered as "aboriginal" (The

Daily, 1993). In this chapter the term *aboriginal peoples* refers to only those people who identify as Indian or Metis.

Prior to the arrival of the Europeans, aboriginal peoples were self-governing. Each of the 52 "Indian" nations had its own language, laws, customs, and territory in different parts of Canada and extending into the United States. The culture and traditions of aboriginal peoples nearly were destroyed as European settlers arrived and forced them to live by European laws and religion and required them to adapt to the European ethnocentric culture in order to survive.

The aboriginal peoples of Canada continue to be governed by the rules of the Indian Act, which has been condemned by many as paternalistic, discriminatory, and outdated. The Indian Act was enacted by the Canadian government in 1876. It defines, by law, who is "Indian," where "Indians" are to live (reservations), and to what they are entitled (rights).

Various methods were used by the dominant society to destroy customs and traditions that had been practiced and handed down from generation to generation by word of mouth. For example, children were physically beaten in residential schools if they spoke their language (Woodward, 1989), and laws, such as the anti-potlatch law, which forbade the practice of this spiritual ceremony, were made as early as 1885.

Life in aboriginal communities is conducive to the development of violence. The economic reality, lack of services, and loss of traditional lifestyles significantly contribute to daily frustrations resulting in apathy or violence.

Aboriginal peoples are among Canada's poorest. The percentage of aboriginal peoples receiving social assistance is 2.5 times that of the Canadian rate (Department of Indian and Northern Affairs, 1989). It is documented that in some aboriginal communities, the unemployment rate is as high as 95% (Royal Commission on Aboriginal Peoples, 1992a).

Many families in aboriginal communities live in substandard, overcrowded, unfit, and unsafe dwellings that lack basic water and sewage facilities. Many suffer poor health, often because they do not have the financial means to buy nutritious food. Aboriginal peoples living in larger urban areas find affordable housing in the "poorer" sections of the city.

Alcohol and substance abuse is another critical problem for Canada's aboriginal peoples regardless of where they live (Royal Commission on Aboriginal Peoples, 1992b). In a study conducted for the Indian and Inuit Nurses of Canada, alcohol was cited as a major contributing factor to violence (Dumont-Smith & Sioui Labelle, 1991).

Racism toward aboriginal peoples remains a problem in Canadian society. Aboriginal peoples encounter racism from people representing every segment of Canadian society. They experience overt and covert racism and discrimination. Aboriginal peoples in this country have been stereotyped for generations as "lazy, stupid, and drunken."

The imposition of foreign laws, rules, and customs and the erosion of traditional customs and practices over time have resulted in a society that is burdened with many social ills, violence being at the forefront.

## VIOLENCE IN ABORIGINAL COMMUNITIES OF CANADA

It is estimated that 80% of aboriginal women are abused (Ontario Native Women's Association of Canada, 1989). Aboriginal women and children suffer many forms of violence. They are victims of physical, psychological, sexual, and spiritual abuse. *Spiritual abuse* is defined as breaking down and destroying one's cultural and spiritual belief system. Violence was found in many instances to begin in childhood and continue into the adult years (Canadian Panel on Violence Against Women, 1993).

Acts of violence against women and children are regarded as private family matters in many aboriginal communities. Community individuals witnessing these acts, including relatives, are reluctant to intervene, and the abused woman and her children have very few sources of support, especially in the smaller aboriginal communities.

### Social Services for Battered Women

Living conditions, frequently compared with those in the Third World (Alphen, 1992), make violence a particularly brutal reality for aboriginal peoples, especially women and children. The majority of aboriginal communities in Canada are small, located in rural or remote areas, and have very few health and social services.

Aboriginal communities often have a nursing station/clinic staffed by one or two registered nurses who provide basic health care. In most situations the nurses are nonaboriginal and have not been adequately prepared to understand the culture, traditions, and lifestyle of the people they are to serve. The turnover and burnout rate for nurses working in aboriginal communities is very high. The nurses can offer only temporary Band-Aid solutions to victims of violence because most of their time is spent on treatment, as opposed to preventative aspects of nursing.

Every aboriginal community has one community health representative who works closely with all other health professionals. The community health representative is always a member of the community. Training for this position is minimal, and the health care worker lacks the necessary skills to deal effectively with emergency situations brought on by violence and may, therefore, avoid dealing with such matters altogether. This problem is exacerbated if the worker is a friend or relative of either the victim or the perpetrator, as is often the case in small communities (Dumont-Smith & Sioui Labelle, 1991).

In addition, few communities have internal social services, including those needed for intervention with family violence, and must rely on outside social service agencies and nonaboriginal social workers. Even when services are accessible, issues such as fear of being revictimized by the institution, fear of having children apprehended, racism, lack of understanding and culturally appropriate services, fragmented services, and jurisdictional problems between the federal and provincial governments make people reluctant to seek help (Frank, 1992). Social services in the larger, more populated communities sometimes are provided by an aboriginal agency employing aboriginal social workers.

Some communities have their own police force, but many must rely on outside, nonaboriginal police agencies for protective services. There are problems with both types of police services. One woman from a northern area of Canada stated: "When a woman calls the police here, at first they'll ask her if she's been drinking. And if she says yes, then they'll probably say, 'you brought it on yourself' " (Canadian Council on Social Development and Native Women's Association of Canada, 1991). Outside police agencies prefer to remain on the "outside," especially in situations of "domestic" violence. It has been documented in some northern communities that police will arrive one or more hours after the initial call for help has been made (Canadian Council on Social Development and Native Women's Association of Canada, 1991).

If a community has its own police agency, the officers are, in most instances, male members of the community. It is quite possible in a small community that an officer is related to the victim or the perpetrator or is a friend and thus knowledgeable of the couple's relationship. Further, the aboriginal police force works under the administrative authority of the band council. The band council is made up of the chief and council members who are mostly males. If the perpetrator is the chief or a council member, it is unlikely that he will be charged with assault, especially in cases of domestic violence. Very few officers can remain impartial and fair under these "abnormal" working conditions.

# CHILDREN GROWING
# UP IN VIOLENT HOMES

Children who witness violent acts against their mothers or other family members suffer long-term emotional problems and may develop serious behavioral problems affecting their school performance and their relationships with other children and family members (Canadian Panel on Violence Against Women, 1993). Data collected so far on the mental state of aboriginal children indicate that childhood depression and failure to achieve is alarmingly high for this group (Health Canada, 1991).

Aboriginal women have two times more children than their Canadian counterparts (Health Canada, 1988), and children up to age 14 account for 39% of the total population (Department of Indian and Northern Affairs, 1989). From these facts, it can be surmised that more aboriginal than non-aboriginal children are witnessing their mothers being abused and/or are being abused themselves. Of the 200 active cases at the Native Child and Family Services agency in Toronto, 80% are reported to experience and witness some form of family violence. A leading Canadian specialist on child abuse has stated, "Many aboriginal children are suffering horribly, physically and emotionally, in their settings and in families that are dangerous" (Kopvillem, 1992, p. 15).

The problems of growing up in a violent home can be compared to, and was influenced by, living in a residential school. Aboriginal children in these institutions, operating from the mid-1900s to the mid-1970s, suffered years of emotional deprivation and physical and sexual abuse by church representatives who administered the schools as mandated by the federal government. The experience of the residential schools created a generation of aboriginal peoples who grew up without good parental role models and with repeated reinforcement of abusive behavior. Once released from these institutions, these children, in turn, became the abusers.

Aboriginal children come into the world disadvantaged. They are most likely to be born into poverty, to witness or be victims of violent behavior in the home or community, and to live in an overcrowded or substandard house. A recent federal report on child sexual abuse stated: "The chances for an aboriginal child to grow into adulthood without a first-hand experience of abuse, alcoholism or violence are small. The tragic reality is that many aboriginal peoples have been victimized and the non-aboriginal community has largely ignored their suffering" (Rogers, 1990, p. 105).

Many aboriginal school-age children are socially deprived and have serious emotional and behavioral problems (Royal Commission on Aboriginal Peoples, 1992b). Although studies on the long- and short-term effects of witnessing violence specific to aboriginal children are nonexistent, it is highly likely that the effects of woman abuse on the aboriginal child witness are similar to those experienced by the nonaboriginal child. Left untreated, these children may grow up with continuous feelings of depression, sadness, anger, and low self-esteem; fail to achieve their maximum potential; and, as is the case for many aboriginal peoples, turn to alcohol and drugs for comfort and become abusers themselves. Moreover, many aboriginal children and youth attempt suicide; unfortunately, many succeed.

In the current Liberal government's Platform for Aboriginal Peoples it is stated:

> A nation's greatest resource is its children. Yet many native communities are losing their children at an alarming rate. Aboriginal young people are committing suicide at a rate of six times the national average and many are falling into a life of hopelessness characterized by a lack of education, alcohol and substance abuse, and for too many, incarceration in our prisons. (Liberal Party, 1993, p. 6)

## TRADITIONAL HEALING: A SOLUTION

The aboriginal concept of health can be envisioned only in a holistic sense. That is, the physical, mental, emotional, and spiritual components are interconnected and must be in balance with each other for optimum health. Sickness will result if an imbalance in any one or more of the elements is present. Healing then is required to restore balance or harmony. Keeping the four elements healthy can be achieved only by living in harmony with nature. One must respect Mother Earth because it is Mother Earth that produces food and medicine from plants, water, animals, and even oxygen in order to be healthy. In aboriginal cultures, all things—culture, language, land, people, spirituality, animals, plants, and even rocks—are part of a whole (Assembly of First Nations, 1992). Therefore, to be in good health, one must live in harmony with oneself, family, community, and all living and even nonliving things of nature.

For aboriginal peoples, the solution to ending violence cannot be achieved by punishing the abuser. Aboriginal peoples believe in more conciliatory ways to resolve conflicts. The primary goal of "traditional healing" is rehabilitation. Rehabilitation is focused on restoring "health"—balance and harmony—in both the victim and the perpetrator. Violence is the result of disharmony in all four aspects. Both the victim and the perpetrator are in a state of imbalance.

The people most knowledgeable about healing in the traditional sense are referred to by aboriginal peoples as "healers" or "medicine people." They can be either male or female and are deemed to have extensive knowledge about traditional healing methods and special abilities to heal others. They heal individuals who seek their help through spiritual ceremonies and use medicines or herbs that come from Mother Earth. The traditional healer strives to restore balance in any or all of the four components: spiritual, emotional, mental, and physical (Malloch, 1989).

Traditional healers use many methods to treat or heal an individual. Prayers to the Creator are always a part of healing ceremonies. Pipes, rattles, and sacred plants such as red willow bark, sage, calamus root, sweetgrass, poplar leaves, and tobacco also may be used in healing ceremonies. Each has a certain significance for the traditional healer and in the healing process.

Fasting for several days is seen by many aboriginal healers as a way to cleanse the body and the spirit. The healer will conduct a special ceremony before the fasting period and will assist the person throughout and immediately following this spiritual event.

Sweat lodges are special structures built of special materials where a person can go to heal spiritually, for purification purposes, and in some cases to fast. Red hot stones from a fire outside are placed in the center of the lodge. The stones periodically are sprinkled with water, causing steam to rise. The person or persons in the lodge will commence to sweat. This is part of the cleansing and purification process a person must undergo to heal.

Healing circles are another part of the healing movement. Healing circles are held in communities, in homes, in workplaces, and even in penitentiaries. Healing circles function very much like a self-help group. Group members provide ongoing support and display understanding and respect for another person who has chosen to heal in the traditional way.

Several social service agencies in Canada currently employ traditional healing as part of their intervention with children (Royal Commission on Aboriginal Peoples, 1993). In Halifax an aboriginal agency is incorporating a program for preschool children to teach them aboriginal culture, language, and traditions as a means of developing positive self-esteem. A healing model for aboriginal child sexual abuse victims is being developed in Toronto at a native child and family service agency. The model will be disseminated to other agencies across Canada that may want to adapt this model in their center for child victims of sexual abuse and other forms of violence.

The advantages of traditional healing are numerous, and it would greatly benefit aboriginal child witnesses of violence. The primary goal of traditional healing is to restore balance and harmony of the spiritual, mental, emotional, and physical elements of a person and with his or her environment. It is based on aboriginal spiritual beliefs and philosophy and therefore restores or strengthens aboriginal culture and thus raises self-esteem. It is culturally appropriate. It encourages active participation of the person throughout the healing process, and, perhaps its greatest asset, its fundamental tenet is to live in harmony with oneself, with others, and with nature.

## CONCLUSION

The issue of violence in aboriginal communities is being addressed more and more by politicians, aboriginal leaders, and health and social service providers. Yet violence continues to be the most serious of all health and social problems affecting aboriginal peoples in Canada.

To stop violence in aboriginal communities, issues such as poverty, employment, education, housing, and racism must be addressed. In addition, all forms of therapy must be made available to the aboriginal person who needs healing. This therapy includes the traditional way of healing, which should be given the same respect and recognition given to Western forms of treatment and medicine in our society. Special healing centers or lodges should be opened to serve the needs of aboriginal peoples and made available to all aboriginal peoples who choose this form of therapy. Funding to open and operate such centers must be provided by the government in much the same way that funding is provided for psychological counseling. The cost associated with initiating these centers is minimal, compared to the hardship and suffering that aboriginal peoples, especially children, endure on a daily and continuous basis.

## REFERENCES

Alphen, T. V. (1992). Natives left to live in squalor. *Toronto Star, 15,* 1.
Assembly of First Nations, First Nations Circle on the Constitution. (1992). *To the source* (Commissioner's report). Ottawa, Ontario: Department of Indian and Northern Affairs.
Canadian Council on Social Development and Native Women's Association of Canada. (1991). *Voices of aboriginal women.* Ottawa: Author.
Canadian Panel on Violence Against Women. (1993). *Final report.* Ottawa: Ministry of the Status of Women.
The Daily. (1993). *1991 census of Canada—Highlights.* Ottawa: Statistics Canada.
Department of Indian and Northern Affairs. (1989). *Highlights of aboriginal conditions 1981-2001.* Ottawa: Author.
Dumont-Smith, C., & Sioui-Labelle, P. (1991). *National family violence survey.* Ottawa: Indian and Inuit Nurses of Canada.

Frank, S. (1992). *Family violence in aboriginal communities: A First Nations report.* Vancouver: Minister of Women's Equality.

Health Canada. (1988). *Health indicators: Derived from vital statistics for status of Indian and Canadian populations, 1978-1986.* Ottawa: Author.

Health Canada. (1991). *Agenda for First Nations and Inuit mental health.* Ottawa: Author.

Kopvillem, P. (1992, September). The end of the silence. *McLean's, 37,* 14-16.

Liberal Party. (1993) *Platform for aboriginal peoples.* Ottawa: Author.

Malloch, L. (1989). Indian medicine, Indian health. *Canadian Woman Studies, 10,* 105-112.

Ontario Native Women's Association of Canada. (1989). *Breaking free: A proposal for change to aboriginal family violence.* Thunder Bay, Ontario: Author.

Rogers, R. (1990). *Reaching for solutions* (Report of the Special Advisor to the Minister of National Health and Welfare on Child Sexual Abuse in Canada). Ottawa: Health Canada.

Royal Commission on Aboriginal Peoples. (1992a). *Framing the issues (public hearings): Discussion paper 1.* Ottawa: Ministry of Support Services.

Royal Commission on Aboriginal Peoples. (1992b). *Overview of the first round (public hearings).* Ottawa: Ministry of Support Services.

Royal Commission on Aboriginal Peoples. (1993). *Focusing the dialogue (public hearings): Discussion paper 1.* Ottawa: Ministry of Support Services.

Woodward, J. (1989). *Native law.* Toronto: Carswell.

# 16

# Conclusion

EINAT PELED

PETER G. JAFFE

JEFFREY L. EDLESON

A sober look at our world reveals too many parents who do not provide their children with a nurturing and stable environment; all too many children struggling to move forward, but are being diverted, or even blocked by the adults who surround them.

Ten years ago child abuse was considered to consist of physical or sexual violations of children. If no bruises were seen, society felt that a child was not really affected. Understandings have changed as the short and long-term effects of emotional and psychological maltreatment have been uncovered.

Abused women and front-line staff in shelters have spoken out for over a quarter century about violence in the lives of women and children. Gradually, social scientists have "validated" these observations with increasing evidence that witnessing violence is neither a benign nor passive event. Violence and the misuse of power and control may gradually traumatize even the most resilient hearts and minds among our children.

Not everyone is taking an active part in the appalling display of violence witnessed by children, but we all are part of the community which enables and, sometimes, even promotes violence. It is our moral obligation, as a community, to do everything possible to give children a violence-free start in life.

## ONLY A BEGINNING

This book documents initial efforts to prevent violence and help children heal from its aftermath. In drawing conclusions from these writings, some common themes emerge. First and foremost is the need for a greater awareness in communities and among front-line professionals regarding the intricacies of violence. Many women are trapped in violent relationships due to poverty, fear, and isolation, but some choose to live with their abuser in order to provide basic necessities for their children. The myth that "a bad father is better than no father at all" and that a woman must "maintain a relationship at any cost" must be reexamined. Such an awareness must spread to all institutions, especially the criminal justice system. If battered women and their children are to be empowered to make choices about personal safety, then they will require courts and police that do not minimize the violence or find ways to revictimize them.

The London Family Court Clinic regularly receives calls from women across North America who have attended custody proceedings only to find a judge who feels that their husbands were abusive *only* to her and *not* to her children. In many other cases battered women disclose the violence committed against them only to be blamed by child protective services for "failing to protect" their children. There can be no real safety for battered women and their children as long as influential decision makers draw arbitrary and erroneous conclusions about who is getting hurt in the terror at home.

Traditionally, the needs of white, heterosexual mothers and their children are discussed. The diversity of populations and the greater vulnerability of minorities and recent immigrants have not been fully acknowledged. Women and children who have to disclose violence to persons in authority from another culture face additional barriers and less sensitive and responsive services. Due to the silence on these issues few clinical and research insights exist, and almost no dialogue between minority communities and service providers is taking place. These and many other issues must be addressed in the near future.

## A MULTI-SYSTEMS SOLUTION

This book is a step toward breaking one cycle of violence in which children in our society are being trapped—one that starts with a child witnessing his or her mother being abused at home. This volume's structure reflects our strong belief that stopping violence and healing from its effects are possible only through a coordinated, multi-system response.

A multi-system community response to children witnessing violence starts with an understanding of the roots of violence in our cultures and the complex social structures that mirror and reproduce it. Intervention consists of efforts to prevent future violence from happening, to teach victims how to survive it while it occurs, to teach perpetrators how to end their violence, and to help all heal from the aftereffects.

While the child witness has been the focus of this book, a multi-system response maintains a perspective that situates the child within his or her family and the larger social networks. Hence, intervention is provided not only to the child but also to parents and others who take part in shaping the child's life. Further, situating the child within his or her social network illuminates the role that we—teachers, counselors, advocates, nurses, police officers, social workers, court personnel and others—have in modeling nonviolent, tolerant, egalitarian, and humanistic values.

Finally, a multi-system response must attempt to change society's attitude toward violence, and help victims/survivors of violence within a multitude of relevant social settings. These settings include but are not restricted to shelters, schools, community centers and youth clubs, religious and spiritual centers, health and mental health organizations, child protection services, courts, and the legislative system.

These intertwined dimensions of a multi-system response to child witnessing of woman battering have been woven into the 16 chapters of this book. The many innovative programs described in these chapters suggest that we have the the power to decrease violence in our society in general and improve the ways child witnesses of violence are treated in particular.

# Name Index

Palmer, P., 88
Papp, P., 101
Pardo, C., 3, 228
Parental Kidnapping Prevention Act
    (PKPA), 155, 156, 166
Patterson, G. R., 133, 260
Patterson, S., 87
Paymar, M., 268
*Pearson v. Caudle,* 158
Peled, E., 3, 4, 78, 79, 80, 94, 121, 123, 124,
    129, 176, 179
Pence, E., 214, 268
Pennington, H. J., 152
Pepler, D., 173
Peterson, C., 48
Pines, A. M., 139
Pirog-Goode, M. A., 260
Pitman, R. K., 72
Pleck, E. H., 5
Poiner, A. M., 107
Polikoff, N. D., 149
Pollock, S., 195
Popkin, M. H., 107
*Porter v. Porter,* 151
Powlishta, K. K., 256
Pransky, J., 267
Pressman, B., 173
Prothrow-Stith, D., 108, 210
Pruitt, C., 52
Pugh, R., 52
Putnam, F. W., 44, 49, 50, 51, 52, 54
Pynoos, R. S., 28, 29, 32, 40, 44, 48, 49, 52,
    54, 55, 56, 62, 68, 134

Ragg, D. M., 44, 62, 68, 78
Ralphe, D. L., 52
Ramsey, E., 133
Raquepaw, J. M., 139, 140
Rauch, S. H., 161, 165
Rawlings, E. I., 44
Regan, K., 203, 205
Regoli, M. J., 163
Reid, J. B., 260
Reitzel, D., 138, 235, 249, 256, 260, 261,
    271
Ritchie, K. L., 5
Ritvo, E., 28
Roberts, A., 122

Roberts, A. D., 129, 133
Roberts, B. S., 129, 133
Rogers, R., 255, 279
Rogler, L. J., 40
Rooney-Rebeck, P., 260
Root, M.P.P., 70, 71
Roscoe, B., 214, 257
Rose, D., 49, 64, 66
Rose, D. S., 47, 54, 64, 66
Rosenbaum, A., 4, 5, 121, 172, 173, 217
Rosenberg, M. S., 4, 123
Rosencrantz, P., 199
Rossman, B. R., 123
Roth, S., 49, 54, 64
Rothbaum, B. O., 44, 47, 48, 54, 55, 68,
    72
Rothman, B. K., 196
Roy, A., 81
Roy, M., 147
Royal Commission on Aboriginal Peoples,
    276, 279, 281
Ruddick, S., 197
Rumptz, M., 125
Russell, D., 28, 164
Rutledge, E. M., 123
Rutter, M., 218

Sadalla, G., 211
Sanday, P. R., 14
Satterfield, M., 171
Saunders, D., 187, 194
Saunders, D. G., 80
Schechter, S., 135, 162
Scherman, A., 117
Schlenger, W. E., 49
Schofield, R., 107
"Schools Try to Tame Violent Pupils," 230
Schur, E. M., 82
Schwartz, H. J., 54, 68
Schwarzenegger, A., 16, 19
Seagrove, S., 245
Seeger, P., 230
Seeley, J. W., 5
Sela-Amit, M., 131
Seligman, M.E.P., 48
Serbin, L. A., 256
Shanok, S. S., 28
Sharpley, C. F., 107

# Subject Index

Aboriginal Canadians:
  child abuse among, 276, 277-278, 282
  social services for battered female, 277-278
  traditional healing as solution to violence among, 280-282, 283
  violence in communities of, 277-278
Abuse, state definitions of, 160-161
Abused children, 194
  and children who witness domestic violence, 172-173
  behaviors of, 18, 172
Active Parenting, 107
Adolescent relationships:
  family and peer environment and violence in, 260
  personality/behavior and violence in, 260-262
  risk and protective factors in, 258-262
  social environment and violence in, 259
  *See also* Dating relationship violence
Advocacy, definition of, 124-125. *See also* Children's advocacy
Amish, 15
Antisocial behavior:
  among traumatized adolescents, 31
Assessment of children who witness domestic violence, 27-41
  closure phase of, 38-39
  cultural considerations in, 40
  family interview in, 39-40

interview preparation in, 34-35
opening phase of, 35-36
trauma phase of, 36-38
Avoidance behavior, 49, 52
  among school-age children, 46

Battered mothers, 193-195
  as child abusers, 194
  as clients, 98
  developing empowered vision of motherhood in, 102-103
  development of extended family network by, 104
  development of new family rituals by, 103
  handling of economic changes by, 103-104
  making up for absent father, 99-100
  parenting issues for, 98-100
  raising children's similarity to father by, 100
  use of children as confidants/allies by, 100
  use of power and control by, 99
  *See also* Battered women
Battered women:
  empowering as mothers, 97-105
  harassment of at work by batterer, 151
  rights of, 147-166
  therapeutic goals for, 98
  who lose their jobs, 162

# About the Contributors

**William Arroyo,** M.D., is a Child and Adolescent Psychiatrist and Clinical Assistant Professor of Psychiatry at the University of Southern California School of Medicine, Los Angeles. He also manages the Child/Adolescent Psychiatric Clinic at the Los Angeles-University of Southern California Medical Center.

**Joan Bilinkoff,** M.S.W., M.P.H., is the Therapy Program Director at the Domestic Abuse Project in Minneapolis. She has worked with battered women since 1977 and lectures on gender issues in social work practice and on parenting issues for battered women.

**Claudette Dumont-Smith** was an Aboriginal Circle Member of the Canadian Panel on Violence Against Women. She is Associate Commissioner for the National Aboriginal Child Care Commission of the Native Council of Canada and former Executive Director of the Indian and Inuit Nurses of Canada. She is a registered nurse and president of her own business, based in Hull, Quebec, that specializes in health research and assessment of health care services for aboriginal peoples.

**Carole Echlin,** M.S.W., has run groups for child witnesses of wife assault for the past 6 years. She is currently a frontline child protection worker in a child welfare agency in London, Ontario, Canada, and has facilitated a school-based violence prevention program.

**Jeffrey L. Edleson,** Ph.D., is a social worker with extensive experience in conducting groups with both adults and children. He is a Professor in the University of Minnesota School of Social Work. He has conducted intervention research at the Domestic Abuse Project in Minneapolis for the past 11 years and serves as its Director of Evaluation and Research. He has provided technical assistance to domestic violence programs across North American and in Israel and Singapore. He has published more than 50 articles and several books on domestic violence, group work, and program evaluation. His books include (with Richard M. Tolman) *Intervention for Men Who Batter: An Ecological Approach* (1992, Sage) and (with Sheldon D. Rose) *Working With Children and Adolescents in Groups* (1987).

**Spencer Eth,** M.D., is Associate Chief of Staff for Ambulatory Care at the Veterans' Administration Medical Center in West Los Angeles. He is also Associate Professor of Clinical Psychiatry at the University of California at Los Angeles School of Medicine and Clinical Professor of Psychiatry at the University of Southern California's School of Medicine.

**Denise Gamache,** M.S.W., is the Program Director of Women Hurt in Systems of Prostitution Engaged in Revolt (WHISPER). She coordinated the secondary and elementary school prevention projects of the Minnesota Coalition for Battered Women, helped establish a battered women's shelter in Minneapolis, and organized collaborative projects with local criminal justice systems to improve the response to victims of domestic violence.

**Robert Gough** is the Founding Director of Changing Ways, the abusive men's program in London, Ontario. He has worked in the area of violence against women for the past 10 years. He is a past Chairperson of the London Coordinating Committee to End Woman Abuse, and he received the 1992 John Robinson Award for contributions toward ending violence against women.

**Elaine Hastings** is a Clinical and Research Services Coordinator at the London Family Court Clinic in London, Ontario. She was Assistant Director of a shelter for battered women prior to joining the clinic in 1988. Her experience includes advocacy and group work with battered women and their children, work with offenders, addressing custody and access issues and child welfare, and preparing child witnesses for court testimony.

**Honore M. Hughes,** Ph.D., a clinical child psychologist, is a Professor in the Department of Psychology at Saint Louis University, St. Louis, Missouri. She has published more than 20 articles and chapters on children of battered women and worked extensively with children of battered women and child survivors of sexual abuse. She teaches courses on family violence at both the undergraduate and graduate level, as well as supervises graduate students providing services to families in which violence is occurring.

**Peter G. Jaffe,** Ph.D., is Director of the London Family Court Clinic and a trustee for the London Board of Education. He is an Adjunct Associate Professor in the Departments of Psychology and Psychiatry at the University of Western Ontario. He has published widely on the topic of violence against women and children and is co-author (with David A. Wolfe and Susan K. Wilson) of *Children of Battered Women* (1990, Sage). He received his undergraduate training from McGill University and his Ph.D. in clinical psychology from the University of Western Ontario. He recently served as a member of the Canadian Panel on Violence Against Women, a federally appointed committee that examined solutions to violence against women across Canada.

**Jane Karyl,** M.A., is a doctoral candidate in clinical psychology at the University of Colorado, Boulder. Her research is focused on the assessment of long-term sequelae associated with child emotional, physical, and sexual abuse, especially the measurement of post-traumatic stress disorder. Her clinical interests include the treatment of women survivors of sexual assault and battering.

**Toby Y. Landis,** Ph.D., has conducted research about post-traumatic stress disorder among children in battered women's shelters. She received her Ph.D. in clinical psychology from the University of Colorado and has conducted clinical work and provided consultation on the effects of witnessing violence as a child. She is currently in private clinical practice.

**Larry Marshall,** M.S.W., is a social work supervisor in a child welfare agency in London, Ontario, Canada. He supervises a group work program for children of battered women. He also has worked in both medical and child mental health settings. He is a past Chairperson of the London Coordinating Committee to End Woman Abuse.

**Michele Marshall,** M.S.W., is currently a doctoral candidate in the George Warren Brown School of Social Work at Washington University, St. Louis, Missouri. Since 1985 she has worked at St. Martha's Hall, a shelter for battered women, in 1987, became St. Martha's Children's Program Coordinator, and in 1992 began serving in the same position at the Kathy J. Weinman Shelter for Battered Women.

**David J. Mathews,** M.A., presently coordinates adolescent programming at the Amherst H. Wilder Foundation's Community Assistance Program in St. Paul, Minnesota. During his 8 years working on domestic violence issues at Wilder, he has coordinated the children's program, men's parenting, and men's domestic abuse programs.

**Martha McMahon,** Ph.D., is on the faculty of the University of Victoria Department of Sociology. She has worked as a social worker for the blind and in community-based adult education programs. Her dissertation research resulted in the book *Motherhood: Gender Identities and Gendered Selves* (1994).

**Myriam Miedzian,** Ph.D., is a Professor of Philosophy and a journalist. She received a master's degree in social work from Hunter College and a Ph.D. in philosophy from Columbia University. She has written extensively on male socialization, criminal behavior, ethical values in contemporary society, and on a variety of women's issues. Her book *Boys Will Be Boys: Breaking the Link Between Masculinity and Violence* (1992) has received national attention.

**Einat Peled,** Ph.D., is a Lecturer in the Bob Shapell School of Social Work at Tel Aviv University in Israel. She has conducted research and published several articles on both American and Israeli battered women and their children. She is co-author (with Diane Davis) of *Groupwork With Children of Battered Women: A Practitioners' Manual* (Sage, 1995). She received her bachelor's and master's degrees in social work from the University of Haifa and her Ph.D. in social work from the University of Minnesota.

**Ellen Pence** is the Training Coordinator for the Domestic Abuse Intervention Project in Duluth, Minnesota. She has been an activist in the battered women's movement for 15 years and currently works with the Visitation Center in Duluth.

**Deborah Reitzel,** M.A., is currently a doctoral candidate in clinical psychology at the University of Western Ontario. She worked as a research assistant at the London Family Court Clinic on projects concerning police responses to wife assault and high school programs aimed at primary prevention of wife assault and dating violence.

**Louise Silvern,** Ph.D., is an Associate Professor at the University of Colorado, Boulder. She teaches and supervises child psychotherapy in the doctoral training program in clinical psychology at the University of Colorado. She has conducted research on the psychological effects of child abuse and of witnessing parental spouse abuse and currently conducts individual child and adult psychotherapy with specialized interest in survivors of child abuse and other traumatic events. She received her Ph.D. from UCLA.

**Sarah Snapp,** M.A., is currently a therapist at the Amherst H. Wilder Foundation's Child Guidance Clinic in St. Paul, Minnesota, and the Director of Cool 2B Safe: A School Violence Reduction Project. She received her undergraduate degree in history from Grinnel College and her graduate training in family environment at Iowa State University.

**Marlies Sudermann,** Ph.D., is a researcher, clinical psychologist and Adjunct Professor of Clinical Psychology at the University of Western Ontario, Canada. She is Director of Violence Prevention Programs at the London Family Court Clinic in London, Ontario. She has been actively involved in large-scale implementation and evaluation of violence prevention programs in school systems and, together with Peter Jaffe and Elaine Hastings, has initiated a Canada-wide dissemination of such programs. Her research interests also include dating violence, family functioning, and groups for children who have witnessed violence.

**Christine Wekerle,** M.A., is a doctoral candidate in clinical psychology at the University of Western Ontario. Her research and writing focus on family dysfunction, child abuse and neglect, and the study of parent-child interactions.

**David A. Wolfe,** Ph.D., is Professor of Psychology and Psychiatry at the University of Western Ontario and Senior Research Consultant at the Centre for Research on Violence Against Women and Children located in

London, Ontario. He is an award-winning researcher and author whose works include co-authoring *Children of Battered Women* (Sage, 1990) and authoring *Preventing Physical and Emotional Abuse of Children* (Sage, forthcoming).

**Joan Zorza,** J.D., is the Senior Attorney of the National Battered Women's Law Project of the National Center on Women and Family Law. The project is funded primarily by the Ford Foundation to serve policymakers and advocates on legal issues relevant to battered women. She has represented more than 2,000 battered women and is the author of numerous publications, including *Guide to Interstate Custody: A Manual for Domestic Violence Advocates.*

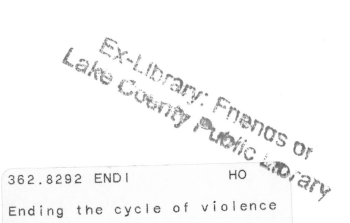